Keepers
of the
Flame

INTERVIEWS WITH ELDERS

OF TRADITIONAL WITCHCRAFT

IN AMERICA

MORGANNA DAVIES
& ARADIA LYNCH

Dedication

As all things come in threes in Nature,
so this book has a three-part dedication.

First and foremost, this book is dedicated to all those Traditional
Elders who have passed from this Earth. The flames from their
torches still light the skies and rival the Moon in their brightness!
May they ever Blessed Be!

This book is also dedicated to all those Elders who
currently tend the flame. May they Blessed Be!

Finally, this book is dedicated to those who will come after
and whose task it will be to tend the flame in their own time.

May the sacred flame warm you as you read this,
and may you, too, Blessed Be for all your days.

Cover Design: Ogmios MacMerlin

Davies, Morganna and Lynch, Aradia.
Keepers of the Flame: Interviews with Elders
of Traditional Witchcraft in America
ISBN-13: 978-0-9709013-0-9
ISBN-10: 0-9709013-0-5

Printed in the United States of America

First Edition, March 2001
Second Printing, February 2006
Third Printing, November 2006

Olympian Press
P.O. Box 29182
Providence, RI 02909
www.OlympianPress.com

Table of Contents

Acknowledgments

THIS BOOK WOULD not have been possible without the help of the many people who gave their time, efforts, and encouragement. Morganna would like to thank Theitic for his on-going love and support, and for being such an important part of her life; Antigone for her loving support of this project; and Gaia, Indigo, Iymlad, and Uinen of Phoenix Rising Coven for their dedication and their work on this project.

Both authors would like to thank Lenura of Beach Coven, Rhiannon and Tuan of Coven Hensiarad and Chloe and Sparrow for their very generous expenditure of time and hard work in bringing this book to fruition. Both authors also wish to offer gratitude and thanks to Maxine and Alex Sanders who first opened the door to Craft for them and so many others. Finally, a very important thanks goes to all the individuals who have shared their experiences and thoughts which helped to create this book.

Foreword: Traditional Witchcraft in America

*K*eepers of the Flame: Interviews with Elders of Traditional Witchcraft in America, in contrast to other recent surveys, seeks to cover one part of the Neo-Pagan movement in depth, not all of it in its full breadth. Excluding practitioners of all other varieties of magical and earth religion, this volume presents to an interested public only those Witches who, in the editors' view, count as Elders of Traditional Witchcraft—those who have been born or adopted into a particular family or initiated into a particular lineage that has preserved traditions of the Craft over an extended period of time. There is also a chronological limit: with a few exceptions, each of these Elders became a High Priestess or a High Priest before 1980.

Morganna Davies and Aradia Lynch have grouped their contributors under the following traditions: Alexandrian, Celtic, Gardnerian, Georgian, Keepers of the Ancient Mysteries (K.A.M.), Mohsian, New England Covens of Traditionalist Witches (N.E.C.T.W.), Ravenwood, the Strega Tradition, Tuatha de Danann (T.D.D.), and finally, "Other Traditional Witches." Some of these traditions have been well documented in a variety of publications, both popular and academic; others are less well known even within the community of Neo-Pagans.

What, then, is a tradition of the Craft? Are *traditions* more or less the same thing as *denominations* in Christianity? Some Witches use the word in this way, but by doing so they blur the difference between those kinds of Witchcraft that have a history spanning several generations and those other kinds of Witchcraft that simply reflect the personal inspiration of a still-living founder. As Davies and Lynch use the term, *traditions* pass down doctrines and practices from one generation to the next, refining them over the long years in the fierce fires of Time and Nature.

Often a tradition is embodied in documented successions or lineages of initiators, for example the branching lines of High Priestesses and High Priests who descend in alternation from Gerald Brosseau Gardner (1884–1964) to each living initiated Gardnerian Witch. In such cases the principal remaining question is simply this: when, where and from whom did the founder of each lineage receive his initiation, or what were his or her other credentials as an initiator? Gardner, for example, maintained that he had been initiated in 1939 by Traditional Witches whom he met in the context of the Rosicrucian Theatre at Christchurch, Hampshire, England. Because of Gardner's importance in the subsequent history of Witchcraft and Neo-Paganism, this claim of his is now being critically examined in academic circles. The most impressive work so far is Ronald Hutton's *The Triumph of the Moon: A History of Modern Pagan Witchcraft* (Oxford University Press, 1999). The data that Hutton has brought together provide a rich historical background against which Gardner's claim can be judged, and they also suggest that he told his initiates and others, at the very best, only a small part of a rather complex truth.

Yet in other cases, even in traditions where initiation is now practiced, the founder's credentials may not depend on any initiation at all, but simply on her (or his) birth into a family where some her close relatives had long cherished and handed down a variety of esoteric, magical and spiritual doctrines and practices within the close privacy of the family circle.

Even the very existence of such unconventional families is now controversial, both among Neo-Pagans and in academic circles, but it ought not to be. It would be relatively easy for a historical genealogist to document a number of such families in North America, who for many generations have eagerly sampled the rich array of alternative religions, spiritual movements and magical practices that have flourished in North America ever since the *Mayflower* landed at Plymouth in 1620. [Some work along these lines has recently been undertaken by several scholars who are researching the earliest history of the Mormon Church. They have been able to show that the founder of that religion, Joseph Smith Jr., was born into just such a family and raised in an environment where he was exposed to many of these religious and magical alternatives. See D. Michael Quinn, *Early Mormonism and the Magical World View,* revised edition (Salt Lake City: Signature Books, 1998), and John L. Brooke, *The Refiner's Fire: The Making of Mormon Cosmology, 1644–1844* (Cambridge University Press, 1994).]

For generation after generation members of these unconventional families have been alchemists, fortune-tellers and cunning-folk, followers of Emmanuel Swedenborg, adherents of Mother Ann Lee and her Shakers, Freemasons, Rosicrucians and Druids. They have been Spiritualists, Christian Scientists, students of New Thought, Theosophists, Hermeticists, and members of Gleb Botkin's long-forgotten Church of Aphrodite. They have been crystal-gazers, seers and sex magicians who studied the teachings of Paschal Beverly Randolph, Reuben Swinburne Clymer, or Pierre Bernard. And so forth. Indeed, a few of them have even served as Deacons, Elders or Ministers in Christian Churches; others have been inventors of new heresies within Christianity.

Of course, to claim that many of one's ancestors held a variety of unconventional religious views, or used a variety of unconventional magical or spiritual practices, is not quite the same thing as to claim that one's ancestors included a lineage of Witches. Yet neither is it an altogether different thing, since the word "witch" has been used to refer to so many sorts of real or supposed spiritual "outsiders" in the past. Moreover, real outsiders have occasionally even applied the word to themselves as an act of defiance or rebellion against the pressure to conform to religious orthodoxy, as did the very influential nineteenth-century Spiritualist medium and all-round occultist Emma Hardinge Britten, who in her *Autobiography* (1901) wrote that she had been "born a witch," that is, a clairvoyant, "ghost seeress" and spirit medium.

Whether it has ever gone beyond this sort of heritage—whether any such family also has included generation after generation of women and men who handed down ancient practices not just of folk magic, but also of how to work with certain other-than-human Powers believed to dwell here and there in the Land and to shape its destiny—men and women who perhaps even claimed to be *Witches* as they carried out these practices—this remains to be documented more fully. There is a small but growing body of testimony that traditions of this sort about the Land and its Powers have been handed down in secret in certain parts of Europe, including England, for a very long time, though what has so far been published is more suggestive than conclusive, and the word "witch" does not often appear in this testimony. [See David Clarke and Andy Roberts, *Twilight of the Celtic Gods: An Exploration of Britain's Hidden Pagan Traditions* (London: Blandford, 1996), and John Matthews, "Breaking the Circle," in *Voices from the Circle: The Heritage of Western Paganism,* edited by Prudence Jones and Caitlín Matthews (Wellingborough: Aquarian, 1990), pp. 127–136.]

Keepers of the Flame puts on record the views of living or recently deceased Elder Witches from some, at least, of these kinds of tradition; it preserves their words against the ravages of life; and it forestalls a possible future in which the only remaining Witches would be those who have no long history behind them, but have simply taken a liking to the word "witch" and have used it to cover any and all products of their own imagination or inspiration. Although such Witches also have their place in the crucible that is our World, it would be a great loss if they ever became the only kind of Witch that there is, or if Witchcraft in general forgot its history and became a present that has no past. Herein lies the importance of the volume that Morganna Davies and Aradia Lynch have now given to the world.

Robert Mathieson, Ph.D.
Brown University
Providence, RI

Preface

SOME TIME AGO my Elder, Morganna Davies, was talking with the owner of a New-Age bookstore who told her that Traditional Craft as Morganna knew it was non-existent. Furthermore, that it never had existed, only having been invented in the past fifty years, and that the only real Craft today is what is being offered by the public Pagan community at large. She was also told that there is no longer a need for traditional training since so many fine books are available today. At first, Morganna was taken aback by this attitude and disheartened, but then realized that as long as she still drew breath, Traditional Craft continued to live. She began to wonder how many other Traditional people were having similar experiences. During this same period of time, a number of hereditary Witches who had been working "underground" began to surface.

Morganna and I felt it was time that Traditional voices were heard again and, with that in mind, we decided to publish a book based on interviews with Traditional people. While similar books have been published, the focus has not been solely on Traditional Craft. We realize that there are different ideas as to what constitutes a Traditional Craft practitioner. For the purpose of this book, we have agreed to define Traditionalists as those people who are either hereditary, initiatory or both. With this in mind, we put together a questionnaire which we sent to the "Old Guard"

Elders we were able to find. An unprecedented thing occurred: Traditional Craft people decided to speak out and be heard. In breaking their silence, those Elders shed light on their Traditions and set right the misconceptions currently in print regarding Craft practices. We believe that there are people in the Pagan community who are looking for a deeper level of commitment than what that community has to offer. To those who genuinely seek, we hope this book will let them know we are alive and well and that it will be a beacon of light to help them connect with Traditional Craft. We offer this book to all those who are yearning for something deeper than what they have been able to find.

Some of the Elders have passed on and there are some we could not find. To those Traditional Elders who are still underground, we want you to know that you are not alone. We are as alive as ever, and we still Keep the Flame.

Aradia Lynch
2000

Passíng the Torch

J N THE EARLY 1950's Great Britain repealed the Witchcraft laws and for the first time in centuries the practice of Witchcraft was no longer a criminal offense. Almost immediately, individuals who had been secretly practicing the Craft began to take on students, and many new covens sprang up all over Great Britain. There were many Witches who were instrumental in this movement; Gerald Gardner, Sybil Leek, Alex Sanders, and others laid the foundation of what has become modern Witchcraft. Their students became the second generation of "legal" Witches, many of whom started their own covens and thus passed on the traditions of the Craft. The organized practice of Witchcraft spread quickly throughout Great Britain and Americans who had traveled to England to study with Gardner, Leek, or Sanders brought their training home to the United States and formed covens here.

Gerald, Sybil and Alex have all passed but their American students, now recognized Elders in their own right, have also made significant contributions to the development of modern Witchcraft. Most of their names will not be familiar to you. Even though Witchcraft itself is no longer a crime, popular opinion and prejudice are slow to change. Individuals who call themselves Witches continue to be persecuted in a variety of subtle and insidious ways. Courts have removed children from homes because one or both parents called themselves Witches. People have lost jobs, personal relationships have been destroyed, and some, even today, have paid with their lives. It is understandable then that many have preferred to remain anonymous, quietly practicing their Craft and passing on the Traditions to their students while deliberately avoiding all the fanfare and media hype that some who call themselves Witches seem to covet.

The importance of such work as this cannot be underestimated. These Elders are growing older and the torches are being passed to a new generation. Morganna and Aradia recognized several years ago that something had to be done to give these Elders an opportunity to be heard before it is too late. Some who contributed their input to this volume during the past few years have already passed. This book is not "about" the Elders; it is a record of their opinions, views, comments, and ideas of what the Craft was, what it is today, and what they think it will be in the future. There are many common threads throughout their responses. You will find, in some cases, that there is a diverse range of opinions on a particular topic. This is not to say that one view is more correct than another. Nor does it necessarily mean that there is disagreement regarding the fundamental principals of the Craft. The responses are formed as a result of the individual's experiences of life in the Craft and are as unique as each Witch.

Read this book. Open yourself to hear their words. These are the voices of the Elders, the Keepers of the Flame.

                                        Donna J. Leveillee, Ph.D.

Introduction

*"The Wheel is ever spinning,
and a time of change is upon us..."*

WHILE MUCH HAS BEEN written about Witchcraft in Britain, very little has been written about those who took up the torch and brought the Craft to this country. Courageous men and women who stood fast in the midst of much hostility and endured persecution of many types in order that the Craft survive are profiled in this book. How much easier it would have been not to dare to swim upstream against the tides of popular opinion, not to be ostracized, not to place self and family in physical danger, not to have shops set on fire and rocks thrown through windows, not to lose relationships with family members and friends, not to lose jobs, and not to be persecuted in the courts and lose custody of children because of one's beliefs. And how many today would be willing to put themselves at that level of risk for the Craft? This book endeavors to recognize some of those who were at the forefront of that movement, for without them there would be no stronghold of Craft today, no Pagan movement, no New-Age Wicca. The modern day resurgence of Witchcraft reached America close to forty years ago. There were families who were practicing underground, but for all intents and purposes, there was no visible active Craft in this country before that time. These individuals, now in their elder years, will not be here with us forever; others have already passed. The voices and experiences of these Elders must be heard before it is too late to do so. They are the torchbearers, the Keepers of the Flame. Many tears of joy and sorrow have been shed throughout the birthing of this book. Old friendships were renewed, new friendships were gained, while others were lost due to death. I know that there are still disbelievers and detractors, but I have seen the heart and soul of the Craft, and I know with certainty that the Craft is alive and will continue on.

All of the individuals profiled in this book are Traditional Craft. Just what constitutes a Traditionalist or Traditional Craft? Webster cites the following among the definitions of "traditional:"

"A cultural continuity transmitted in the form of beliefs, principles and conventions of behavior deriving from past experience and helping to shape the present. A convention established by constant practice. A belief, legend, etc., based on oral report, usually accepted as historically true though not verifiable. The transmitting of cultural continuity, beliefs, etc. A religious law or teaching, or a body of these, held to have been received by oral transmission."

My personal feelings and beliefs are in agreement with all of the above. For the purposes of this book, Traditionalists and Traditional Craft are defined as follows:

"Traditional Witches are those who have been born into, were adopted or initiated into a family and/or culture that practices those teachings defined as Traditional Craft. Traditional Craft is the practice of teachings that have been personally handed down to them by another qualified individual who came before them." We have chosen to focus on those who kept to the Old Ways becoming, with few exceptions, High Priestess or High Priest before 1980. Some of these people are well known to the public eye, while others are not.

It is easy to forget that even twenty years ago, information about Craft was not readily available, nor were teachers as forthcoming as they are today. One struggled, often for some time, to find a teacher and a coven with which to work. When I first came to Craft, the only choice was a teacher with whom one happened to connect. The seeker leapt at whatever he or she was fortunate enough to find and, for the most part stayed with that teacher. The student studied what was taught, learned, and then taught others. There was very little in print, or allowed to be printed. There were oaths of secrecy and loyalty given freely. Those oaths were heartfelt and held sacred between the student, the coven and the Gods. All were oath-bound, and it would have been unthinkable then to break those oaths.

Things are very different today. Many books can be bought, some good and some bad. Contact addresses for further information are readily available, and most people can read and distinguish between the different traditions before making an initial contact.

Yes, the Wheel continues to spin and all things change, as they must. It is natural and even desirable to move on and move ahead. But I would caution that we are also in danger of losing the wisdom of the past. The day will come when there will be a need to know about the experiences of those who came before, and about what was learned yesterday. The time may come when that knowledge could help you tomorrow.

Morganna Davies

Part 1
Profiles

ART ONE IS A COLLECTION of profiles of Witches from various traditions. Individuals belonging to a specific tradition are grouped together in so far as possible. Some of these individuals understandably wish to remain anonymous and only their public Craft names are used. Their anonymity will be upheld and respected. Others are willing to be in the public eye and answer questions from serious seekers.

An introductory statement about each tradition begins each profile group. Some individuals have associations with more than one tradition. When this occurs, they are listed under their chosen tradition.

Alexandrian

THE ALEXANDRIAN TRADITION is descended from Alex and Maxine Sanders. In addition to the United Kingdom, where Alex and Maxine lived, the tradition has taken root in Australia, the United States, Canada, Belgium and the Netherlands. According to Maxine Sanders, it was Stewart Farrar who first coined the term "Alexandrian." Initiates trace their lineage back to Alex and Maxine. In the United States there were primarily two lines of Alexandrians in the early 70's. The first known to practice were members of the DuBandia Grasail coven in Massachusetts, the second were from the New York coven headed by Mary Nesnick. Most of the early initiates in the States came from these two lines.

Alexandrian covens are autonomous so workings may vary from coven to coven. Covens meet at least at New and Full Moons and for the Eight Sabbats. The three-degree system is utilized, and, in some covens a preliminary degree of Dedicant is given. There is a strong emphasis on training which includes a great deal of ceremonial magic. For the most part, the tools and the ceremonies are very similar to those of the Gardnerian Tradition.

Maxine still lives in the United Kingdom. Alex died from lung cancer on April 30, 1988. The English Witch, Vivianne Crowley wrote a most informative and moving memorial to Alex which was published in *Children of Sekhmet*, Beltane 1989.

DR. HANS HOLZER is an extremely well-known writer, screenwriter, and a leading authority on psychic phenomena. He is a professor of parapsychology and lectures at colleges and universities throughout America.

I had been commissioned by Doubleday to write a book entitled *The Truth About Witchcraft* in 1969. I had already become familiar with Witchcraft through my friend Sybil Leek, but it was not Sybil who brought me into it. I came to Craft through doing research for my book. When the book order came, I met a lot of people in America and in England. I interviewed them and became involved because I never write about something unless I get involved. I went to Los Angeles and met a lot of people who were practicing the Craft and took part in their rituals. I became initiated, actually three times, and so I'm a High Priest three times over. Later, I wrote a second book called *The New Pagans* which was illustrated by Fred Adams who was a very fine artist. After that, there was some controversy. I didn't think that controversy among Pagans was the right thing. I felt that you do not imitate the Christian churches by fighting each other as they do, so I decided to tell the world that these differences are really not necessary. I wrote *The Witchcraft Report* which made some Craft people very happy and others very unhappy. I also personally thought that, being in the mid-West particularly, there were a lot of Puritanical attitudes toward the business of whether you do ritual skyclad or not. And if I look at antiquity, I never heard of anybody dancing around with a robe on. You know, that's the American way of life, and so that's the way it happened.

When I first came to the Craft, people took themselves very seriously, and many had that "holier-than-thou" attitude—the "we do it better than the other coven" attitude. Then I met Alex and Maxine Sanders. You know, I was very close with them. They are in a documentary film I am now putting together. I learned a lot from Alex. It's a pity that he passed on, but I'm still in touch with Maxine from time to time. Craft was maybe more serious than it is today.

I don't run a coven. I'm not "underground." I am never underground; I don't even take the subway! These days I teach by lecturing to larger groups, and I do a lecture on the Craft with slides. I have even spoken about Witchcraft at the University of Zurich, and if you don't know the Swiss—they are the mid-Westerners of Europe. I showed the slides and, of course, I could just see how shocked they were. It did them a lot of good! If someone comes to me wanting help, to be directed towards a group, that's what I would do. I would check out whether this group is doing things that I can accept. I have some questions about some groups, so I would try to be very careful where I sent someone

I think that people who want to join the Craft should be told exactly what it entails, and my personal point of view is not shared by every Wiccan by any means. The tradition is very old, and I think that the weakening of every element of the Craft is wrong. I do think that Alex Sanders and Gardner before him have restated it, but I don't like it being adapted to avoid any criticism from the outside. I don't believe in that. It's no one's business outside of the Craft.

CORBY INGOLD is the Magus of the Coven of Stang and Shield in Seattle, Washington.

I cannot claim to be from a Hereditary tradition, in that I did not receive my Craft teachings from my parents or other blood relatives. The first teachings that I received from another Witch were in the sixties, in the 1734 Tradition. I have since become an initiated Witch, practicing in the Alexandrian tradition, as well as in my own American-Celtic blend.

I announced myself as a Witch, or at least an aspiring one (I had not, at this point, been officially initiated, only self dedicated) to my family at the age of fourteen. I don't think they took it very seriously. Witches were pretty fanciful, fairy-tale stuff in those days. They were fairly tolerant, no doubt considering it to be another of my eccentricities and a passing phase. That I am still a Witch today in my mid-forties probably reveals something about the nature of Craft involvement back in the sixties. I think we tended to see it as a serious commitment, not just something you could easily pick up for a while and then put back down again. My family, while not exactly encouraging, certainly never has interfered or been in the least critical of my Pagan beliefs. This acceptance made it pretty easy for me to express my religious convictions, even maintain a working altar in my room.

The Craft was quite different in the early and mid-sixties. Much less accessible; back then you really had to work at it if you wanted to be a Witch. I think there was much more dedication on the part of those who did become involved. There wasn't the plethora of books available today.

Hardly anyone had heard the term "Wicca" (which really didn't become current until the early to mid-seventies), and if you told people you were a Witch, you ran the risk of being locked up in a mental hospital. There were no supply stores where you could buy ready-made Athames and robes; you pretty much had to make these things yourself. So there really was much more craft in Craft. My first Athame was a Malaysian dagger from a waterfront import shop (interesting in terms of what I later learned about the Malaysian magical influences on Gerald Gardner). We all bought incense from church supply houses back then and added our own herbs. It was really a matter of "make it yourself" or adapt. There were no legal defense funds for Pagans, or social network to speak of. It was all very much underground. It was definitely a secret society, a mystery cult, and it wasn't easy to get in. There was no question of choosing between different traditions. Whatever you were fortunate enough to find in the way of a coven, if you found one, was what you ended up joining. (This is still somewhat true today, but to a much lesser extent). Above all, when I first began practicing Craft, it was very much a Nature religion, which is how I have always thought of it. Unless it was pouring down rain I always tried to celebrate the Moons and Sabbats outside, usually in the woods or an isolated stretch of beach. I was appalled later when I learned that many held their meetings indoors. To me this is a deviation from the original Traditionalist and hereditary Craft teachings.

Our coven tends to be somewhat more underground than public at present. My High Priestess and I provide standard Craft training for advancement through the degrees, as well as a great body of lore, accumulated over the years of experience, that is probably fairly unique and idiosyncratic. It is this part of Craft training, drawn from the lifetimes and experiences of Elder Witches, which truly constitutes an oral tradition and will probably never be standardized. I am personally much more comfortable in an informal, anecdotal learning situation, and the best of my teachers were like this also.

JIMAHL is an Alexandrian High Priest of the Na Fineachan a'Gutha Sinsirrean coven in Boston, MA. He authored the critically acclaimed book *A Voice in the Forest, Conversations with Alex Sanders*.

Although I came formally to the Craft late in life (my 30's), I have always known instinctively that I was a Witch. This memory pervaded my childhood years and left me with a longing to find my own kind.

When I found a copy of *Eight Sabbats for Witches* by the Farrars, I knew I had finally come home. I met my teacher and initiator that same year.

I never told my parents about my Craft involvement. Not only are they Pentecostal, but my dad is a minister. They could never understand my own religious path. Some things are better left unsaid. I have one son who, in the beginning of my Craft involvement, was very open-minded. Then he married a born again Christian and converted. Now the Craft is a sore spot between us. We have hardly spoken in the last few years because of it.

When I came to Craft the New Age had just descended, so Wicca was already finding its ground. There was a climate of acceptance, especially among the young. Ironically though, I was never drawn to mainstream Pagan crowds. I stayed close to my teacher and set my feet upon a traditional path. I'm currently training my second group of students. My first coven has hived off to form their own, although we all still meet as Elders whenever possible. I personally teach all my students and make the necessary commitment of time to get them through the degree system. I love to start with beginners and provide them with a clear, consistent learning experience. I take great pride in my teaching. I have always been and continue to be public.

As I get older in both mundane and Craft terms, I realize how important it is to identify and train new students. This presents a unique challenge to the teacher. We must selectively pass on the knowledge so that it will survive us; yet at the same time we must protect the secrets of our individual traditions to maintain its integrity. Although this is not an easy task, it is one that I personally embrace wholeheartedly.

MORVEN is an Alexandrian High Priestess of Na Fineachan Glice Coven west of Boston. She was co-founder and Managing Editor of *Harvest* and has contributed to *Living Between the Worlds* (edited by Chas Clifton) and *A Voice In The Forest* (by Jimahl).

When I was in high school at the end of the late sixties, I became interested in yoga, reincarnation, ESP, Tarot, and astrology, which were all very popular then. About 1970, I found Sybil Leek's *Diary of a Witch*, and was totally fascinated by the Gypsy lore, the accounts of ESP, and all of the supernatural. Leek was the first Witch I read about who wasn't involved in devil worship, and there was a warmth and sense of responsibility that shone through her writings.

At first I was content to just read, but eventually I wanted to learn more and to meet people of like mind. I lived in the suburbs and never even considered trying to find anyone in my own town. I wouldn't even have known where to begin. In 1974, I saw a Personal Ad in the *Boston Phoenix* from someone claiming to be Wiccan. I knew what Wicca was from another book I had read, Paul Huson's *Mastering Witchcraft* (one that would be considered ethically incorrect these days, but not then), and knew that it wasn't devil worship. Still, I was cautious. I contacted the person by mail, using a post office box. Instead of some lunatic, a nice man answered. He asked me what I read, what I knew of Wicca, and how I became interested in it all. I replied, and after more correspondence, he asked if I would like to come and talk to the members of a coven he knew.

The group he first introduced me to was more a magical order than a Wiccan coven. Their energy and elaborate rituals were just too much for naive little me. I wasn't scared or turned off by what I saw; I just realized they were too advanced for me.

When the man who brought me asked me what I thought of the ritual, I said that it was nice, but not exactly what I was looking for. He said he had one other option. The group I had just met had formed from an Alexandrian coven that had recently disbanded. Some of the other members of the initial coven were thinking of reforming, with a definite Wiccan slant.

After some discussion on his part with the group, I was invited to their Samhain '74 ritual. I felt a little more at ease because these people were less intense than the other group. The only thing that made me feel even slightly uncomfortable about this group was the fact that once again, they all seemed so intelligent and so learned. Here I was, bumpkin from the 'burbs, trying to hold conversations with people who were quoting Greek myths and Celtic legends. At that time in my life, it was news to me that Celtic was pronounced with a hard C! Much to my surprise, they accepted me, and I was initiated into the coven in January 1975.

Craft was so different then. There weren't many books available and only a few occult shops in the entire country. I remember that when we needed to buy books on the coven's required reading list, everyone gave their money to one person who happened to be going to New York City so that he could stop at The Warlock Shop (which became the Magickal Childe) to get our books. Other than ordering direct from a publisher, there was no other way to get them! For supplies we went to religious supply shops, antique shops, and made things ourselves. Now even the small suburban city next door of 35,000 people has its own shop.

There were no open rituals, or at least any that I knew of. You had to be invited personally to a ritual, and, except for a one-time exception as a guest, you couldn't attend unless you were initiated. There weren't a lot of different traditions around, either. On the East Coast, we knew of Gardnerians, Alexandrians, and a Celtic Traditional group, but that was about it. Those that existed were hierarchical and secret. No one would think of starting his or her own tradition, and I don't remember any general Pagan groups available to those not interested in the magical side. Things started to open up, though, about five years after I was initiated.

My parents were never aware of my Craft involvement. Some time after they died, when I had been active in the Craft for a couple of years, I told my brother. I gave him a book to read, asked him if he had any questions, and that was it. He's been very accepting and even greets me with the appropriate holiday greeting around the Greater Sabbats.

Today, I'm still the High Priestess of my original coven but my initiates have now all reached Third Degree. Four of them have hived off and formed their own separate covens. When time permits, the rest of us still work together as an Elders' coven, but lately we haven't been meeting. At the time of this writing, three groups are actively training students. I'm not training any students now because I just don't have time. I'd love to train a group again, but not now. Maybe I'll have some time after I retire. Sometimes I am soooo tempted, but it would be irresponsible to start another group if I couldn't carry it through to completion. My husband is not Craft, which makes it more difficult because the time I would spend preparing for classes or rituals, or spending with students, would be time apart. After a while, it puts a strain on the relationship. There's nothing like it, though: the shared sense of purpose, the energy you raise, the minor miracles! Someday, maybe... Someday...

MARY E. NESNICK served as Alex Sander's representative in the United States during the early seventies. She was responsible in large part for the spread of the Alexandrian Tradition both here and abroad. She later founded the Algard Tradition which she continues to practice and teach.

During the early sixties I was introduced to Ray and Rosemary Buckland and was initiated into their Gardnerian Coven on Long Island. In time I left and wrote to Alex and Maxine Sanders. Our correspondence led to a visit by Patrick Sumner, a High Priest, and my initiations into the Alexandrian Tradition. I began to teach the many students who were hungry for the knowledge and wanted to become Craft. At Alex's request, I became his representative here in the States for some years. When Alex received letters of inquiry, he forwarded them to me to contact.

The Craft was very different in those early years. Everything was very secretive. People could lose their jobs, and even their children, if their Craft involvement became known. It required a great deal of courage and perseverance to reach out and make connections. Many of those early students have gone on to become High Priests and High Priestesses and are still practicing today.

I still teach, although mostly privately, preferring to remain underground. I am aware that I "ruffled a few feathers" along the way. But, always, my uppermost goal has been, and is, the growth and survival of the Craft.

STARSPAWN is an Alexandrian High Priest, healer and herbalist. He is renowned for his oils and incenses. He began his life in Craft as a member of Du Bandia Grasail, the first Alexandrian Coven in America. He teaches and practices in San Francisco.

ℐ was a senior in college and my Psychology professor, knowing I had an interest in psychic phenomenon, introduced me to a fellow student who was conducting a telepathy experiment. We met and she excitedly told me of a recent discovery of an actual Witch's coven to which she was applying for membership. Over the course of the next few months we dated, did the psychic experiment and she filled me in on the details of this thing she called "Wicca." She had acquired several books from both archeological perspectives and a ceremonial viewpoint, as well as a few that were recently published. One was from England by June Johns entitled, *King of the Witches* about the life of Alex Sanders. The coven my friend had made contact with was led by an American Historian who had traveled to England where he had encountered both the man and this ancient religion and had brought back the teachings to America.

Later I met this historian and was questioned by him as I showed interest in attending a Witch's Sabbat. On Beltane night, 1972, I was allowed to attend. I remember being very nervous. A friend had taken me out drinking that night to calm my nerves and to attempt to talk me out of this madness. His fear was that they were really Satanists, and I would be dead by morning.

Something inside me refused to hear such nonsense and to attend at all costs, even though I knew the ritual was to be done "skyclad." I was very hesitant, still being a good Christian boy. I was also told that no metal was allowed in the circle, so my framed eyeglasses were removed for the night. So, naked, blind as a bat, and very frightened, I was brought into the circle. All I remember from that night, other than meeting a wide assortment of men and women, was a strong overwhelming sensation of "coming home." It felt as if nothing else in life was real, except for the short time I spent in circle. Something deep within my soul was rekindled like a lost memory triggered by the sounds of invocation, the smell of incense, the sight of candles (blurred by lack of sight), and everyone dancing the Witch's Rune. I was home, and I never wanted to leave again.

I applied for membership and began the intensive study and preparation for initiation, which took place October 26, 1972. I have wondered what my life's path would have been if not for this re-birthing into the Craft, but have never looked back in regret. I was truly re-born!

I was raised in a strict Roman Catholic family. My father was Protestant, until he met my mother, and converted to Roman Catholic so that she could marry him. He later became deeply involved in church activities. My brother entered the seminary while in High School and trained to be a missionary. My sister married young in life and has remained married for over thirty years. My family was very aware of my interests in psychic abilities, but not aware of the extent. They never knew of my growing involvement with the Craft or of the extent to which I threw my life's work into it. About ten years ago, I had another secret I needed to tell them and thought it was best to let everything be revealed at once. So at that time, I came out both as a Witch and as a gay man. The reaction was fairly predictable. It was a very rough period in my life. These days, my parents are very supportive of all phases of my life. My sister still does not approve. My brother passed on a while ago but knew and supported me in my choices.

When I first began to practice, the Craft consisted of small isolated covens working in supreme secrecy for fear of exposure, ridicule or even possible imprisonment, as some laws were still enforceable. There was some networking among selected groups who grew to trust one another. Written texts, instructions, open circles, and contact points were very rare. I remember Paul Huson's book, *Mastering Witchcraft*, as being the main information point of reference at the time. There was also Sybil Leek's *Diary of a Witch*, an autobiographical account of one woman's coming to terms with her hereditary lineage as a Witch; it was such a joy to read. There were other books, but most were written in what seemed code, so that uninitiated would not gain the secrets. There were times when it was not safe to come out of the broom closet for fear of losing jobs, spouses, even children in bitter custody battles. One needed to be very resilient to be known as a Witch.

I have been a solitary practitioner for many years now. In recent years I have begun to identify with the term "Shaman". I now say that my religion of mortal birth was Catholicism, my religion of choice is Craft, but my spirituality is Shamanic. Years ago I heard something that seems applicable to my path at the moment: "Religion is for those who are afraid of Hell, Spirituality is for those who have already been there." So I deal now with spirituality. When I am approached to teach, I offer it freely. All I ask of my students is to have an open mind and be of good faith. Listen to what is being handed down to them, as my teacher (and the teachers before them) handed it down to me. I also stress that I am only here as a guide. "A teacher opens a door, but it is the student who must pass through it."

TANITH began in the Craft as a member of Du Bandia Grasail, the first Alexandrian coven in America and, in time, became its High Priestess.

If I had to pick my most important push in the direction of the Craft, it would be very early self-awareness, a sense of being someone stuck in a small, powerless body at the mercy of the large and often clueless. Even as young as age two, I remember being so frustrated and sensing that I had not always been in this helpless situation, that I had come from somewhere else to here. As a slightly older child, I always felt I carried to situations a perspective not shared by my friends. A good example is getting into an argument over the meaning of the word, "pebble." We were trying to build something in the backyard, and I asked the others to bring me some pebbles. They came back with handfuls of little stones. I said, "No, no—pebbles—you know, BIG ROUND things!" Of course, they thought I was crazy. I went to my mom to ask her to set them straight, and I remember the sense of disconnection and bafflement when she supported them. It stuck in my mind for years until my husband, hearing the story, suggested we look up "pebble" in the Oxford English Dictionary and we found that it's an obsolete term for cobblestone. All this fell into place when I first read of reincarnation. I had never paid much attention to the Catholicism my family tried to teach me except to disagree from personal experience. (Thank the Gods my mom was a Unitarian Universalist, although she was not allowed to officially teach me that.)

I always loved animals, Nature and the country, and when I read Sybil Leek's *Diary of a Witch* at the age of thirteen, I knew that was it. Plain and simple, I was a Witch, and I just kept banging on this door and that, determined to learn. I read everything I could find on Witchcraft, and when I was fifteen, I called a radio show that featured Louise Huebner, but was told I was too young. Then, in 1971, at seventeen, I found and answered an ad in the *Boston Phoenix*. After exchanging letters for a time, I met with the High Priest and another member of the coven in a coffee shop. We talked for over an hour. Towards the end of the conversation, the High Priest asked me if I still wanted to join the coven. I did. I was instructed as to the time, place, and what to bring with me. I was also assigned a list of books to read. These included works by Margaret Murray, Gerald Gardner, T.C. Lethbridge, and Justine Glass. By that time, I'd already read Hans Holzer's *Truth About Witchcraft*, which included a chapter about Alex Sanders, so I had an idea of what that tradition was about.

At the appointed time, I told my mom I was going to meet some friends to see a movie and got on the "T." Many train changes later, I found myself in a part of Boston I didn't even know existed and made my way to a basement apartment. Of course, in retrospect these people could have been dangerous, and I could have possibly been maimed or killed. But I wanted so much to be a part of Craft, I was willing to take whatever risk necessary. As it turned out, the apartment was filled with fascinating people, frankincense smoke, evocative music and books of all sorts (most of the coveners were librarians and academics). After some introductions and conversation, the furniture was pushed back to make room for the circle. Men and women disrobed in separate rooms, since this was a "skyclad" tradition, and I was blindfolded along with another initiate. There followed a then-typical Alexandrian initiation, made more powerful to my mind by the strangeness of the locale and all the people I had never before met. This sort of immersion initiation is virtually never done any more, but it was pretty common back then.

The first degree was considered a learning degree, and the initiation was considered to protect the group more than expose it, as the times were such that no one would think of talking about their experience in public if they had been a full participant in this way. Everything was very secretive then. Llewellyn hadn't published Lady Sheba's *Book of Shadows* yet and no one had Craft information unless he or she had been accepted into a coven. Craft was also very heterosexually oriented then, as that had been the structure at that time in England, from whence our tradition came. Most covens practiced skyclad. Magic was permitted and encouraged. Coveners chose a particular specialty to study and gain expertise in. I chose herbs.

I no longer run a coven, although I will give advice and information to the occasional seeker. I did take one aspirant to a few circles a year or so ago, but encouraged him to make contacts beyond me after that.

Over the years, despite the changing and eventual demise of my original coven connection, I have maintained contact with friends in its various daughter groups and I still guest-Elder occasionally at Sabbats. In 1986 a friend formed a primarily-women Pagan celebratory group in the Southeastern Massachusetts area, which I joined and to which I still belong. I also took the Unitarian Universalist Goddess-awareness course, "Cakes for the Queen of Heaven" in 1988 to network with like-minded people in the Cape-South Shore area. This has changed my focus to a more contemplative, free-form style of working. Still, I am, and will always be, a Witch.

Celtic

HE WORD "CELTIC" has different connotations for different people, and is used as an umbrella term to describe various peoples who lived throughout Europe. Though these tribes were independent, they were all considered Celtic *(Keltoi)* by those who encountered them. The word Celt and the society it reflected didn't become popular in European literature until the sixteenth and seventeenth centuries.

Unlike modern Celtic Reconstructionalists who focus on scholarly research to reconstruct a lost oral tradition, the Celtic Traditions described in this section are as diverse as the Celts themselves. These Traditions have been poetically inspired by the deities, customs and ceremonies from Wales, Ireland, Scotland and Britain. They have survived in these family-oriented groups as brilliant testament to the wild Celtic spirit.

As the diversity of the Celtic people suggests, there are no training systems common to all of them, nor do they all originate from the same sources. Some of these practitioners may have a degree system and some may not. Some worship a specific pantheon which is different from others. Each practitioner hands down information as it was taught to them. Some call themselves Celtic for no other reason than that was what they were taught to call what they did.

MARTHA ADLER (SELENE) was known by many in the Craft community. She was a High Priestess who lived and practiced in Florida until her death on November 11, 2000.

I first came to the Craft when I read Gerald Gardner's first book in college and went to an occult bookstore to try to find a coven and teacher. That visit led to a contact and eventual meeting with the coven that accepted, trained, and initiated me. When my training was complete, I started practicing and in time started my own coven. My family thought that I really was not only weird, but also not completely all there, and refused to discuss the Craft with me. Neither of my children were interested in Craft teachings or, for that matter, in any religion at all and still are not.

My experience in Craft was very good, none of the weird stuff and people that later came to profess to be of the Old Religion.

During World War II my husband Fred and I worked for the U.S. Army and were stationed in England. Fred worked in legal services, and I was a nurse. We met the "old" Witches during that time. We were taught by Ruth Wynn Owen who belonged to The Plant Bran, a Family Tradition based on ancient Welsh pre-Christian religion. We brought those beliefs and teachings back to the United States. Here in the States I belong to a Celtic coven.

When I began my studies, the year-and-a-day training was a minimum requirement. One of the teachings emphasized was the Tenets of the Craft. These Tenets are based on honesty to self, others, and to the Craft itself, and obeying the Laws was required of all who practiced the Old Religion. Anyone who did not adhere to the Laws was no longer considered a Wiccan and would no longer be accepted in any group. My training included learning Craft tradition, history, and legends, as well as the Laws by which we all live and practice. I was also taught herb-craft, mental and psychic abilities, and other related subjects. In short, I was provided with all that is needed to develop into a sound, knowledgeable Crafter able to stand on my own and to, in time, begin my own coven.

I feel the Craft today has gone far from the way it was in the sixties and seventies. In some ways it has changed for the better but in many ways it has not. I feel many of the most important aspects the student needs to be a good Wiccan are lacking.

Though it's been a number of years since I have headed a coven, I am often consulted by others for advice and counsel. As an Elder, I am always willing to help whenever possible. I would also like to say to all those who truly want and who should be Craft: Be not discouraged at the length of time it may take to find those who you belong with. When it is right, it will happen.

CHAS S. CLIFTON edited Llewellyn Publications' *Witchcraft Today* series and collaborated with Evan John Jones on *Sacred Mask, Sacred Dance.* In 1999 he contributed to the centennial edition of *Aradia: The Gospel of the Witches.* He is actively involved with the Nature Religions Scholars. He lives with his wife and High Priestess, Mary Currier, in the foothills of Colorado.

I was raised an Episcopalian. The parishes I was most active in were what we called "Broad Church," neither highly ritualistic nor evangelical. One, however, had occasional "High Church" events, such as sung Masses on certain festival days. I sang in the choir before my voice changed and was an altar server at both churches. For a couple of years I used to get up early and serve at one of the 6:30 a.m. weekday Masses. Usually the priest's vestments and altar cloths were in the color of the liturgical season, such as deep purple for Advent or green for trinity. But one morning I arrived and the young curate who usually celebrated those Eucharists told me that a family had requested a Requiem Mass for a departed relative. He pulled open the bottom drawer of the big chest in the sacristy and came up with a gleaming embroidered black chasuble, lined with red satin, and the other vestments to match it. All through that particular service I pondered its implications. What we were doing was somehow going to benefit someone on the Other Side. The thought was spooky, fascinating, and although I did not know it at the time, my first conscious experience of High Magic.

By my sophomore year in high school, however, I was drifting away from the church. It just stopped making complete sense. For one thing, Christianity always seemed to stop at the edge of town. As a young backpacker, hunter, and mountaineer, I always wondered what my religion was supposed to be when I was up in the hills. Then, during my undergraduate years, I was exposed to bits and pieces of a Pagan worldview, but I would not have known it by that name. I learned to read Tarot cards and to do other forms of divination. I read Charles Leland's *Aradia*, but I had no idea that there were Neo-Pagan Witches. In the summer between my junior and senior years, I found Robert Graves', *The White Goddess*. By summer's end, I had decided that if I was the only Goddess-worshipping Pagan in the world that was fine by me.

I lived a year in Portland after graduation. In 1974 I took a beginning astrology class, which met at a small metaphysical center, and there I bought Hans Holzer's book *The New Pagans*. Apparently there was this whole national Pagan scene that I was unaware of. I think it was there that I found the address for *Green Egg* Magazine, as well as the text of a Pagan Way self-initiation ritual. I performed the ritual one night in my apartment, using my dining table/desk for the altar. For a brief moment, I was flooded with fear that the heavens would part and the Christian God would strike me dead, but the fear passed. I also picked up a reprint of Gerald Gardner's *Witchcraft Today* but knew next to nothing about the contemporary Gardnerian Tradition.

The following winter I returned to Colorado. After a year and a half of solo Pagan practice, recognizing the quarter and cross-quarter days, I began to meet people. A friend introduced me to a group of would-be ceremonial magicians, who lived communally and practiced on Golden Dawn/Thelemic lines. At the same time, through a letter sent to the *Green Egg* Forum, I met Michael and Judy Myers, two Colorado Witches who had moved from Denver to rural northeastern Colorado near Fort Morgan. Their coven is described in Chapter One of Margot Adler's book *Drawing Down the Moon*. Looking back now from two decades later, I suspect that one ingredient in the teachings was the "1734" Tradition spread by Joe Wilson and ultimately derived from Robert Cochrane (d.1966) in England. I suspect this because of some of the teaching methods used: the encryption of doctrine in riddles, and the reliance on *The White Goddess*, directly or indirectly.

A large difference between the 1970's Craft and today's was the scarcity of written material. That was even truer in the 1960's, according to people like Raymond Buckland. There were very few "how-to" books on the market. Gerald Gardner's *Witchcraft Today* was still in print, and Llewellyn had published Lady Sheba's *Book of Shadows*. Stewart Farrar's first book, *What Witches Do*, was available, as were Sybil Leek's, but Starhawk, Margot Adler, Scott Cunningham, and the rest were all in the future. People relied more on privately circulated material, such as the Cochrane-Wilson letters, which were widely circulated. And, of course, there was no Internet, which made the few publications of the time, such as *Green Egg* or Herman Slater's *Earth Religion News* or the NROOGD (New Reformed Order of the Golden Dawn) *Witches' Trine* all the more precious.

There wasn't much coven-to-coven interaction in those years. In 1976 several of us went to the Church and School of Wicca's "Samhain Seminar" in Amarillo, Texas. Before the first big outdoor festivals, the early Pagan gatherings were hotel conventions, based on science-fiction conventions, such as Carl Weschcke's "Gnosticons" in Minneapolis in the early 1970's or the Samhain Seminars of the late 1970's. Many people there felt that their ritual secrets would be compromised if performed in front of other Witches. Two covens coming together was a big deal, an event that had to be carefully negotiated.

My family was completely unaware at first of my Craft involvement. I have two older sisters, and I took them into my confidence after a while. Mary and I did invite family members to our handfasting—and then my devoutly Episcopalian mother invited my devoutly Episcopalian grand-mother, who in turn invited various other relatives, including the Baptist cousin who loudly pronounced the ceremony to have been an "abomination" after it was over. (Since we're still married 23 years later, he has softened a bit.) Mary's father and stepmother also came along with some of her co-workers. Her father was mainly happy to see her "married off" and inspected the license carefully to make sure it was authentic. Once he saw that it was he was a good sport about the rest. Her stepmother was an ultra-Irish-American, and once we told her that the ceremony was "Celtic," she was fine with it.

Mary and I ran our coven based in Manitou Springs, Colorado. We had a "congregation" bank account and started Artemisia Press, which published *Iron Mountain: A Journal of Magical Religion*, later absorbed by *Gnosis*. Then in 1984 I started graduate school, and after I had finished, Mary started. After several moves and changes of employment, we ended up living in the Colorado foothills teaching at the college level. We no longer head a coven but do get together with others sporadically or at festivals. My first couple of years in the Craft had a heavily "book-Celtic" flavor but has also been heavily influenced by work with English Traditional witches. Mary and I had been married by the Myerses in 1977, and in 1978 we took a month-long honeymoon in Ireland, visiting the Farrars and the Fellowship of Isis, among others. We had an excellent time, but I always felt afterwards that I now had an inkling about what it would take to be a North American Witch, one whose heart was here in this country, instead of giving allegiance to some other place and time.

ALEXANDRIA FOXMOORE was the first initiate of Ravenwood and the first to become a High Priestess. She founded and remained High Priestess of Foxmoore Covens until her death on April 23, 2000. She was owner and proprietor of the original Crystal Fox store in Maryland, and owned and operated "Trinket's the Magickal Kat*" in Delaware. She authored *Eternal Ice* and published *Foxtales*, a Craft newsletter.

My mundane family had members who were Witches. My spiritual mother was Gardnerian/Celtic and my spiritual father was Druid. Although it is popular to make a distinction between hereditary and initiatory, I was taught that one was initiated into a family tradition. The tradition gave the new initiate "lineage" and thereby was the key to heredity. A child of an initiated Witch was in no way a "hereditary Witch" nor was that child automatically an initiate. That was part of the right and honor bestowed only upon initiated Witches. There was no birthright to Witchcraft. Each individual given an opportunity for initiation worked through the disciplines and studies as a Neophyte. It was also an accepted prerequisite that this Neophyte had natural abilities that qualified him or her to be considered for initiation.

When I began to practice Craft, the majority of covens were very tribal and secretive. One networked through coven officers called Summoners. There was protocol involved in communicating with other groups. There was little changing from group to group. Once initiated into a Craft family it was your tradition for life. No one would have considered reading a book and starting a coven on his or her own. There were traditional path workings to become teachers and leaders within the individual covens. An initiate was a first degree (a practitioner of the Religion and Crafter). The initiate could elect to remain as a first degree in good standing for the

---

* Lady Alexandria's store, Trinket's the Magickal Kat, is still open for business and operated by members of Foxmoore.

rest of his or her life and many did. The second degree within a coven was the office-holder and teacher. Their training was long, testing and tedious. If a coven became too large or had reason to expand, one of the female second degree initiates would petition (or be chosen) to work toward gaining her third degree initiation and would then become a High Priestess. Only then would she be released to start a coven of her own within the tradition while still maintaining allegiance to the Mother coven (original coven). The covens were Matriarchal in nature with the High Priestess as the center of each. She was the "law", having final word on all decisions. The High Priest (who was chosen from among qualified second degrees by the High Priestess) was the head teacher, and if there was anyone who had a public persona, it was him.

Paganism today is in the midst of tremendous transition. Popular Paganism exists because there are no heavy rules and regulations and because it speaks to the heart of freedom. I believe that as Crafters, we are leaders in a world struggling. If we fight amongst ourselves over theology, theosophy or structure, we run the risk of destroying ourselves. We must not fall prey to the mistakes that have been made by so many structured religions since the beginning of time. As an unstructured religious movement, we have a unique opportunity. If we learn not only tolerance but an appreciation for all our diversity and a sharing of our wisdom, we chance survival as a world with freedom of religion.

CHRISTINE M. JONES (ATHENA) is a High Priestess in the Celtic Tradition. She was Sybil Leek's last student and initiate. Christine is a regular guest speaker at the World Religions class at Brevard Community College in Florida. She is the author of *A Handbook of Sacred Truths, Magic of the Archangels*, and *A Witch's Workbook*. She is also the subject of a forthcoming movie, *January Witch*.

I was raised in England where I grew up in a strict Roman Catholic family, so I was completely unfamiliar with the concept of a Mother Goddess. After coming to America I lived in New Jersey for a time where, following a year of serious illness, I went through an out-of-body experience that entirely changed the course of my life. I found myself in the presence of the Mother Goddess and Father God. The last words I heard as my spirit returned to my body were, "You are so loved." I was very still for some time after thinking about what had just happened to me. Then I slowly walked into my living room where I found the world went on as usual. I remember the TV newscaster was talking about world events, but what had just occurred in my life over-shadowed anything he had to say. It was after this experience that I moved to Florida to meet and study with my mentor, Sybil Leek.

In 1977, Sybil introduced me to the Craft and to the wonders of the unseen world. I owe this Lady an eternal debt of gratitude, for it was she who rescued my spirit and set my feet on the right path. Later I researched my family roots back to Thirteenth Century England and discovered some of my ancestors were Witches.

Sybil was colorful and flamboyant and was all things to all people. She was a hard taskmaster who did not suffer fools gladly. Her mental abilities were phenomenal; she had a quick wit and was a master of the mind—she called mind-to-mind communication "think talking." She was a wonderful cook and made an excellent New England clam chowder. Her knowledge of herbs was extensive. She made all her oils and incenses—and they worked! With her help I gained my knowledge of herbs, candle making and burning, and use of sacred oils. I cherish all these gifts from her, but her greatest gift to me was the knowledge of the Guardian Angels.

It was a mid-winter night when Sybil suggested I seek the help of one of these holy beings. Up until this time my knowledge of angels was limited to my Catholic training, and I told her I was very surprised that Witches had anything to do with Christian angels. She said rather tartly that "Angels are non-denominational."

I do not remember the exact date of my first encounter with an angel, but I do know it was a Saturday night at 10:00 p.m. Sybil had visited toward evening that day. We had tea and talked of various and sundry things. The headline news at that time concerned the Atlanta murders which, until then, remained unsolved. Sybil had been showing me various techniques to enhance psychic abilities for use when solving crimes. She gave me instructions on how to invoke the Archangel Cassiel and obtain information about the murders, and then left for a dinner date. That evening I had my first experience of many with angels. I gave the information I received to the police; I was able to tell them exactly where to look. A week or so later, the police made an arrest.

Before her death, she asked me to continue her work with the angels. Sybil died on October 26, 1982 and I continue to keep that promise to her.

I know that, from the first day on this earth to wherever I evolve to in eternity, I will always remain a Witch. And I believe that, if in this land of America, our homes could become a sanctuary for the Archangels and a holy shrine for our Creators, however we perceive them, order would be restored in our lives and peace would return to our family unit.

TIMOTHEA is a teacher and former High Priestess of Moonstag Coven in Denver, Colorado. She was a founding member and last president of the Denver Area Wiccan Network (D.A.W.N.).

My search for the Craft began in about 1960 after reading Gerald Gardner's books, only I couldn't find anyone who was involved. I didn't know how to begin to look. Then I saw a tiny ad—I think it was in the *Atlantic Monthly* magazine. Gwydion Penderwen answered and directed me to Bonnie (Ishtar) Sherlock in Lander, Wyoming. He told me that Bonnie was the "only real Witch" he knew of in my area. I made contact with her soon after and arranged to visit with her to talk more.

I asked Bonnie to give me directions from the point where I would leave Interstate 80 at the western end of Wyoming. As Bonnie concentrated, thinking of landmarks and left or right turns, I received a strong picture of the area. It was like turning on a television set inside my head, and I SAW where I was to turn left, over a little bridge, and into her yard. This was the strongest telepathic communication I had ever known. I did not even require her words describing the area and later drove right in as though I had done it many times before. I never forgot this unconscious demonstration of Bonnie's abilities. After that visit, I knew I'd found my people. I studied and worked with her until her death in October of 1976.

Craft people then were extremely secretive about their activities to non-initiates. You knew NOTHING when you took your initiation—truly a leap of trust on your part! You had to really want it with all your heart. Tools were mostly hand-made; they certainly weren't available in stores.

Books on Craft were nearly non-existent. In coven workings the emphasis was more often on spell-working. I was taught early on to work with mental powers enhanced by ritual to bring about change. I guess the apple doesn't fall far from the tree because I remember seeing my mother "visualize" money and objects during the Great Depression. They came!

I practiced underground out of necessity. My husband worked his entire career for a company that did advanced aerospace research and so my Craft could not be known for professional and social reasons. I was only able to become more open after his retirement.

D.A.W.N. came into being in the early eighties in response to the need by Wiccans in the Denver area to have some communication between groups as the Craft was emerging into public view. D.A.W.N. held monthly meetings in a rented hall above a fire station where discussions resolved many issues between our own groups and others and aided public education and liaison with police officers. Each registered coven had one vote and members could choose to be open or not as to their affiliation. As Craft grew in the area, supply stores began to open and teachers became available through those stores. The need for D.A.W.N. dwindled until it was happily put to rest, having fulfilled its mission.

Gardnerian

GARDNERIAN WICCA is a Tradition (or branch) of British Traditional Witchcraft, founded by Gerald Brosseau Gardner and his associates. The Gardnerian Tradition is lineage based.

Although each coven is ultimately autonomous, coven leaders normally maintain close, respectful and loving relationships with their own elders. Covens are typically led by a High Priestess, with the support and counsel of a High Priest. Initiates work through three degrees of initiation, which both facilitate and celebrate stages of spiritual and magical growth.

Gardnerian Witches see the Divine as immanent in Nature and personified as the God and Goddess, whose loving creates and sustains the manifest world. Gardnerians celebrate the cycle of life through eight seasonal festivals known as Sabbats, and also gather at the Full Moons for advanced learning, magical working, coven business and worship.

RAYMOND BUCKLAND was High Priest of the first Gardnerian Coven in America. He is a well known lecturer and author of books on Witchcraft and related subjects. Some of his more recent books are *Buckland's Complete Book of Witchcraft, Advanced Candle Magic* and *Doors to Other Worlds*.

I first came to the Craft as a result of corresponding with Gerald Gardner and his High Priestess, Olwen. In 1963 I was initiated into the Gardnerian Tradition by Olwen in Perth, Scotland.

At that time, my father was deceased. My mother became aware of my involvement a few years later and was very interested. Had my father still been alive, I feel he might well have become involved. My elder son was initiated in 1965 when he was just seven years old. Over the past twenty years he has ceased to be active, but he is still interested. My younger son was never involved enough to be initiated, though in recent years his interest has grown.

In those early days, the Gardnerian Tradition was the only visible aspect of the Craft. In many ways the Craft was extremely strict, and there was very, very little written material available.

I am no longer involved in running a coven. After over thirty years of doing so, I now prefer to operate as a solitary. While I don't personally teach students anymore, I continue to provide teachings through my writings and the occasional lectures and workshops.

JUDY HARROW is High Priestess of the Proteus Coven of the Gardnerian Tradition. She is a member and past officer of Covenant of the Goddess (CoG). Judy authored the Wiccan section in the Military Chaplain's Manual for the U.S. Army in 1991.

As a Witch, I consider myself a dedicated member of a Pagan religious order, a Priestess. Two strong, lifelong interests drew me to this spiritual Path: a love of Nature, particularly of the local deciduous forests, and a feminist orientation. I also enjoy participation in ritual, but this is less important to me than the meaning of the ritual.

In 1976 I was thirty-one years old. I was reading a great deal about Witchcraft and Paganism, and finally got brave enough to ask a friend, whom I knew practiced this religion, how I might learn more. She took me to the Samhain celebration at the local Pagan Way grove. This led to my Initiation into the Gardnerian Tradition in September of 1977. In time I was elevated and started teaching a study group. This group evolved into Proteus Coven. Proteus is still active, and I am still its High Priestess, more than nineteen years later, as I write this.

We are decidedly lineage-oriented. Our family has grown to include several daughter and granddaughter covens. We bring the process and insights of liberal theology to the practices and symbols of Gardnerian Witchcraft. We seek lifelong growth in priestly skill, understanding and wisdom. We offer our personal creativity in service to the Old Gods, Pagan community and culture, and most important of all, our wounded and threatened Mother Earth.

The years have been busy and productive. I served as First Officer of Covenant of the Goddess (CoG) and held a variety of other offices on the CoG Board of Directors. For two years, I did a weekly radio feature on progressive religious activism of all faiths. I also served as Program Coordinator for the Interfaith Council of Greater New York in 1997.

Throughout the years, the Craft has been a central organizing principle of structure for my life. It has provided an outlet for my creativity and gives me a sense that I'm doing something worthwhile with my life.

MORDA is High Priestess of the Coven of the Sacred Stones in Chicago.

My first husband and I both came into the Craft in the sixties. We were both from a Jewish background, but did not identify with that spiritual path. We found what we were seeking when we discovered the books written by Gerald Gardner.

I was initiated in England in 1968 by Madge Worthington and Arthur Eaglen through the lineage of Rae Bone, who was initiated by Gerald Gardner. It was much more difficult to get into Craft then. There was less going on at that time; there were fewer books and everything was more secretive. Most of the books that were available dealt with spells or the Witchcraft trials; one had to learn from others.

My family was, for the most part, aware of my Craft involvement and reacted very positively. They were highly secular Jews, but my father was kind of a spiritual searcher. My mother thought the Craft was a great religion, but reacted negatively to the 'W' (Witch) word. Various relatives, at one time, would call and request a healing or some type of working. My father's family produced some good psychics and many believers in things metaphysical. Even my husband's twin sister, a nun, accepts it—she has no choice. I never told one aunt and uncle—otherwise, all my relatives knew, and respected my choice. Though I never had children, if I had, I would have wanted them raised in the Craft.

My coven has been in existence since 1974. We are relatively, but not totally, public. Though we have never been underground, I am very protective of my own identity, preferring to use my Craft name in books and articles. As the saying goes, "Just because I'm paranoid does not mean that they are not out to get me."

RAOKHSHA, formerly of New Hampshire, is a Witch Queen and High Priestess of the Gardnerian 'Circle of the Emerald' Coven.

As a child raised in rural central New Jersey, I was free to roam the fields, forests, meadows and swamps of an undeveloped area. I had been told many times of my Native American 'blood' inherited from my great-grandmother, and so I enjoyed pretending to be her and investigating the wild in my own backyard. I was raised a Baptist, and the Jesus that I loved was someone who loved children, Nature, freedom, and being a caretaker and teacher. There were no hierarchies in my religion. You got to talk to the 'big guy' in prayer, no intermediaries needed.

My grandmother was what one could have called a spiritualist in that she went to séances. My mother had a Ouija board that told her of my father's location and health as he fought through Omaha Beach and other World War II battlefronts when I was an infant. All of these spiritual practices—self-styled Native American, Baptist, occult—seemed interwoven in my world.

When I had finished college and was working for a government agency, I got a mailing from the 'Universe Book Club.' I was able to buy book club editions of works by authors such as Stewart Farrar and Paul Huson. Then I was fortunate enough to find books by Sybil Leek in the bookshop. All the while, in the 60's I was studying astrology and Tarot, palmistry, graphoanalysis—anything I could get my hands on and my teeth into. I was in my early thirties in the 70's. Craft books were only to be found in New York City, and tools were either handmade or purchased at one of the few "festivals" of the era.

I was reading a Craft-oriented book in a 'brown paper wrapper' on break in my office when the wife of a friend came in to use my calculator. She asked what I was reading and I told her it was about Witchcraft. I expected that she would think I was weird. Instead she said, "Oh, are you interested in learning about Witchcraft? I can put you in touch with a real Witch." Now remember that this is in the early 70's and the chances of her really knowing a Witch were next to zero!

After the exchange of letters through P.O. box addresses, I was interviewed as a candidate for training. There I found that the woman in my office not only knew a Witch, but was a Witch! I came to find that the Craft was a religion, something we still have to prove to the public, I'm afraid—and not just spell-casting and sexual license. I also found that most of my fellow coveners had at least undergraduate degrees. I felt so at home in this group. And I was a valued participant in skyclad rituals because my hair was 40 inches long then and 'somebody had to go for coffee!'

I found ways to tell my young daughter what I was doing without using the "W" word. I told her of our meetings to learn how to heal people and how we felt about Nature. Later I told my mother who said, "I certainly hope you're not doing anything you're going to be sorry for….and, by the way, I could use a little good fortune." I guess that meant I should cast a spell to help her win at Bingo. She had told me many times of a dream she had a couple of nights before her own mother died. In it she saw a woman dressed all in black knocking at Grandmom's bedroom door. Grandmom, who was frail and almost seventy-five, answered the knock saying "Katie Marvin, is that you?" And then she followed the woman in black down the stairs from her room. For decades I thought that "Katie Marvin" was Death calling for my grandmother. During her own terminal illness, Mom corrected that impression and told me, matter-of-factly, "No. Katie Marvin was a Witch." While going through Mom's things after she passed, I came across a flea market purchase of a brown-edged old paperback, *Witches;*

The Sixth Sense, by Justine Glass, so that would have been the picture my mother carried of her daughter, the Witch.

Even now, I have never told my father. He uses the "W" word to describe his estranged second wife, and has absolutely no 'worldly wisdom' when it comes to anything outside his closed world. His racism of my adolescence has subsided and he actually buys gifts for my 'mixed' daughter and her children, but I can't expect him to step much farther outside of his safety zone. We didn't speak for thirty-some years because of my choice of husbands, and I have no reason to revisit that period, or to reintroduce it to my world.

Setting the concept of reincarnation aside for a moment, I believe that, despite the validity of past life experiences, we were incarnated in our current gender and ethnicity for a specific purpose this time around. My own daughter is 'mixed,' her father having been Afro-American. While we had a pretty healthy mix of black and white influence in her formative years, and she has always been aware of my Craft involvement and respected it, she has never expressed a desire to study. Her own spirituality connects to an Afro-Baptist path and through it she has had some pretty extraordinary religious experiences. As it is my ethnic heritage, with a bit of Native American ancestry, I am comfortable with my Celtic path. She would not be. As for my teenage granddaughter, she asks questions about my 'meditation' work, but doesn't quite have a handle on the concept of deity as feminine. Yet...!

The Craft was far more secretive in those early years! We told no one what we were. We wore minimal 'Craft' jewelry (partially because it was so hard to find). There was no media coverage to speak of and so very few books on the market. Our numbers were few, and we were geographically spread out.

There were Craft "courtesies" to be observed. One group didn't just ask another Witch to join it for a Sabbat. One High Priestess/High Priest would almost formally invite the other High Priestess/High Priest. Later full covens might be invited. Secrecy was observed as a matter of safety. We only knew each other's street names and home addresses if we formed friendships and exchanged that information. I think it made covens tighter 'organizations.' When one joined a Gardnerian training group, it wasn't part of a smorgasbord of inquiry. One had to show that he or she was serious about that path and that path only.

Only the High Priestess and High Priest could speak for the Craft then; i.e., do interviews or write articles. This ensured a more consistent or 'official' picture of the Craft coming from a 'veteran' rather than a novice, and it prevented a myriad of interpretations being broadcast. Nowadays everybody is an authority!

'Then' we showed up at every meeting because it was our felt duty, not a social occasion. More recently, I've seen that theater tickets can take precedence. Today it seems that people bounce around a whole lot more until they decide on a tradition or group. A couple of years ago a woman asked me to be her teacher. I told her that I was relocating some 500 miles away. She then decided to simply start her own group!

I found personally that there was power in being 'the hidden children' of the Goddess, for power shared is power diluted. Attend any open Pagan festival and find a plethora of vacuous-eyed groupies who 'wannabe' a Witch and tell me why we should have to battle that level of idiocy to defend our desired image of being serious practitioners. I never expected or wished that there would be a 'Pagan temple on every corner.' More often than not, I'd like to have it the way it was! Those who wanted to follow the Path found it—sometimes with difficulty—and learned from a teacher, not a 'pulp-fiction' how-to book by either a plagiarist or a fraud. (Gads! I'm jaded!)

ROGER PRATT is both a hereditary Witch and an initiate of the Gardnerian Tradition. He teaches Tarot and other metaphysical subjects in the New York area.

I was ten years old when I returned home from bowling with friends, convinced I could influence the bowling balls. I told my mother that I was a "Witch." Knowing that I was about to announce that to everyone I knew, she sat me down and told me, "Yes, in fact, you are, dear. So am I." My mum was concerned that I might have "a big mouth." She was a triple Scorpio and that may explain part of her "secrecy."

Eventually, after training with her (to my mum, the Craft was a solitary path), I began in 1970 to train with Marged Nichols in England. She introduced me to Donna Cole Schultz, and I was initiated as a Gardnerian at age twenty-one.

You know, in those days one could read EVERY new book on the market—AS it came out! In the 1960s—especially around 1968, thanks to Sybil Leek, psychedelics, and a big article in *Time Magazine* and a Hippie magazine called *Eye*, Craft began to rise in popularity. But pop-Satanism was often confused with the Craft. I was always most comfortable with the British Witches. My mum was from Edinburgh, Scotland, born in 1913, and my dad from Liverpool, born in 1904. I was also at home with the country Witches, often farmers, and people living in Middle America.

These days I am a solitary. After many years with the coven we separated, due to careers and distance coming between us. I went back to my mother's solitary type of practice. I am, however, quite public about my involvement. I guess my mum's "big mouth" prediction came true!

I do continue to teach in classroom situations, and personally and privately, more as a consultant. Tarot and divination skills are my specialty. I've achieved some fame as a reader, and I like teaching skills that everyone can use. I sometimes give personal teachings regarding circle casting, consecrations, psychic protection, and meditation techniques. I also teach a course in Celtic Magic.

Georgian

THE GEORGIAN TRADITION was founded in 1970 by George (Pat) Patterson, Zanoni Silverknife and Tanith. It began as a small coven in Pat's home, at 1908 Verde Street, Bakersfield, CA. Soon after forming the group, Pat applied to the State of California for legal status as an incorporated church and through the Universal Life Church had a charter (1971) and Ministerial credentials for himself and Zanoni.

Pat received early teachings from members of a Celtic Coven in Boston. When World War II began, Pat enlisted in the Armed Forces and served for four years. On his return to Boston, he found that family members had destroyed his Book and ritual items. He could not find the family he had studied with. He did not find any other Witches for a long time, but he never gave up hope of finding his brothers and sisters of the Craft. In, 1970, at 52 years of age, Pat began a magical calling that resulted in Zanoni and Tanith finding him and helping to found the Georgian Tradition. Their first student, Bobbie Kennedy, came along shortly thereafter.

Pat gathered information, lessons and lore from many helpful sources. These included Doris and Sylvester Stuart of England, Lady Gwen of the New England Covens of Traditionalist Witches (N.E.C.T.W.), Ed Fitch of the Gardnerian Tradition and others. The Georgian Tradition is based on Gardnerian and Alexandrian practices, and Etruscan lore, using those rites and rituals shared by the Sylvestrians and N.E.C.T.W. as well as material from New York Covens of Traditionalist Witches (N.Y.C.T.W.) Lord Hermes, Ed Buczynski and Lady Siobhan (Order of the Silver Wheel) were most helpful.

Pat produced the Georgian Newsletter which was read throughout the United States. He devoted his life to teaching the Craft until his death in 1984.

Georgians are now world-wide and growing; many are in the Armed Forces, carrying the Tradition with them. Recently, there has been an upsurge in those interested in reconnecting with or learning about the Georgian Tradition.

ZANONI SILVERKNIFE was one of the founders of the Georgian Tradition in the USA. She is Head Mistress of Starborn Sothis and a founding and charter member of Covenant of the Goddess (CoG). Zanoni was one of the earlier contributors to the magazines *Green Egg, The Crystal Well* and *Magickal Times*.

I was always considered "weird" by my family, due to the things I knew and could do. At seven my remembrances and visions began and I knew not to speak of them. I began to experience out-of-body Goddess contact at eleven years old. By fourteen I danced to the moon in an abandoned field near my home and, at sixteen I began to recall past lives with some detail. I knew that I was not the same as other people and felt I would be forever alone and apart.

When I was about twenty-four years old, I was dating a DJ who took me to a friend's home to play cards. There they began to tell me about a man they knew who considered himself to be a Witch. It frightened me, and I didn't want to discuss it with them. About a year after that I came across an article in the *Coronet* magazine on Witches featuring Sybil Leek, Ray and Rosemary Buckland and Louise Huebner. I was intrigued with the three spells they presented, though one included the use of a

Tonka bean, and I hadn't a clue as to what this was or even how to obtain one. I decided to try the other two spells. I figured "it couldn't hurt"! They worked—amazingly so! I still remember those spells by heart!

I read Sybil's *Diary of a Witch* and Nora Loft's *Little Wax Doll*, the only books I could find at the time. I developed a burning obsession to learn more, to KNOW. I felt that if I did not learn about the Craft I would literally die inside.

I remembered the "Witch" my date's friend had talked about and set out to locate him. I learned his name was Pat Patterson and that he was an engineer for a local radio station. I called the station and asked for him. A deep, male voice came on the line and answered me very cautiously. When I told him I was looking for a Witch, he wanted to know how I had found him. Suffice to say I made an appointment with him, telling him my girlfriend would be coming along as well.

That day in 1970 was the beginning of the Craft for me and my friend, Tanith, and the foundation and formation of the Georgian Tradition. I had finally arrived home. Pat is gone now, and I miss him. I do feel him close every once in a while, and I hear his laughter echoing in my mind. (Blessed Be, Pat. See ya next time!)

My family became aware of my association with the Craft fairly early on. My parents were afraid, repulsed, horrified, angered and disgusted. My father is a minister and refused to come into my home without his bible tucked firmly under his arm. My mother went along with him. They are good people who follow their own path, but cannot understand that I must carve out my own. On the other hand, my brothers and sisters thought it was pretty neat and "far-out" at the time. Now, it's just their big sister's way.

My son and daughter were five and three when I began practicing the Craft. They have not chosen to follow the Craft as their religion, but the philosophy (the important part to me) is well ingrained in their psyches. There are grandchildren now, too, and for them I preserve all the lore and materials against the day when I may not be able to pass it on orally.

Craft, in those days, was exciting and mysterious, steeped in the lore of ages and yet raw and new. There was little literature available to us in those days and we clung selfishly to every scrap of information we could dredge up. There was a vitality to the growth of new avenues of learning, new ways to do things, new groups springing up like weeds in a garden of flowers (and believe me, many WERE weeds). It was all about discovery, both inner and outer. It was a birthing out of stale and meaningless morays, through the pain of familial disapproval and social ostracism. It was a time of pioneering in the Spiritual realm. It was a time of persecution by the ignorant, fearful and stupid, a time of fighting for tolerance in an unbending world. To quote the famous line: "It was the best of times; it was the worst of times," as is each new time of change.

We had very few people to network with in the beginning, and those few became extended, beloved family. Many of those early contacts have either been swallowed up in the mists of time or have gone to Summerland. Some of the people I was in contact with in those early days were: Gwen Thompson, Doris and Sylvester Stuart of England, Fred and Martha Adler, Rolla Nordic, Ed Buczynski, Ed Fitch, Leo Martello, Bonnie Sherlock, Gwydion, Dana Corby, Joe Wilson, Tony Kelly, Etidorhpa, Bill Mohs, Tommy Zielinsky, Victor Anderson, Siobhan, and many lovely people I met during the forming of CoG. There are others, but they are very private people. A great deal of sharing went on in those early days; sharing from the heart.

Though we lacked the materials and books to work with that are available to modern Pagans today, what we did have was a strength of knowledge that comes from actually delving inside ourselves, practicing the Craft in the way it was meant to be practiced. We had a depth of feeling, a sacredness of Circle.

Keepers of the
Ancient Mysteries
(K.A.M.)

K.A.M. IS AN ALEXANDRIAN-based tradition that was formed in 1973 when initiated members of recognized traditions were brought together by Fate and circumstance. Gwen Thompson was also an influence in the teachings. The founder and head of K.A.M. was Morganna Davies, an Alexandrian High Priestess. In time new covens were born and K.A.M. was incorporated in the State of Maryland as a Witchcraft Religion.

The K.A.M. Newsletter was published for several years with subscriptions world-wide and copies of the Newsletter available in Maryland public libraries. Each coven within K.A.M. follows a specific emphasis such as Greek, Celtic, Egyptian, etc. A basic training coven has also been retained to ensure that the basic teachings are passed on to all involved. On completion of training and advancement through the degree system, the initiate may found a new coven. The inter-connectedness allows a free exchange of information between covens in a family atmosphere. The system was designed to maintain the Alexandrian base and to ensure a quality training system universal to K.A.M. covens.

Morganna remained at the head of K.A.M. until 1979 when she turned it over to her daughter, Ayeisha, who remained at the helm until her death in 1998. Before her passing, she turned the responsibility for K.A.M. over to Trivia Prager. At Imbolc of 2000 Morganna formed the New England K.A.M. (N.E.K.A.M.).

AYEISHA was High Priestess of the Keepers of the Ancient Mysteries (K.A.M.), and a renowned Tarot teacher and reader. She taught classes on Craft and lectured at East Coast schools and universities. She was a frequently featured guest on television and radio programs. Before her death on August 27, 1998 she turned over the responsibility for the Mid-Atlantic K.A.M. to Trivia Prager.

I came to the Craft over twenty-five years ago. Before that time I was not as interested in the Craft as I was in magic, a magical lodge. My mother, Morganna Davies, was initiated into the Alexandrian Tradition a year and a half before me. At first, I wanted to investigate the Craft to find out whom my mother was involved with and whether they were all crazy. But once I connected with the spirituality, I realized that this was what I needed along with the ceremonial magic.

My mother has been pursuing her spirituality ever since I can remember, and my family has always been very tolerant of many traditions. So they were very pleased about my involvement with the Craft. After my son was born, I thought long and hard about whether or not to teach him the Craft. I absolutely did not want my child brain-washed into a particular system. I think that the challenge of whether or not to teach children the Craft is an on-going debatable struggle. I felt it was important to expose him to many different philosophies. He attended Circle up until the age of sixteen, but I also made sure he had trips to ashrams and monasteries and other spiritual religious centers as well. I definitely made sure he wasn't exposed to the more frightening, negative aspects of the last 2,000 years or so, which have a big emphasis on scare tactics in order to keep people in line. Just look at the idea of heaven and hell. Hell is a pretty darned negative, scary place. And if young children are exposed to that concept, I think that it influences them in a very profound way which is very difficult to shake later. So I've tried to keep my son away from that sort of thing, but in reality, it's almost impossible. Christianity, Judaism, Islam, whatever—they permeate all parts of our lives, our society. I believe they're insidious. Even in a courtroom people used to swear on a Bible that had to do with that particular system. But you know, I think that if I had it to do over again, I would have my son in more Circles and would probably work more actively with him. I wanted him to be free to choose, and that's at least something that has been achieved. In a traditional Wiccaning ceremony, you don't indoctrinate a child into that particular religion, and you don't promise that they will be adherents of that tradition. What is done is that you ask for blessings of health, intellect and wisdom that will serve the child. The doorway is opened to the fact that there are many paths to the Gods. So, we celebrate choice and ask for blessings and protection for the children until the time when they are grown so that they can take on their own journey.

When I began, the Craft was very specific. It said exactly what it was, that it was an apostolic initiatory tradition, and people took it a lot more seriously and worked harder than they tend to do today. There is so much "pop-Wicca" available with very little effort. It's rather like taking people out of high school and putting them in college. There's a great deal more work to be done and demanded of you there. Certainly, even down to the fact that people had to work hard to make contacts and often travel through several states to be with teachers and to receive the Craft. I think people were just geared to work harder and more was expected of you. Also, when I began, there weren't Witches on television programs and on every corner wearing big tee shirts. There were only a few spiritual shops that were mostly holding forth with Christian magical traditions or the Eastern traditions like Hinduism or Buddhism. It wasn't as easy as just driving to the corner to find a teacher. You had to do a legitimate spiritual search, and when you were ready a teacher would appear. Becoming ready meant doing a lot of personal work. Today's Pagan culture is very diverse and generally that culture is much more interested in exploring and even creating new forms than in building on existing traditions. There's so much emphasis on the public role and how to present it to the public at large that I think it tends to dilute our traditions and to also force our traditions on an unwilling audience. The Neo-Pagan community today pretty much generally prefers media figures and rapid growth. This is not compatible with Traditional Craft, which has a relatively slow method of training and initiation. Traditional Craft places great emphasis on personal growth and your ability to live in harmony with the world at large and all the different creatures in it.

When I was first initiated, most Craft traditions kept to themselves. It was very difficult to make contact with anyone else in Craft, and traditions did not mix with one another. K.A.M. was unique in that people who were living in Maryland, who were all initiated in their own specific traditions came together. And most of them still had to travel some distance to receive training from their mother covens. But these people "happened" to connect with each other in a really interesting, magical way. It was very unusual to have people from different traditions practice together; it simply wasn't done. But these people became very close, and in the end, each of them brought a little bit of their own traditions and they put together a ceremony that included parts of each of those other traditions. It was an amazing thing to happen at that time, and there were very real suspicions about whether or not this ought to be done, and whether this was moving further away from Traditional Craft. But K.A.M. is still here, still functioning, and is still very traditional.

PATRICIA POTHIER (ANTIGONE) began her Craft journey in the Elefsinian /Mediterranean tradition and later came to the Keepers of the Ancient Mysteries (K.A.M.), where she remains an Elder. She was High Priestess of the Coven of Nea Elefsis.

I was born in San Francisco in 1933, the year that Hitler came to power. Hitler was to have a great influence on the course of my life, but I am getting ahead of my story.

San Francisco in the 1930s was peopled primarily by immigrants from Ireland, Italy, and China. But "Witch blood", if I have any, I got from my mother who came from an old family from Transylvania. (Yes, Virginia, there IS a place called Transylvania.) She never used the "W" (Witch) word, but whenever I had a problem of any sort, she would say, "Put it out of your mind and I will meditate on it." The problem always worked out in my favor.

My mother sent me to church on Sundays (the 9:00 a.m. "Children's Mass"), but she never accompanied me. I became friends with a group of Italian children; we were all motherless in church together. We talked about the things we were taught in church. Did one male God really create the heavens and the earth, the whole universe, just for the use and edification of MAN? And was the objective of all our striving really a heaven where there were no pussycats or puppy dogs because animals have no souls? Instant Darwinism.

My friendship with the Italians continued through high school. I was almost "family," and I was welcome at the full of the moon to attend the rituals of *la vecchia religione*.

In 1956 I left San Francisco and resettled in the District of Columbia. It was there, during the course of a brief hospitalization, that I met the person who became my teacher and friend for the rest of her life. I was lying on my bed with my pentagram boldly displayed on my hospital gown. (By this time I had read Gardner and Murray and considered myself Wiccan.) A nurse came into the room, saw it, and said, "Is that wise?" (Remember that Joe McCarthy was still in the U.S. Senate.) Her name was Barbara Leipelt, and she was High Priestess of the Coven of Nea Elefsis.

Barbara was born in Munich, Germany and had come to America after the Second World War. She was the sole survivor of her family, her two siblings having been murdered by the Gestapo for their part in a gallant but futile resistance movement. There were many such movements in Germany, formed around a revered priest or teacher. Most of them will never be known because Germany, unlike France and Poland, had no organized resistance; probably because there was no free German government in exile to direct it. Witchcraft, like astrology and all the other occult arts, was banned in Germany; not because the Nazis did not believe in them, but because they did. And if the stars were going to tell the Führer where to attack next, better that knowledge was not generally accessible. Barbara and her friends belonged to a group that had reconstructed—as far as possible—the teachings and rituals of the ancient mysteries of Eleusis, and these teachings she brought with her to America.

By the mid-sixties, the Coven of Nea Elefsis was flourishing. I had experienced the Mystery and gathered together the bits and pieces of knowledge from which I later taught. But Barbara was falling into the abyss. She begged me to go to Germany and find the graves of her friends, so that they might be reburied with proper rites. But people murdered in Gestapo prisons do not have graves. She had dreams that "so-and-so" was about to be arrested and I must warn "him". When she finally understood that "he" and all the others were twenty years dead, she turned the horror inward: She had survived and left her friends to die. One morning in April she said to me, "It is so much easier to be a ghost if one is dead." I never saw her in the sunshine again.

The Coven melted away, leaving me with only the name to honor and hold. Then a friend introduced me to Merlin, who lived close by in suburban Maryland. Merlin was an initiate of Gwen Thompson of the New England Covens of Traditional Witches (N.E.C.T.W.). With Gwen's permission I traveled to Connecticut to meet and begin study with her. It was during that time that Gwen learned of Morganna Davies' Alexandrian coven in Baltimore. Gwen contacted her and asked if Merlin could attend Sabbats there, rather than having to travel the long distance to Connecticut. Morganna agreed to this and Merlin introduced me to her. She accepted me as a student, despite the difference in traditions. Morganna opened whole new worlds for me and the mixture of traditions proved to be an asset, rather than a liability. It was around Morganna's dining room table that the Keepers of the Ancient Mysteries (K.A.M.) was born, nearly thirty years ago.

The K.A.M. flourished and grew. After receiving my Priestess degree, armed with new knowledge and more confidence, I decided to revive Nea Elefsis. For a number of years, Nea Elefsis was a wonderful place to be, and many daughter covens were born of it. But in its very success lay the seeds of its destruction. Coveners who were not even half-trained came to me, saying, "I've been here a year and a day; when do I get my second degree?" They didn't care about knowledge or ancient traditions; they wanted only power. They were like college students who care nothing for learning and want only the final piece of paper.

With a heavy heart I dissolved the Coven, but I learned something from the experience. I learned that the real enemies of Craft are not the fundamentalist Christians, who have always wanted to burn us at the stake, but the directionless mass of "New Age" Pagans, who will lose irretrievably the truths our ancestors died to preserve. They will not do it deliberately; but in their eagerness to assume the trappings, symbols and outward appearances of the Craft, they will not take the time to study its deeper meanings. And what they do not learn they cannot pass on. They will not even know what they have lost. Our ancestors died for the Craft but we must live for it, that it be passed on, whole and untarnished, to future generations. That is the challenge which confronts us now.

TRIVIA is High Priestess of the Mid-Atlantic K.A.M. She is an accomplished artist and Tarot card reader.

I came into Craft through the back door, through my art. If I had to put a date on it, it would be the ceramics course I took in the summer of '74. I met a woman named Rebecca and we became friends. She offered to read my cards and I thought I'd humor her and agreed. I found myself thinking, "Gee, she doesn't know me that well; there must be something to this card reading stuff." Rebecca considers herself a Witch although she isn't traditionally trained and initiated. In another time she would be considered a Hedge Witch. (She's since moved to California and become a master gardener.) She gave me my first deck of Tarot cards and taught me basic candle magic. (I realized I'd been doing that since I was old enough to put the dime in the slot and light a candle in front of the Virgin Mary.)

About the same time I was discovering that men and women had different reactions to my painting. Men would complement me on my use of color, while the women would get excited about my images. The work I was doing at the time evolved into what I called my "High Priestess Series" even though I didn't know any High Priestesses at all. I decided to find out why there was a gender variation in the reaction to my work.

I began haunting the 31st Street Book Store, which was a well-known feminist bookstore in Baltimore. I discovered Judy Chicago's "Through the Flower" and began collecting everything I could find on women artists. From there I worked my way through books like "The First Sex" and "Ancient Mirrors of Womanhood." I found Z. Budapest's mimeographed book and started doing simple rituals. Then came the fateful day that the proprietor slipped me a copy of the K.A.M. Newsletter. I read it and finally got up the nerve to write for more information. An application for student status followed, and I labored over my answers to the questions. I was privileged to be accepted as a student by Ayeisha.

As they say, the rest is history! I was a student on what I call the "ten year plan"—that is, I spent ten years going from Pagan student to Third Degree Initiate. In theory you could do it in three years and three days, but I truly think you need the time to process the information, practice it and make it your own.

I am for the most part still in the broom closet. I didn't want to upset my parents at their age and I earn my living teaching in a public school. I don't need bible-waving parents threatening my livelihood. A funny incident: one of my coworkers approached me one day, asking, "Are you a witch?" I lied and said, no. Then I realized what I was doing. This woman has some psychic skill, and she knows I'm lying. Ah, but she has common sense, she knows why I'm lying! We went along for some years, every so often she'd come to me and say, "I saw this person on TV and she said she's a Witch and she says they do thus-and-such. Do you?" And I'd answer her questions. I did finally come clean with her after my Third Degree Initiation. We're still good friends and keep in touch even though she's retired now.

Family was another story. Dad died the year before Ayeisha. I figured what he found out on the other side was what he found. When Ayeisha's obituary appeared in the local newspapers including mention of her Craft involvement, my mother hit the ceiling, "But I thought she was a nice person!" Yes, Mom, she was a nice person. You met her and you liked her. My mother hung up on me. I never said I was a Witch, but I didn't say I wasn't. My husband went ahead and told Mom the lie she wanted to hear. My youngest niece on the other hand cut right to the chase, "Does this mean that you're the head of K.A.M. now?" My sister didn't want to get caught in the middle; you can't tell what you don't know. She waited until after Mom's funeral to ask me if I was a Witch. So, now I'm out to my immediate family.

I have no children, so there was no issue of raising them in the Craft. From what I've seen, raising children in the Craft works if both parents are Craft. It can get messy in divorce cases and custody hearings.

As I've gotten older, I've become more conservative. When I was a beginning Pagan I wanted to tell the world. With each degree of initiation I found myself becoming more humble, more inclined to secrecy. It's as if the more I've learned, the more I want to protect the integrity of the Craft. I teach and have had a number of people come through my living room. Very few of them did I initiate. Those in a hurry didn't like my "ten year plan." Some were put off because I failed to see the greatness in them. I am left with a core group of relatively sane, stable adults who are prepared to teach the Craft as they had been taught.

The Keepers of the Ancient Mysteries began so that traditionally initiated Witches could find a common ground to practice together. As such it was a blend of traditions. After almost thirty years it has evolved into a tradition in itself.

Mohsian

THE MOHSIAN TRADITION began in California. It has particular roots in the European Mystery Traditions and consists of a combination of three main traditions: 1734, The Plant Bran and Gardnerian. Mohsian has also been influenced by the Boread Tradition through Thomas Giles. This combination of traditions into one harmonious whole gives the tradition its distinct flavor.

It is important to note that 'traditions', as are known today, did not exist at the time the Tradition began. The Elders knew, worked and shared with each other. The strong boundaries of separate 'traditions' did not come about until later. The Mohs were running a coven in 1965. They began using a "tradition" name around 1969: American Tradition or Eclectic American Tradition. In 1973–1974 the term "Mohsian" began being used in Corax Coven; the term stuck and has been in use ever since. The Moshian American Tradition is not the same as the Scott Cunningham American Tradition and bears no resemblance to his.

The influence of The Plant Bran brings a great depth of beauty to the tradition. 1734 Tradition adds a strong connection with European Shamanism and vision work. Most working Mohsian covens at this time are working with the Celtic pantheon and Celtic Patron Deities. The Gardnerian lineage came into the tradition in around 1969. Mohsians celebrate the Sabbats and the thirteen Esbats of the year. Initiation is usually preceded by an Outer Court rite of dedication. The three degree initiations are Gardnerian based and cross-gendered. Initiates are oath-bound; self-initiation is not practiced. Third Degree Elders and their covens are wholly autonomous. There is a strong feeling of family that runs through the tradition.

DANA CORBY is the senior-most practicing High Priestess of the Mohsian Tradition, with all known existing Moshian covens descending from her. An accomplished musician, she was featured in Gwydion Penderwen's *Songs for the Old Religion*. For the past two years, Dana and her husband and High Priest, Darrell Robyn, have headed up TERRA, a Wiccan/ Pagan community-building organization in Tacoma, Washington.

Remember that scene in the first Batman movie, where Bruce Wayne acknowledges to himself that he's obsessed but recognizes that without his obsession his usefulness would cease? Well, I'm like that about the Craft. Literally every facet of my life has value to me primarily in terms of my vocation as a Witch and Priestess.

I was twenty-four when I came into the Craft by a long and circuitous route. I always had a feeling that there was a thin veil between this reality and some other one. As a child, I loved old places for their atmosphere and the feeling that at any moment the dead might step through the veil and I would be able to see into the past as it had happened in that place. I also came from a family where the idea of psychic ability was not scoffed at; my parents often exhibited a marked degree of telepathy between themselves, but not with others. I can recall sitting on the sofa with my mother watching TV while my father was out in the garage working, having her remark, "Gee, I wish your father'd come in; this is a good show," and then having him burst in a moment later asking if she'd called. So when a teacher brought in a set of Zener cards for the class to play with, I was intrigued. And while I tested out flat normal, it awakened in me the knowledge that it was possible to develop psychic ability, and a desire to do so.

In my teens the family converted to Mormonism. Within about five years I realized that I couldn't conform to that belief system, largely on the basis of their views on sexuality and their treatment of women, and left not just Mormonism but the entire Christian world-view. For the next several years I experimented with various alternative beliefs, from spiritualism to Zen. I began feeling that I was a Witch with no real idea what a Witch was, except that all the various threads I was following led there. I knew that Nature was holy and that magic was possible. Then in about 1970 I stumbled upon the first edition of *The Witches' Almanac* and within weeks, a book on Witchcraft by Hans Holzer. It took another year and a lot sending out energy to find a teacher, but at last I found Sara Cunningham's now-legendary Stonehenge shop in Pasadena, California. My then-partner and I attended one of her classes, were thoroughly grilled by the existing students, and joined the student group. We were members of Sara's First Church of Tiphareth for about a year and a half. And it was actually at a joint Yule ritual with another coven that we met the people who would eventually become our initiators, Bran and Moria.

The Craft in the late sixties and early seventies was still, on the whole, very much as it is portrayed in Paul Huson's *Mastering Witchcraft*. There was much more emphasis on magic and less on theology. And there wasn't this present-day timidity about exercising power; one angered a Witch at one's peril. The Witch expected to take her Karmic lumps if she blasted someone who didn't deserve it, but she believed she had a right to make that kind of judgment because she was a Witch. The Craft was based primarily on folklore, rather than on anthropology and ethnography as seems to be the case today. Not that I'm disparaging the anthropologists; without them there might not have been a modern Witchcraft, and with them our understanding has been broadened and enriched in many and wonderful ways. But Witchcraft was an art of the people, not the intelligentsia. Its values of simple living and being creative with what was available, of acting powerfully but subtly to change one's life for the better, are being lost in a welter of scholarly discussions of Indo-European language root words and culture comparisons of Great Mother archetypes.

There are some things about the Old Ways that I'm glad are mostly gone, like the tendency of coven leaders to keep their people isolated from other groups and to control their access to information. Today's information "banquet" is a godsend to the Neophyte. Yet, at least on a leader-to-leader level, what information there was, was shared open-handedly with no regard for copyright or recompense. Herman Slater's publishing of *The Pagan Way* material broke an unspoken contract of long-standing, and ended what had been a utopian, collectivist ideal that was at the root of the modern Pagan movement.

The times being what they were, there was more experimentation with drugs in a ritual context as well as more sexual experimentation, both as a means to express spirituality and/or to raise energy. I understand that some in the wider Pagan movement are experimenting both with drugs and sexual practices that most of us old Traditionalists wouldn't even recognize as sex. But I'm old-fashioned; I hope to hell their wards are up.

LORAX is a Craft Elder and Druid who teaches meditation, traditional martial arts and Physical Culture. He is a filidh (ritual poet) in training. He has written and lectured extensively on theological realities of the Craft and Craft histories. With his wife and High Priestess, Erynn Rowan Laurie, he is co-founder of the Inis Glas Hedge School and Celtic Reconstructionism.

I am from an initiatory path. I feel that all paths are initiatory, regardless of how one gets there, because one is always a beginner, whether by birth or acceptance into a group. It would be possible to be born within a family and rejected, or leave. While in high school I had the experience of the numinosity of the trees and forests that convinced me to pursue this Craft. I found my first and best teacher right after high school. For a number of years, my family was unaware of my interests. When they did find out, they reacted with shock and horror, and at one point tried to have me committed to an institution.

Looking back, I would say that the Craft was possibly more pompous, secretive and abusive within a coven structure than it is today. However, the scale of the power games that are now played by national organizations would have been inconceivable then. The amount of money that seems to be required (by some) for study would have sickened teachers who have passed on. Today, the Craft (generally called Wicca, though it wasn't then) is often sold as a political movement, or therapy that can make one feel good, fight the patriarchy, or be something meaningful to do with one's life. While all of these things can be the results that follow good ritual, and a spiritually guided life, there is a surprising silence on the part of many national leaders as to the reality of magic, magical results, or deity. I would like to hear more discussion in these areas.

Twenty, even ten years ago there was less focus on environmental concerns and the implication that divinity within Nature, or Nature as divine, held for Crafters. While the impulse may have been there to respect and preserve nature, I think that reflection on our economy, our lives, and the insights of the ecologists have improved our understanding of the interconnectedness of things and have given us good tools. Another difference was that magic and the transpersonal existence of deities, not just archetypes, were commonly accepted as being real and capable of impacting the world. Many people came to the Craft after a transformative experience of personal deity, or a similar numinous experience. Today, there seems to be almost a push for the Craft as a political statement.

Both my wife (my High Priestess) and I continue to teach. We provide training in meditation, devotional and trance techniques, culturally relevant materials form Insular Celtic cultures, and a Celtic world-view that is appropriate to this era, and this place (the Pacific Northwest). I also provide a certain amount of impersonal teaching by making some materials available through festivals and/or the Internet. I would assume that I reach far more people than I ever could in person. However, one sacrifices depth of understanding and the all-important dialog in impersonal teaching.

New England Covens of Traditionalist Witches (N.E.C.T.W.)

THE NEW ENGLAND COVENS OF Traditionalist Witches (N.E.C.T.W.) was brought into the public in the late 1960's. The Tradition was originally named by Gwen Thompson, a hereditary Witch from New Haven, CT. Gwen's family tradition blended with popular occultism and was handed down through many generations to its present form. The origin is pre-Adamic and emphasizes magic, spirituality, legends, and lore. Gwen's teachings have founded or influenced many Traditions in the United States. A book on Gwen and her life is forthcoming.

The N.E.C.T.W. is a center for Covens of Traditionalist origin. It is a place for men and women to be trained as priests and priestesses of the Craft. The need for diversity within groups of the Tradition is recognized, but basic common principles and practices are taught to all in order to maintain the common thread between groups.

The practice is informal and Initiates think of themselves as a family group. The eight Sabbats of the year are observed as well as the thirteen Full Moon Esbats. Circles are held outdoors, weather permitting. Initiates are robed, and ritual worship and magic are practiced in circle The Tradition is Goddess oriented but recognizes the triad of the Goddess and the God. The Tradition emphasizes interest in ecology, herbal lore, astrology, Tarot, and divination, and an extensive reading list is maintained.

MARSHA BARD (LENURA) is High Priestess of the Beach Coven in Florida. She was raised in a family tradition and as an adult was initiated into the New England Covens of Traditionalist Witches (N.E.C.T.W.) She is a member of the Ceremonial Magic Tradition, the Order of the Evening Star, a branch of the Society of the Evening Star (S.O.T.E.S.)

J was initiated into a family tradition as a "daughter" of Chris Carpenter, High Priestess, although I was not her genetic daughter. It was a curious thing that Chris and her husband, Christopher, had the same name. The woman who lived upstairs from my grandmother was a Witch, and from the time I could remember anything at all I remember being involved with the Craft. At the time it was simply a way of life until I was about six years old. I remember playing outside in my grandmother's garden when the little boy next door yelled over the fence, "You're living with Witches—you must be a Witch too," and threw a stone at me. I didn't know what offended me, but I knew I had been offended and jumped over the fence and beat up that little boy. I think I've been in the position of defending the Craft ever since against the misinformation that runs rampant through our society.

My father was oriented toward the American Indian culture and always insisted that the one God of Christianity was not a believable theory. He often pointed out the work of the Sun God, or the Lightning God, and he communicated with the God of the Winds and Mother Moon. My mother, on the other hand, had been raised a devout Christian. Although she never tried to turn me in that direction, she never really understood my beliefs until much later in life when she fell ill with cancer.

I spent a great deal of time with the Carpenters. Once when I was badly hurt and bleeding, Chris carried me up to her apartment and laid me on her kitchen table. She began to sing as she put a pan on the stove and put some "huge" leaves in the water. Then she took the leaves from the water and wrapped them around my arms and legs, all the time singing her song. Then she told me a story about the Goddess. I remember feeling so warm and protected. I healed with no visible scars or marks.

When Mr. Carpenter died, he was not sent to a funeral home, but was "laid out" in their living room. Chris insisted I attend the funeral. Only the coven and friends were there. At one point, Chris asked everyone but me to leave the room. Chris told me it was my turn to say goodbye and instructed me to touch Mr. Carpenter's face as I said my words of farewell. When I touched his cheek, it was hard and cold, and I was taken aback. Chris held me gently in her arms and told me the Craft story of death and the Summerland. Then she told me that my touch had brought Mr. Carpenter back so that I could see him one more time and know that he was okay. She told me to look over in the corner at his chair and as I looked, I saw him there, smiling at me. He told me that he wasn't going away, but that he was changing. He said I would feel him always, not in the apartment, but in the trees and in the flowers that bloomed in the spring. I turned to look at Chris and when I looked back, he was gone.

The Craft I grew up with had an oral tradition. To my knowledge, there was nothing written down. There was no Book of Shadows, although from time to time, I do remember people signing pieces of paper. I was initiated at age twelve, just before I turned thirteen, and I never had to sign anything. To this day, I don't know what was signed or why, but those pieces of paper were placed under various items around the Carpenters' apartment—sometimes under or behind a mirror, sometimes under a statue. I remember very well the healing circles that were held and the flowers that were used. Chris had a greenhouse in the back yard and grew the beautiful flowers that were used. In the winter, we all made paper flowers. I was taught to sing songs into the flowers and then dip them in hot wax to seal in the energy. These were made into bouquets and delivered to those who requested them.

I still honor those teachings I received from the Carpenters and will continue to sprinkle them liberally throughout the teachings I pass on to my initiates.

DEVON is High Priestess of the Coven of Minerva in Rhode Island. She also founded Starseed Coven. She remains a member and officer of the Ceremonial Magic Tradition, the Order of the Evening Star (S.O.T.E.S.).

My first experience with actual Craft working and actually finding a word for what I was doing was through books. In the late fifties and early sixties, there were precious few of those. I practiced solitary for quite a number of years partly because of constant moving (my family was military) and partly because I never found anyone who could tell me something that I couldn't find in books. Peripherally my family knew but never saw any harm in it. I think they thought it was "a phase" that would pass.

Those early years were bleak. There were very few public Craft people. There was a system of knowing someone who knew someone who knew someone else in the Craft. But if you were tenacious and patient you could, through a series of introductions, finally get to the people who could help you. A lot of the Craft in the state was very underground.

Then I finally met people who seemed to have a pretty solid background in Craft and in time I was initiated. I'm a part of N.E.C.T.W. which is based on the teachings and traditions from Gwen Thompson. I believe that Gwen's decision to initiate people and pass on the teachings, stories, and practices of her hereditary tradition was one of the greatest things that any Elder could do. It ensures that our Craft and beliefs will not fade away through time.

I teach initially as much basic training as is necessary—magical workings, herbs, cultural mythology, astrology, etc. What I can't personally teach, I generally find other Craft people to help with the training. As a person progresses, the training becomes adaptable to the individual, with deeper emphasis on certain subjects.

I feel it is up to all of us as Priestesses, Priests, and Elders to carry on our practices and traditions in a responsible manner. Changing with the times is inevitable and promotes mental growth. But the Old Ways should not be set aside. They should be remembered and honored for what they have given us and the teachings should be passed on with respect. There is so much to be learned by all of us, and the ability to communicate not only with our peers but with the world remains an awesome responsibility. My heart, body and spirit are Craft, and may it ever be so. May we walk the Path together.

ETIDORHPA was High Priestess of the Crystal Coven for many years. She founded and published *The Hollow Hassle Newsletter* and over the years has been featured in various publications including *Fate Magazine*.

I had been exploring different religions for quite some time but hadn't found the right one for me. Then I found a book by Sybil Leek. It was published sometime during the sixties and talked about growing herbs and her life and little touches of her religion. It was enough to pique my interest. I found other books after that, one of which was June John's *King of the Witches*. I knew of no one here in the States, and if they were here, they were underground or very low key. Finally I was able to locate Alex Sanders in England and wrote to him. He forwarded my letter to Mary Nesnick, an Alexandrian High Priestess in New York City. We corresponded for about a year before she would agree to meet with me and others she had been corresponding with. She flew to San Francisco to meet with all twelve or thirteen of us who flew in from different areas of the country at our own expense. I remember we stayed at the Sheraton Hotel. Mary's Priest was a law partner with a well-known firm, and we were taken aside separately and questioned by them. The questions were "grilling" and I really didn't think any of us would pass muster. In the end, she sent most of them home, except for myself and a clinical psychologist who later became my first High Priest. We were both initiated in San Francisco. I lived in West Los Angeles and he lived in Thousand Oaks, but we managed to overcome the distance in order to work together.

It was about eight years after my initiation that I learned that my paternal grandmother and great-grandmother from Ireland were involved in the Craft. Unfortunately, I never knew them. Both of my children were eventually initiated. While they don't actively practice, it is still their religion of choice. (Of course, anytime something goes wrong, it's "Mom, we need you to help...")

I came into the Craft in the late sixties, and it was quite different from today. The only public people I knew of were the Priestess who initiated me, the Bucklands, and a very few others like Martha and Fred Adler. Information was hard to come by. I believe that those of us who came in during those times had to be very dedicated because it took us a long time to be able to learn what we needed to know. When I think about our initiations—you know, I had to fly from Los Angeles to Baltimore at my expense for both my second and third degree Alexandrian initiations from Morganna Davies. It wasn't as though you had someone down the street to go to.

I ran an Alexandrian Coven for some years. During that time, I married Tom LeVesque. Morganna flew out for the wedding, and she and Rick McGrew who was a friend of Sybil Leek, stood for us. Then, at Sybil's invitation, we all four went to visit with her at her home in Las Vegas. I hadn't met Sybil before, and I must say she was impressive (I hadn't realized she was so tall). After staying the night and next day, we left and went back to California. It was Morganna who later introduced me via correspondence to Gwen Thompson, who headed the New England Covens of

Traditional Witches (N.E.C.T.W.). Gwen and I corresponded for some time, and I eventually flew to New Haven, Connecticut to meet her. We learned we were born on the same day but different years. We became close, and I was eventually anointed into that Tradition, which I practice to this day. Gwen is gone now, and she is sorely missed.

I don't run a coven anymore, but I do think that if someone very special came along, I would teach on a one-to-one basis. When I was running a coven I wasn't as open to the public as many others were. I'm more apt to want to be underground, but I believe we also need those who will take the public forefront and teach others.

 **GWION is High Priest of the Triple Star Coven in New Jersey. Originally initiated into the New York Welsh Tradition, he traced the sources of this Trad, and form the Welsh Rite, a branch of NECTW. The components which comprise the Welsh Rite are descended from the family practices of Gwen Thompson. Gwion reconciled the philosophical differences between the Celtic and Welsh branches of the line, thereby grafting the Welsh Rite Traditionalist Gwyddoniaid back onto the "root" NECTW lineage.**

I came to the Craft at a early age. My interest started as a young boy of 10 years old. Like many I was drawn in part because of the glamour associated with Witchcraft. My thirst for knowing what it was to be a Witch would eventually lead me to a local used book store in Brooklyn when I about twelve years old. I frequented the bookstore as often as possible spending hours going through their occult section, acquiring as many books as I could. Eventually, I worked up the nerve to ask the shop owner if he knew of any Witches or warlocks. To my amazement, he looked in his rolodex and came up with a number for a "warlock." This same (as I was soon to be corrected) Witch recommended that I contact Herman Slater at the Warlock Shop/ Magickal Childe. Within six months I joined the outer court of the Welsh Tradition, Earth Star Temple Coven. My mother was frantic. She absolutely forbade me to go to the Magickal Childe. She would search and find my hidden grimoires and destroy them. I persisted, however, and after two years of training there, I was initiated at age sixteen. My initiation at such a young age was unheard of at the time, and there was a great deal of controversy in the Traditional community because of it.

During that period of Craft, homosexuality was very much frowned upon. It was very difficult being gay, much less being "out." So at age nineteen I was given initiation into the Minoan Brotherhood by Edmund M. Buczynski. I continued with the Brotherhood until 1990. I believe that most Minoans in the USA are descended from me. However, Welsh Trad was always at the heart of who I am, and so in 1990 I returned to my roots. Knowing that Gwen Thompson had a great influence on the Welsh Tradition, I sought out the N.E.C.T.W. to solve the ritual and philosophical differences between the two traditions. After meeting and working with the N.EC.T.W. the Welsh Rite came into being.

The Craft then was more strict than it is today. Books were few and far between and there were no "self-initiated" or "eclectic" people out there. One typically spent time in an outer court before being initiated into a coven that was traditionally based. My coven, Triple Star Coven has gone through as many changes as I have over its life. Since its birth in 1990, it has grown and changed to better fit the needs of its members. We are a small coven concentrating on the "high magic" of Circle. Ritual and the experience of it is given precedence above all else. Our training includes both folk and scholarly teachings, but the why and how of Circle are stressed over all other teachings.

My advice to all who are new to the Craft is to take your time to find a language that you understand. Surely if you don't take this time you will fail.

OWEN ROWLEY was High Priest to Gwen Thompson of N.E.C.T.W. in the early 1970's.

I always knew I was a Witch, but I also knew I was NOT the kind of Witch that was the common misconception in the era of my youth. I felt deeply that my personal spiritual path was rooted in the Occult and I began formulating my own magical rituals before puberty. In the late 1960's I became aware that Witchcraft was not the same as Satanism or Devil worship, that it was still alive as a remnant of an ancient faith. I determined that I would find my way to the Craft. My search eventually led me to Gwen Thompson and the N.E.C.T.W. I count myself fortunate to have found my way to her door, and even more fortunate that she took me in and taught me the ways of the Old Tradition.

My mother was aware of my interest in the Occult. She even had some interest in it herself and when I took initiation, I thought she would take it in stride so I told her about it without hesitation. I don't ever remember my mother going to church on her own, so it was a complete shock to me that she was upset about my initiation into the Craft. Next thing I knew, she had a bible in her hands. I don't know where she got it from; I never remembered her even owning a bible! It was kind of funny!

My Priestess, Gwen, was the epitome of Magic. She wielded the power of the spoken word with natural ease, and opened the gates between the worlds at will when she had need. While a few media-mad Witches made public spectacles of themselves with rote repetition of public domain material, Gwen moved behind the scenes seeding gems from her family tradition and changing the landscape of the Neo-Pagan revival which flourished in the last quarter of the twentieth century.

I've recently undertaken the training of one student, but it is training in a form that does not follow my own initiated tradition. This student is an extraordinary individual who has a very high public profile in the technical/internet industry. He is acclaimed as an Internet visionary and futurist author. He is also an accomplished author and wields enormous influence on the shape of future technological directions. We weave a Techno Pagan web as the fulfillment of ancient promises. Our task today is to keep the secrets sacred not to keep the sacred secret.

THEITIC is High Priest of the Coven of Minerva in Rhode Island and serves as Historian for the N.E.C.T.W. Tradition. He is a founding member of the Order of the Evening Star (S.O.T.E.S.), a Temple of Ceremonial Magic since 1977 and is also an initiate of the Alexandrian/K.A.M. Tradition.

I was interested in Nature, plants, animals, and magic as far back as I can remember. I began reading about the Craft during the late sixties and early seventies. I searched for the right group from 1973 to 1975; then had to wait until I was of age before I could be initiated. My initiation took place in 1976 into the family tradition of Gwen Thompson.

My family was aware of my interests, and I tried to keep my involvement above board without being pushy. Most of them had little or no negative reaction. Coming from an Old World Italian family, some of my Craft practices fit right in with what other members of the family did every day. This made things a lot easier. My aunt bought me my first book on the Craft and my grandmother helped me make my first robe.

In the early seventies, the Craft in New England was still very much underground. There were no open circles, public groups, new age tapes (or videos, CDs, computer programs, etc.); in short you had to really search to find a contact. I began by hanging around the occult section of the local bookstores watching for someone who was wearing black and might also be wearing some silver jewelry. At that time, the occult section of a large bookstore would typically have a dream dictionary or a couple of books by Sybil Leek (usually including *Diary of a Witch* and *The Complete Art of Witchcraft*), Dr. Rhine (various titles on ESP), Paul Huson (*Mastering Witchcraft*), Leo Martello (*Ancient and Modern Witchcraft*) or Hans Holzer (a vast collection of materials on unusual phenomena and people).

I can't remember when or how I found them, but I did write to *Green Egg*, *Earth Religion News* and *Gnostica News*. (Does anyone remember when Llewellyn published something for free?). People really took their time writing back in those days. There was no e-mail, the fax machine hadn't been invented yet, and stamps cost five cents.

After searching for a very long time, I finally found a functioning coven in Rhode Island. The members of this coven, just like most Witches of the time, faced many problems. People lost their jobs, had car windows smashed, received Christian hate mail and were rejected by family and "friends." They also faced many of the same problems that other minorities faced. Imagine what it would be like to be a black or homosexual Witch in 1971! Our religion has always attracted the minorities and the unusual. This is probably because so many of the mainstream religions reject different or non-conforming people. For many of our kind, survival became the first law of the land.

In the mid-nineties I received initiation and cross-training into the K.A.M. where I also serve as High Priest to the Phoenix Rising Coven.

I am presently the Priest of two very active covens. As an individual, I am public. The Coven of Minerva is mentioned in some source books, but is basically underground. We aren't easy to find in the Rhode Island community. I do teach students, but I would prefer to call it "coaching." The Craft is handed down from teacher to student by way of experience and those experiences are individual and unlimited. The Wise Ones guide us through these experiences, they do not provide us with a specific set of instructions. I have found that my coven learns best outside the "classroom" environment: on the beach, in the woods, by a fireplace or over a cup of tea. Although any life experience is worth sharing, our coven focuses its training on divination, magic and meditation.

Ravenwood

Ravenwood Church and Seminary of the Old Religion was founded by Sintana at Samhain 1977 in Atlanta, Georgia as an incorporated non profit religious organization. Since its inception Ravenwood's mission has been focused on public education and awareness of Wiccan beliefs and practices. Ravenwood's open door policy made the church available to any interested parties twenty four hours a day, seven days a week. Though these times were often turbulent, Ravenwood persevered in its public ministry and ultimately won several critical legal battles gaining state and federal recognition for Wicca as an accepted religious path.

Simultaneously Ravenwood has served as an educational institution for those drawn to the Old Religion. From persons seeking basic factual information to those called to a lifetime of study and dedication within the Wiccan priest/esshood, Ravenwood offers a highly individualized training process built upon the Wiccan laws and tenets, the ancient mysteries, and the soul's own experiences. For a very few this path may take them through Ravenwood's initiatory process to become teachers of the Old Religion.

Today Ravenwood continues its original mission under the leadership of its High Priestess and High Priest, Larina and Gaelin with guidance from Sintana, its Elder High Priest, Merlin, and the support of the Craft Eldership at large.

SINTANA is the founder and Queen Elder of Ravenwood Church and Seminary in Atlanta, Georgia. She successfully challenged the system in the Bible Belt South and set legal State and Federal precedents that continue to benefit Craft communities today. She and Ravenwood were the subjects of the book *Living Witchcraft* by Scarboro, Campbell and Stave.

I was always attracted to spiritual energies and teachings from all traditions. Even early on I understood that all were one, different and yet the same. My mother, who was of Christian teachings, told me that when I was very young my chosen friends lived within the cracks of the cement walk. She said she would watch as I called them out to play and proceeded to talk to and for them. I felt myself to be a spiritual misfit, being in the wrong place at the wrong time. It was not until I chanced to meet my first teacher when I was twenty that I experienced that coming together of all that I knew and believed was spiritual truth. I was set upon the Path, and it fit like a velvet glove.

I did not confide my beliefs to my immediate family until I became a High Priestess and founded the Ravenwood Church and Seminary in Atlanta in 1975 and became Rev. Candy Lehrman. By then I was confident in who and what my role would be in life, and my family's opinions were not an influence. Over the years my family became very positive about what I was doing though they never totally understood. Throughout the years they would visit, often for a few weeks at a time. They came to love the Sabbats and were always impressed with the quality of our members.

Life's most precious gift to me has been my daughter Sybil who, though not trained in early years, came to it of her own accord after studying and comparing other religious traditions. She has been my chief supporter and critic. Through her love, blessings and support, the early years of our public teachings were made possible. She is now a solitary Priestess in Atlanta and an Elder of Ravenwood Church. Her son, my grandson, is still upon his quest. He has had a rich and diverse environment with many Wise Ones as mentors. During his early years he saw both the beauty and the horror of religious zealots in our early civil rights battles that went on daily for years in Atlanta. Through his mother and life he has acquired a great sense of values and a noble character. Life has also blessed me with the love and loyalty of others' children who have become our extended family. I believe the teachings they received of the Old Ways have enriched all their lives and souls whether they are of the Old Religion today or not. Each has a respect for the great masters and faiths of today. They are loving, productive members of our society. What more could any parent ask.

My beloved Priest and teacher, Sariel, was initiated as a young man in Italy into the Italian tradition that took his word and also his left little toe. He later studied in England and was initiated into a traditional group on the Isle of Man, which to my understanding was not a part of the Old George group. Sariel was a scholar and learned teacher of the Qabalah. It was his teachings and guidance that formed the spiritual and educational roots of Ravenwood Church and Seminary.

I learned and acquired a love and dedicated commitment to the service of the Old Ones. I learned how important it was for those seeking to teach the inquisitive, eager, and not so honest young power seeker, to walk this path with honor, tenacity and pride.

Sybil Leek who was an Elder of Traditional Craft became my mentor during our early civil rights battles. Through her guidance I learned that as teachers and public figures we had to set healthy examples and be productive and responsible. We had to stand strong and tall with undoubting faith in our mission and above all, live and teach the ethics. She reiterated Sariel's teachings to never compromise the Great Principles.

Sadly, I see nothing remotely similar to what I found when I first came to the Craft. And, indeed, if I were seeking today I do not believe that I would be at all interested in today's lack of roots, tradition, ways of grace and protocol that were taken so for granted in the early days.

We at Ravenwood carry on our mission of education, to create understanding and enlightenment to the sanctity of our beloved Craft. And most importantly, our civil rights to "Be." I give honor to those individuals, especially our adversaries, those who by their deeds taught me what should not be done, and by what was lacking to find the answers and fill the void. We're still working at this one.

Strega

STREGA (or Stregheria) originated in Sicily. Sicilians are a blend of many races and cultures: Carthaginian, Phoenician, Egyptian, Arab, Greek, Roman, and Norman, among others. Strega is an oral family tradition passed down for centuries through Italian family lines. A female Witch is called a Strega, and a male Witch is called a Stregone. The old Italian word for Witchcraft is Stregheria, but the religion of the people is known as La Vecchia Religione, the Old Religion.

LORI BRUNO is a hereditary Sicilian Strega/ Maga and is High Priestess of the Our Lord and Lady of the Trinacrian Rose Coven which is Sicilian in origin. The Coven became a legally recognized body in the Commonwealth of Massachusetts in 1993. Trinacria is the ancient name for Sicily meaning three capes. Lori is also a psychic and a published author.

As a child I witnessed my family doing daily rituals. Rituals were done for everything including cooking and blessing of the food and caring for people who came to the door needing help. I learned to walk in the footsteps of Nature, to feel the very Life Force, and to look for signs. There was always a message there for me. I learned to commune with the animals and to care for them as well as for less fortunate people. My family's door was always open. We lived a humanistic path, and that is what Strega really is, of the heart.

We had to be underground by necessity because of the remembrance of the Inquisition that took members of my family. There was an aunt in the 1300's whose only crime was to have knowledge of how to heal bubonic plague victims and how to use natural antibiotics such as honey and rosehips. She was also accused of having a magic knife, which she did, and it was one made of the finest Damascus steel. For this crime of protecting she was hung upside down in the marketplace and burned alive. In the year 1600 another ancestor was burned alive on February 17th in the Campo di Fiore in Rome, Italy for heresy. This man was the learned philosopher Filippo Giordano Bruno. His crime was that he could see into the future, was a man of science and literature, and a visionary who was ahead of his time. Today many of this theories are being studied in Europe. The Russians named a crater in the moon for him. His statue stands on the place where he was murdered by the Inquisition.

Though my children were aware of their heritage I never tried to force the beliefs upon them as each of us has our own sacred path. We, as members of the Craft of the Wise, do not force. Our children are free to follow their own hearts.

Our coven is a teaching coven. Our focus is on teaching how to live with all humanity and to perform ritual correctly, always mindful to do what you will an it harm none. However, this does not mean that you turn the other cheek. We only have two: slap one and you will not get the chance to slap the other. We have the right to protect ourselves from any and all harm.

We also run a charitable organization for children living with AIDS called Sacred Paths Alliance Network. Our other organ is POWER, the Protective Organization of Witches and Earth Religions. It's a legal arm of our coven for the protection of religious rights.

DR. LEO LOUIS MARTELLO was a hereditary Witch of the Sicilian/Continental Tradition. He published the *Wicca Newsletter* and *Witchcraft Digest* and authored books on the Craft and other subjects. He held the first public gathering of Witches in this country in Central Park, New York on October 31, 1970. In doing so, he won the first civil rights victory for Witches in history. Leo passed over on June 28, 2000.

Though "Witch blood" runs in my family, I must point out that Witchcraft is not inherited. It is passed on in Witch families through teaching and training. Being born into a family of musicians doesn't make one a musician. This knowledge has to be learned. Similarly, being born into a family of Witches doesn't mean that a child is suddenly transformed into a miracle man or wise woman. Then, too, because of the Inquisitional persecutions, most Witches in the past went underground and became separated from other Crafters. This enforced secrecy caused much of their Witch lore to be lost. For this reason many people who are considered Witches in various parts of the world practice limited rites, spells and incantations but are unable to explain their origin.

My ancestors came from Italy and Sicily. Martello is the name of a town located in the Valley of Martello in Northern Italy. My grandmother, Maria Concetta Martello, was the town Witch in Sicily. She read the old *tarocchi* cards. She combined psychic ability with good, old, horse sense. An inborn psychologist, she was shrewd, occasionally shrill, but always sensitive to the needs of others. She healed, helped others and dispensed herbs. The village priest, who considered her the town's chief candidate for Hell, preached sermons against her every Sunday. Maria Concetta loved it and laughed in his face.

The local Sicilians were Christians on the surface but Pagans under-neath. When they told their troubles to the priest, he prayed, but nothing happened. So they went to my grandmother. She provided solutions and produced results. When she was talked about as a Strega (Witch), it was neither in fear nor condemnation, but with respect.

My father, Rocco Luigi Martello, who died at 88, had only a smatter-ing of Witch lore. As in many of the branches of the Craft today, it was the women initiates who were the most active in Sicily. My father went to work at the age of twelve in Sicily and saved enough to come to the United States when he was twenty. He never spoke to others about his Strega mother, Maria Concetta. I learned about her through occasional remarks and slips that he made.

When I was eleven, after having spent time in a Catholic boarding school-orphanage (my parents had separated), I cultivated the friendship of a town Gypsy, Marta who taught me how to read cards. Another Italian Witch, Funzi, took me on herb-gathering expeditions in the nearby woods. There was also the son of a man who once worked circuses as a combination strongman and lesser-grade Houdini. Also, I kept blurting out things about other people that came true—things that made my father open up and tell me long stories about his mother, Maria Concetta, always saying—"I see her in you. I see her in you."

My father gave me free rein to pursue my interests. My grandmother was still living in Sicily, and he wrote letters to her about me and includ-ed some of my own questions. For two years this correspondence went on—then, silence! After a long time we received a letter from Sicily say-ing that Grandma had died. Shortly thereafter, cousins of my father who lived in New York wrote to him. When I came to New York at eighteen, I met them for the first time. They knew everything about me; I knew nothing about them. At first I didn't understand why they were so inter-ested in me. Among other things, they had me read for each member of the family, smeared oil on my hands and took my palm print. I found out later that they had been watching me for years.

On September 26, 1951, I was initiated into their totally underground Sicilian coven. In those days the Craft was totally secret, underground and private. We took vows of secrecy. We were dedicated to each other unto death. Nothing was put in writing … ever! Teachings were handed down orally. Reverence, reason and respect determined all our actions. For almost twenty years I kept secret my initiation into la vecchia reli-gione (the Old Religion) as part of the oath I had taken.

I gave up personally teaching and running covens years ago to devote myself to initiating civil and religious rights for Witches, including the establishment of legal churches, tax-exempt status, paid legal holidays and educating the public. I acted as an apostle for others who wanted to come out of their "broom closets". (By the way, I was the first Witch to use this term. In 1969 the slogan of the Witches' Liberation Movement was "Out of your broom closets and onto your brooms!")

Tuatha de Danaan
(T.D.D.)

UATHA DE DANANN is an Irish Celtic Mystery Tradition created in the mid-seventies as an outgrowth of the main branch of NECTW as given by Gwen Thompson to Kerry. It was created as an umbrella organization by its three founding Groves:Oak (Kerry), Apple (Bethany), and Pine (Althaea). Tuatha De Danann (TDD) was one of the earliest Celtic Revival groups, transforming its Craft roots, and moving in a new direction based on the Mysteries, Myths, and Magics of the ancient Gaels.

The Covens, known as Groves, are named usually, though not exclusively, after the Trees of the Ogham alphabet. Tenets of Druidical teaching were worked into the course of study, with Lugh and Brigid as the central Godforms, consistent with Gwen Thompson's Celtic theology. The Priestesses and Priests are called Bandrui and Drui respectively.

TDD reached its height in the mid-eighties, with six active autonomous Groves, and an Outer Order known as Circle of the Living Earth. During this period, the organization was best known for its exhaustive research into the ancient Mysteries of Eire, the creation of an authentic Bardic Tradition, a unique Druidical School, and the annual Lughnassad Festival, when all the Groves assembled to celebrate. TDD is still active, and has Groves throughout New England, and on the West Coast.

MERLIN AMBROSIAS is High Priest of Apple Grove with his wife and High Priestess, Bethany. They are also members of Elder Grove.

I was raised in a Military family that settled in Rhode Island in the sixties. In the late sixties and early seventies I became very interested in Philosophy, Metaphysics, and Nature as components of a belief system. Having been raised by parents of Jewish decent (my father was then an atheist and my mother was too much a feminist to participate in the strongly patriarchal, organized, Jewish religion), I had very little direct exposure to or influence from organized religion. I was free to explore and believe as I wished. I was in charge of my own spiritual development, without any religious baggage from my childhood. My wife, Bethany, and I had friends (Stock and Kerry) who had been seeing a woman in Connecticut (Gwen Thompson). They had been initiated and elevated to High Priest and High Priestess of a Traditional Craft Coven, New England Coven Of Traditionalist Witches (N.E.C.T.W.). Over many months we learned more about the Craft from them and from many of the books available at the time. I became very drawn to the Nature-based religion and magical traditions of the Craft. Realizing that the Craft was home, the belief system I was searching for, I asked for initiation. After many more months we were initiated into N.E.C.T.W.

I eventually told my parents of my involvement. My father and I had a few discussions about it and related subjects. We generally didn't agree, but he was willing to allow for my point of view. It didn't seem to bother him. My mother didn't really get into specifics, but was supportive in a quiet way. She would buy things for us that she thought we'd be interested in (a book, a box, anything "Witch" like). In the early years when we first started celebrating Yule on the Winter Solstice instead of Christmas on the 25th, there was a bit of confusion on the parts of my parents and in-laws. They eventually got used to it.

When I came into the Craft it was still very underground but slowly becoming more public. A lot of books were coming out on the subject, a lot of people were getting involved, and Pagan festivals started to be more common place. Many of the people involved were young, and it was hard to separate the dabblers from the serious.

After some time in N.E.C.T.W., we were elevated to High Priest and High Priestess so that we could form a new Coven. Soon after, we named our Coven Apple Grove and together with Oak Grove and Pine Grove formed Tuatha De Danann (TDD) a Celtic (Gaelic/Irish) Mystery Tradition. Through the late seventies and early eighties, TDD reconstructed a Gaelic/Irish based Pagan,

Mythological and Magical tradition, created a Bardic tradition that included several live performances of Pagan/Celtic music, and created and ran a more public Pagan group (Circle Of The Living Earth).

Our first son was nine to twelve years old when we were at the height of our Craft activities. He was brought up around the Craft, was present at most non-initiatory events, and regularly interacted with members of our groups. We retired in 1985 to devote more time to careers and our three children (with the addition of a son and a daughter both born in the early eighties). The two youngest have always been aware of our Craft and Pagan backgrounds, and we have always openly discussed our beliefs and philosophies. In addition, we continue to observe many of the Pagan holidays as a family.

Our eldest son has always planned to be initiated and may soon request it. Our two younger children accept their Pagan roots but currently have other priorities in their lives. As a family, the pagan philosophies are just part of daily life.

We have only recently come out of retirement and formed Elder Grove with Stock and Kerry. Both Apple and Elder Groves are underground. We do not teach formally at this time. However, we have, from time to time, helped someone in need or who may benefit from Pagan philosophy or spiritual insight. This is usually just part of interacting with those who come and go in our daily lives. In time we may resume formal teaching again.

Our teachings include Celtic (Gaelic/Irish) based Mythological, Magical, and Bardic Traditions and Mysteries, as well as, Pagan religion, philosophy and spiritualism.

MURTHAGH ADHAMH ANDOILE is a Drui (High Priest) of the Tuatha De Danann Tradition. He is currently the head of Nemed na Morrigna (Grove of the Morrigan) in North Hollywood, California. Murtagh (Tagh) was once known for his "Pan Dance" which he performed at various festivals with his once partner, and still friend, Gwethalyin. He has written for various publications including Obisdian and Fireheart and is on the editorial board of Obsidian Magazine, the Journal of Occult Folklore and Mystery Traditions.

I am originally from Rhode Island but now live in Southern California. When living in Rhode Island I belonged to a Craft/Celtic Reconstructionist group known as Tuatha De Danann (TDD). TDD was an Irish Celtic Mystery Tradition group which goes back to the N.E.C.T.W. founded by Gwen Thompson. I also helped run the outer order of TDD called Circle of the Living Earth, and was a founding member of the Providence Random Assembly (PRA). PRA was a clearing house and Pagan speakers bureau made of individuals from various covens as well as non-affiliated Pagan members.

I guess, in some ways, my first contact with the Craft was when I was about a month old. I was diagnosed with a strange childhood disease where I had a high fever and cried constantly. The family physician, in a time when doctors still came to your home, wrote me off, saying there was nothing to be done. He felt it would be better for me to be home to die at home with my family around me, as opposed to being in a hospital. My family lived on Federal Hill in Providence, which was (and still is) a heavy Italian/Catholic neighborhood.

Roman Catholicism, as practiced by Italians and other European cultures is a mix of Church doctrine, folk magic and entities that are not wholly Christian. My aunt visited a local "Strega" (an old wise woman), who gave her a magic spell to be done over me for healing. The women in my family gathered together and did the ritual which involved oil, water, candles, eggs and such. (Years later I found pieces of the rite in Geoffrey Leland's Etruscan Roman Remains.) As soon as the ritual was completed, my fever broke, my crying stopped, and the doctor, who was called again, was amazed. In some ways I feel, in retrospect, that's where the Goddess took hold of me. For the rest of my life, even when I was growing up "Catholic" I had this undying need for something different.

As a young Catholic, I always lived a dichotomy because I had visions of a female entity that would come to me that I called the Virgin Mary but it was not Mary like the Church knew her. I always prayed to her as opposed to "God," the super Father figure. When young, I always operated within Church parameters because I was told I had the "Call to Vocation," and should be a priest. The parish priest felt this because I heard voices and saw things. Much later in college, my professors in the Anthropology Department, christened me the "Department Shaman." I learned young that my family on both sides had a history of occult and paranormal experiences from ESP and clairvoyance to strange manifestations. My father's side of the family is from Tuscany in Northern Italy, and the legend goes that we are descended from a god or goddess. According to the history, one of our ancestors, a Twelfth Century monk, was burned at the stake for being a heretic and a diabolist. This event is recorded in one of Montague Summers' books. I know Summers should be taken with a grain of salt, but some of his historical research does seem to be accurate.

In my teens I found a copy of the Hills' book, *The Supernatural.* In the section on Witchcraft they talked about "White" Witchcraft (i.e. British Gardnerians). It was here in the sixties that I began to search actively for the Craft, and I began practicing folk and ceremonial magic. I still hadn't found any "real" Witches by the time until I got to college.

As a freshman I became a part of a parapsychology group called Pyro (Parapsychological Investigatory and Research Organization). It was during that time that I met Owen Rowley who would later be the gateway for many of us to join N.E.C.T.W. or one of its incarnations. Owen owned a bookstore in Providence called The Equinox which, so far as we know, may have been the first of its kind in Rhode Island. Owen joined us in PIRO for a time, and we practiced some ghost hunting, ufology, and the like. Owen later became initiated, and with Stockbridge Chandler opened a store called The Old Way. We lost track of each other for a few years after that.

I continued to practice magic privately and continued to work with several of my anthropology professors in the fields of Shamanism and Folk Magic. In order to gain a better understanding of myself and my on-going experiences with the Otherworld, I studied mythology, comparative religion, shamanism and spiritualism. In 1974 I went through a "Dark Night of the Soul" and totally broke from old ways of looking at things. All the Gods/esses I had dealt with previously came back in force, introduced me to other entities in the Universe. It was a strange time for me; as I had not been totally "earthed," mentally or spiritually for about three weeks culminating with my return at Yule. I was different. I remember little of what happened, for a part of me, a part of my soul had gone. It was then that I, or some part of me decided, that it was time to bring myself back together. I was the only one who could heal myself. When I came fully out of it, there were no more blinders (physically or spiritually). I saw the Goddess and. had finally come home.

By 1975 I was doing public pagan rituals with people, holding events and acting as "a priest" in the Pagan sense to a multitude of people. I had still not found the Craft group I was looking for. It was another year before I reconnected with Owen, and in 1976 reconnected with the new TDD. During that period Owen, Stock, Kerry, and Baldur opened up the Cuckoos' Nest, Rhode Island's Pagan bar. I started to visit and get to know people. After an interesting Halloween party at the Nest I knew I was home. The rest is history. I was initiated into Apple Grove at Yule and my future partner, Gwethalyn, was initiated at Imbolc. We had met in connection with what we came to call "The Pan Dance" at the Nest party. We later took the "show" on the road and performed from the late seventies until the mid-eighties at Pagan festivals around the country.

I never had trouble with my biological family over my beliefs. They have all been aware of my magical involvement for some time. My father died at the Imbolc after my initiation, and I know that he knows on the other side. My mother has always known and been supportive of me in whatever I've done. My siblings are all aware of my Craft involvement. My younger brother is a Gnostic and reads voraciously about Paganism and mythology. My nieces have "confessed" that they are interested in Witchcraft, and I've been steering them to the proper books.

TDD (and N.E.C.T.W.) was very underground and secretive in the seventies. We were a Western Mystery tradition with the emphasis on the word, "mystery." The Tradition was a hierarchical system based on an extended family group. The coven/groves operated as nuclear families with a high priest and high priestess holding parental roles. The Elders were like uncles and aunts in the family, the initiates in other covens like cousins. The Matriarch of our line was Gwen Thompson. Our circles were closed, and no one who was not a member of the Tradition could attend.

The rules for the degrees were relatively clear and straight forward. You had to attend thirteen moons, eight Sabbats, and all coven meetings for the first year, no ifs, ands, or buts. Part of this was so the priest and priestess could gauge your development, since most of the training was oral. They looked at how you were taking instruction, and getting involved in the group egregor (group mind). By the end of your first degree, you should have the basics for the rest of your Craft work; how to cast a circle, understand and work with elements, Craft history and the group's mythology and theology, and. some rudimentary magic and spellcraft. In TDD we used the word grove instead of coven because of the Irish Celtic bend.

In later years when we came out from underground, around 1979, festivals began to be public. Owen and his wife Ardell, Gwethalyn and myself were sort of ambassadors for TDD at other festivals around the country and in the growing Pagan community We caused some confusion because of our terminology. When we told people that we were not priest or priestess, or when we said we were in a grove, people wouldn't talk to us. It took a couple of years before we realized that when people heard "grove," they thought we were in a Pagan grove and uninitiated, rather than a Wiccan coven. The fact that we did not call ourselves priest and priestess was due to our Tradition structure. Those terms were never used until one ran a grove. We finally started explaining that in our Tradition this is the way it worked

As an aside, I've read in several places that the chant, "Hoof and Horn" is a "traditional" chant. Well, in 1980 or 1981 we attended the Rites of Spring III, and with Ian Corrigan, who was originally a part of Birch Grove, we did a chant workshop and realized that there were very few God chants. So for the next several months, Ian struggled to put together God chants and finally came up with "Hoof and Horn." At that time we had a musical group called "The Bards." The first time we did it publicly was at an event called Music in the Woods, sometimes known as the TDD concert, which we held at a campground in Rhode Island. It was there that Ian introduced the chant to the Pagan community. When we went to a festival in 1982 in Michigan, the chant had already hit there; in variations and nobody knew where it came from or where it originated, and I have actually seen it in people's books of shadows as saying "traditional chant." Well, it is in the sense that it came from a Traditionalist coven, by a Traditionalist Witch, but at the same time, it was written in 1981-82. It just shows how things can be disseminated in the movement and the community.

In TDD we had a firm grounding in ceremonial, elemental, and planetary magic. We were also encouraged to learn a divinatory system. All members had a specialty. Mine was Celtic mythology and for a divinatory skill, geomancy. I was also well versed in elemental magic. Gwethalyn was the expert on dance extremely good in Tarot.

We were all on a path, The Path, and that's what our Craft was about, not power, not a social group. We were there for personal enlightenment, and working magically on ourselves. In this way we would change and help the world at large. We always knew we would not stay together forever, but would go on to create new covens for the survival of the Craft. I remember us all joking that one day we would have branches around the world in the British Isles, the Western United States, and in Zimbabwe. While we don't have covens abroad, we are in the Western United States and elsewhere, and continue to grow.

During the last sixteen years in California I have continued to develop my unique Celtic form of magic. When not teaching magic I spend a lot of time doing healing work, and Southern California, Hollywood, the plain of Maya, needs lots of healing.

STOCK is High Priest of Oak Grove with his wife and High Priestess, Kerry. Both are also members of Elder Grove.

After years of interest, I was seeking initiation into an authentic magical lodge. A friend of mine with similar interests made contact with Gwen Thompson. He told me about her, and I requested a meeting with her. Although she did not represent the traditional magical lodge I had been searching for, her "presence" was overwhelming. I asked for initiation into N.E.C.T.W. and after some time she agreed. Kerry originally became interested because of my involvement, but after her first meeting with Gwen knew without doubt that this was her path as well.

My parents knew nothing of my involvement at first, but once they became aware of my interests in the Craft they became quite concerned. They've been in a state of denial ever since. Kerry's family thought we were crazy, and mine were certain I would eventually "grow" out of it. They were wrong. Both of our children were raised "around" the Craft. Although the philosophy of Paganism was expounded freely, they were not usually present at circles as they grew older. Neither practices today, but both are very aware of their Pagan roots.

My first "dabblings" were in the late sixties and early seventies, but my interest had been in place years before that. Most of the information about the Craft at that time came from people like Ray Buckland, Leo Martello, and Alex Sanders.

Kerry and I ran Oak Grove with thirteen members until about ten years ago. We were very much underground. With six groves in place, we decided it was time to take a "hiatus." Now, however, it's time to finish what we started, and Oak Grove is active again.

Other Traditional Witches

THOUGH MANY OF today's Elder Witches are associated with Traditions such as the ones previously described in this book, others simply refer to themselves as Traditional Witches. Most of these people adhere to teachings which have been taught and handed down through family lines. Although many of these Elders have taught in the past, a number of them are solitary today.

Of these unique Craft Elders two are especially noteworthy because of their significant and transforming contributions to the early development of the Craft in the United States.

**ELIZABETH PEPPER is a Hereditary Witch.
She is (with John Wilcock) co-creator of *The
Witches' Almanac*, co-author of *Magical
and Mystical Sites*, and co-editor of *A Book
of Days*. She is the author of *Love Charms,
Moon Lore*, and *Celtic Tree Magic*.**

ꙮy father's family (the Peppers) came
to this country in the 1600s and there
were English, Welsh, Scottish, Irish, Dutch
and German surnames on the family tree. I
gather that at least one member of each suc-
ceeding generation had interest in or dis-
played an aptitude for Witchcraft. The trait surfaced again and again. My
maternal grandmother was Spanish Basque and she met and married my
grandfather, an Anglo-Irish sculptor whose specialty was gravestone
angels, in London. They immigrated to America, settled in New England
in 1887 and raised seven daughters and one son. I think it's unusual for an
entire family to follow a single occult path but my mother's did. The main-
spring of Craft traditions as I know them comes from them.

I grew up in Providence, Rhode Island, on the East Side. That's where H.P.
Lovecraft lived and it's the setting for many of his tales. He often used the real
names of streets and places, so it was fun to go and find them—strange old
Victorian mansions and walled gardens with gargoyle fountains.

My parents and other members of our family practiced the Craft. All
of them, in one way or another, taught me. I don't think our Craft involvement was generally known in the neighborhood. I do remember sensing
a certain coolness, a kind of unspoken disapproval from some people.
They kept their distance, but that's a typical New England pattern. The
training I had was given in an informal manner. I was an only child; the
only child on my mother's side of the family. Six of my aunts lived within
walking distance. Each one had a particular occult interest or talent. The
Dark of the Moon was the time for healings and forming rings of protection. Tide Turnings (changing a run of bad luck by ritual) took place
after the first quarter of the waxing moon.

Something was always happening; we'd concentrate to make it right,
turning negatives into positives. I think that one of the best things about
growing up in a Craft family was the way commonplace things could be
touched with magic. The Craft educates the heart and the spirit as well
as the mind. Imagination is constantly encouraged and stimulated. I have

so many lovely memories like being given my first kitten or watching the full moon rise for the first time. These were like sacred ceremonies, very solemn occasions.

My teaching is done now through my writings. I work most frequently with John Wilcock. Our friendship and collaboration dates from 1957 when we both lived in Greenwich Village, NY. He worked at the *New York Times* and helped found *The Village Voice*. I was art director for *Gourmet Magazine*. *The Witches' Almanac* is a compendium of history, lore and legend. I wanted to do the Almanac because I wanted to show the beauty and wisdom of the Craft. Like the Tao, it is a way, an attitude toward living. Montaigne described its theme when he wrote that "it is the journey, not the arrival, that matters." In the Craft, we seek to make our journey as rich and lovely as we can.

I enjoy my life this time around. I've known incredible good luck. The happy times more than make up for the rough patches. The occult outlook lends flavor to life, deepens and sweetens the heart and the soul… or so it seems to me.

JOSEPH B. WILSON published the first Craft newsletter in America, *The Waxing Moon,* in 1964. In 1970 he co-founded the "Pagan Way" in America and the "Pagan Movement in Britain and Ireland" in England.

While I was not born into a Craft family, I was taught by those who were—where the Old Religion was practiced in remnants. Once a practice leaves a family, it is no longer hereditary so if it must have a label it should be considered traditional. Initiatory? Even within the families I am familiar with, a form of initiation takes place, though that form is very different from the shallow, theatrical things one finds in New-Age bookstores. I have been "adopted," and I have been "initiated." By the way, not everyone in a hereditary family practices the Old Ways, only those who have been "called" do so.

I received my call, in the form of three near-death experiences within a single week, in 1955, when I was thirteen years old. After searching and stumbling around for seven more years, I finally found my first real teacher. This person explained what happened and assisted me through the crisis and into the practices of the Old Religion as they were observed in that family. I was accepted into that family by spiritual adoption. Later on, those practices were merged with those of two other families, both in England, who accepted me because of my acceptance into the first one.

My parents were not aware of my involvement for another few years. They had no objection to my religious orientation or practices, but did object because I had foolishly been using the word, "Witchcraft," to describe what I did. "Oh! You must not let your grandmother find out about that; it would hurt her so much!"

There is no comparison between the Craft then and now. When I began my personal search for others involved in the Old Religion through my publication of *The Waxing Moon*, there really was no widespread Craft in the United States. Although the Gardnerian movement was in full swing in England, that tradition didn't take hold in the States via Ray and Rosemary Buckland for another couple of years. I found hundreds of people who were interested in learning, but only one or two who knew anything at all. So, I networked people, and freely distributed my own anonymously written papers of Pagan philosophy and rituals that I and some others (Ed "Fitch," Tony Kelly, and "Thomas") wrote. In 1970 I expanded that work further by co-founding "Pagan Way" in the United States and the "Pagan Movement in Britain and Ireland" in England. In both areas we gave out literally thousands of packets of material. I was upset, then amused, in the mid-seventies when I discovered groups claiming to be "traditional" and "hereditary" which were using verbatim portions of rituals that I had written, while claiming that stuff had been handed down in their family for generations.

I have seven children, all but the eldest born since I entered the Old Religion. I raised each of them with an understanding and acceptance for all religious faiths and taught them the basics of love and understanding of the Earth Mother. Five of them have gone their own way and have nothing to do with my beliefs, primarily because their mother was a Fundamentalist Christian. The youngest two have a more understanding mother and may or may not follow my path. Even if they do follow my path, their orientation will be different from my own.

I seldom teach anymore. I'm not interested in time-wasters or those who think they already know it all, who expect me to be their own preconceived notion of perfection, or those who give nothing back in return. But I am willing to do so for the rare individual who is willing to work, capable of learning, and who is not just after a shallow "fast food restaurant" helping of instant spirituality. Many claim to want to learn, but very few who have the courage, strength and determination to face reality and do it. Those who just want to take are welcome to get the information that is freely available in books, on the Internet and on my Homepage.

Part 2
Personal Perspectives

Our initial contact with the Elders included a questionnaire. What follows are their answers to these questions which reflect how they feel about Craft as practiced today. It is interesting to note that some issues show a great deal of agreement among the Elders while others show a great diversity of opinion. As you will read, many issues evoked strong reaction. These opinions are specific to the individuals who hold them. We have tried faithfully to record what we were told for the benefit of future generations.

Do you believe that what you do is based on ancient teachings and writings?

MARTHA ADLER: I most definitely believe the Craft is based on ancient teachings. My tradition is based on ancient pre-Christian Welsh teachings (Bran).

AYEISHA: I absolutely think that what I do is a very ancient tradition. I think that the Craft goes back to the dawn of time. I don't believe that any one particular tradition survived intact, but I think that the concepts and the understanding, and the Gods Themselves are as old as time. I believe the Craft is descended from the ancient Mystery Religions. I want to delineate here that a mystery religion is not like Catholicism or Islam. In those traditions, a priest is the contact point between the worshipper and the deity. Nor is it like any of the Protestant traditions where a sacred book provides the contact and guidelines for being in tune with the divine. Instead, I think a mystery religion is one of personal experience and responsibility. Each worshipper is encouraged, taught, and then expected to develop an on-going positive and direct relationship with the Gods. It is called a mystery because these sorts of experiences are very difficult to communicate in words alone, and are usually distorted when people attempt to tell them. Near and Far Eastern religions like Buddhism, Hinduism, Taoism, Shintoism—all of these—are probably mystery traditions, but the Craft is very Western in its cultural flavor and quite different in many ways.

You hear people spouting the nonsense that "Drawing Down the Moon" was supposedly "invented" by Alex Sanders or Stuart Farrar or

Lady Elizabeth, but the fact of the matter is you can pick up an ancient Egyptian or Greek text and see how old it really is. The mysteries of Eleusis, the Italian mysteries of Rome, Egypt, and Persia before Islam were certainly practicing mystery traditions. And all of those traditions have surviving, intact histories of Drawing Down the Moon. I think it's certainly true that Alex or Stuart or Elizabeth brought them up to date somewhat, put them in more timely phrasings, and they have reminded people about these practices. But they certainly didn't invent them whole cloth; they've been there forever. The thing I would say about that is that the Craft, the concepts, and the practices are timeless. I think Craft is one of the only mystery traditions, and religions for that matter, that is perfectly compatible with Science. Craft flows with the development of people and really with the development of the Earth itself.

All of the ancient teachings are as valid today as they were then. We might use the energy in a different way. Fertility, for example, springs to mind. You can work fertility magic to create, increasing the population by creating pregnancy and more babies. At this point in the Earth's development, we aren't in desperate need of many more citizens. What we do need is a lot of creativity to put into the way we manage the Earth and our resources. Fertility magic that could create a child can just as easily be turned into fertility of the mind or the spirit. You can inspire an artist to create art, or an architect to build wonderful buildings. It's all the same energy; it's been there all along, but now there is a modern application of the energy. And in that way I think that Craft will never be outdated because it essentially works with the stuff that everything else is made of.

MARSHA BARD: I believe I have been many lifetimes in the Craft. Sometimes I don't really know how I know what I know. I cannot discern if what I do is from some subconscious memory from my childhood or from a past life experience. I don't really think that the Craft of the past is relevant to today. We are not an agrarian society; no matter how countrified we feel, we have really become city Witches. As Witches, our common sense is perhaps referenced from a different place than others, and it may be that reference is the ancient teachings, but it must apply itself to today's lifestyle.

LORI BRUNO: Yes. What I do is based on ancient teachings, but the Strega never wrote anything down. It was all committed to memory and orally transmitted. Our rituals are based upon respect for the Gods, upon the fertility and protection of the earth, the fertility not of body but of the mind that our people will be free from the harm we have witnessed past times. We do ritual for healing, for prosperity, so that our loved ones who have gone before us remain at peace and will return to us, and that there will be no wars that will desecrate the earth and humanity. We work for a greater understanding of all the great religions of the world so that there will be no more murder and mayhem or ethnic cleansings in the name of God, or the murder of women in the name of God, or genocide in the name of God, and that all people will come to know that there is a great Mother and Great Father who are benevolent, and that they are loved, not for their pocketbook and not for their station in life but for themselves. The animal kingdom too has rights, and we pray for all of them.

RAY BUCKLAND: I do believe what we do is based on ancient teachings, but not by an unbroken line.

CHAS CLIFTON: Although folk-magical practices, such as divination, are ancient, I do not think that there has been a continual, non-Christian religion handed down from "The Burning Times." By far, the majority of people executed for "Witchcraft" during the late Middle Ages, Renaissance, and Early Modern period (through the 17th century) would have identified themselves as Christians. Trained historians who are sympathetic to Paganism, such as Ronald Hutton of the University of Bristol in England, hold that view, and I suspect that they are right. (I recommend reading Hutton's *Stations of the Sun: The Ritual Year in Britain*.) At most we can claim inspiration from the past and, if you subscribe to reincarnation, the carrying forward of some kind of modern adaptation of ancient tribal Paganism that may have been experienced in past lives. But I think it's unhealthy to spend too much time looking over our shoulders, either back in time or back across the Atlantic.

DANA CORBY: Yes, to the extent that those who created the modern Movement based it on ancient teachings and writings—and it's pretty well proven that they did. It's spirit is both archaic and futurist, as befits those who walk between worlds. Modern Witchcraft is a revivalist/reconstructionist movement based on many threads of fact and myth. Like all else in our cosmology, its creation is ongoing. Isn't that just Grand!

DEVON: I don't know about ancient, but the writings are old and the oral legends are even older. What I do is based on hereditary traditional teachings, and I do believe that these practices were drawn from much older teachings.

ETIDORHPA: I do believe the Craft comes from ancient teachings and writings, but I don't believe there was ever one complete book that was passed down verbatim. Some information was oral and some written. I don't believe you would find the entire Book in any one tradition, but I don't think it's important that everything be ancient. I think the ritual that does what it's supposed to do is every bit as effective as one that has been passed down.

ALEXANDRIA FOXMOORE: I believe that I follow to the best of my knowledge the ancient ways.

GWION: I do believe that the core of my Tradition is based on ancient teachings. However, I do not believe it is an insular tradition that has not been influenced by outside tradition. I think there has been a lot of cross-pollination over time.

JUDY HARROW: Yes, I believe they are, but not necessarily by direct transmission.

HANS HOLZER: I think it is based on truth as well as on ancient teachings. It is Nature based. Spinoza wrote "deus e noctura"—God is Nature.

CORBY INGOLD: I believe that some of what I do is based on ancient teachings. Much else is a modern development woven from the remnants and strands of several different traditions. I believe we need to be honest about this and not say we have some kind of unbroken oral tradition extending back to the dawn of time. Such claims are quite ludicrous, as anyone with a bit of experience knows, and by making such claims we paint ourselves as fools, or at least very naïve. I have worked closely with indigenous tribal peoples who do have very ancient traditions that have survived fairly intact, but even they do not claim that their traditions have not changed. As one Northwest Coast Salish shaman expressed it to me—traditions do change. They have to in order to survive, just as human beings do. So while there are indeed very ancient threads that run through the rich tapestry of modern Witchcraft, I believe that these threads are rewoven from time to time in order to find an appropriate contemporary expression. However, having said that I must also emphasize that I am a Traditionalist, and therefore by definition fairly conservative in my approach to the Craft. I do not believe in changing things for no good reason, and I believe that much harm is done by tampering with the traditions as they have been passed down to us.

We, as Traditionalists, should try to pass on the teachings that our Craft Elders have shared with us in as true a form as possible, by which I mean true to the original. I regard this as a sacred trust, something we must do. And this is no contradiction to my earlier statements about the need for change. I believe the teachings and ways change organically, from the inside as it were, in answer to outer pressures and needs, new understandings, etc. But this should not be brought about through the ego or fickle-mindedness of any individual man or woman. There is beauty in the way the teachings have been passed down, and I believe we should strive to preserve that same precious quality when we hand them on to our students and descendants. Also, I see no need to fix something that isn't broken. I think the Traditional attitude is more to leave well enough alone.

As far as sacred writings go, I don't believe that "Books of Shadows" were anything more than an individual Witch's personal recipe book, which is precisely what the Book of Shadows was understood to have been in the early days of the modern British Craft revival. Also, when British Craft crossed the Atlantic and came to these shores, to my mind, a decidedly non-Pagan, Judeo-Christian element of book worship and literal interpretation crept in. One of these is to decry the value of the Book of Shadows in a modern Craft setting providing it doesn't become the focus of petty inter-Nicene squabbles with High Priestess X or Magister Y quoting chapter and verse to prove that someone is wrong. There's enough of that in the mainstream religious world, and I would hope that we Witches are secure enough in our beliefs to be comfortable with a certain amount of diversity amongst our ranks. Also, most of the people who were likely to have been village Witches or Cunning Men prior to the Twentieth Century were probably not literate enough to have made much use of a Book of Shadows. I think it more likely that they, as Doreen Valiente expressed, got their teachings and techniques directly from the Book of Nature. Today most Traditionalists do have some kind of Book with the rites and traditions of their lineage, etc., and I think this can be a great boon, provided it is understood in light of some of the things I've mentioned above.

JIMAHL: Yes. Absolutely. I am reminded constantly of the ancient roots of the Craft: the Wheel of the Year, the Rites of the Moon and Sun, the veneration of the primal forces of Nature—it all resonates with a time beyond knowing.

CHRISTINE JONES: Of course our Craft is based on ancient teachings. Anyone who thinks otherwise is arrogant and ignorant of history.

LORAX: Traditional refers to the way that materials are passed on, the gestalt of the teachings, their organic and flowing nature when contrasted with a cookbook initiatory and training approach, or a politically driven paradigm. It also requires the passage of much time and experience.

I believe that what I do is based on principles that are almost universal to polytheistic and pantheistic cultures. The specific materials that I have received from my teachers can be traced to oral bits that may predate the last century and written materials that seem to have been gleaned from the Celtic Twilight movement. My sense is that the materials of the Craft I practice were assembled or reconstructed late in the nineteenth century, and then passed within certain families. Modern occultists are generally not familiar with many of the "ground-level" invocatory, social and lodge movements, such as the Grange, that were part and parcel of life for many persons in the earlier part of this century.

Every generation in history has reinvented religion according to its own needs and biases. To deny that the modern EuroPagan movement of the Craft hasn't changed things, even within the past twenty years would be to deny that this is a living movement. We are new trees, offshoots of the Elders within an ancient forest. The cycle of life requires continuity, change, and a certain amount of reflection, sadness, and humor.

LEO MARTELLO: My own research has proven to me that some of our rites have an ancient heritage. Others…who knows? I do know that they are much more ancient than the so-called modern traditions. My ancestors, my grandmother Maria Concetta Martello in particular, would turn over in their graves if they saw some of the things that are being passed off as Craft today!

MERLIN: Yes. Since the teachings & mysteries were always secretively kept among the few, my trust in the source of the teachings and my own spiritual sense about them is enough. Furthermore, my research and that of the people in our tradition have found information in obscure and very old places that corroborates teachings we have received through our tradition. When viewing the big picture of history, the Craft philosophies and way of life, it makes sense.

MORDA: I think some of the teachings are as old as humankind, and the form the Craft takes is modernized and adapted to time, place, and cultural context. I think there are ancient, archetypal ideas combined with modern writings.

MORVEN: I'm not one who believes that everything we do is based on ancient teachings and holy writ, but what I do believe is that it is a system that works.

MURTAGH: My feeling is that what we have in my Tradition's Book of Shadows comes from a period of time probably a little more than 100 years ago. Most of the older sections are pretty much traditional folk information. I believe the earliest modern Craft work comes from the magical revival in the mid-1800's with Eliphas Levi with the French revival and, of course, the British revival in the 1880's with the Golden Dawn and the Theosophists later with Crowley and the A.A. and the O.T.O., and finally, Dion Fortune with the Society for Inner Light. The Celtic material comes from original sources that are at least 1,500 years old and come from oral tradition that is probably older, but again, as in Celtic spirituality we are reconstructionists. We do not know exactly how things were done, or the total reasoning or the mental processes of people 2,000 years ago. We've made a lot of assumptions on how people think. People in other cultures do not think or conceive of concepts the same way. We don't know what the Ancients did. To say that the Book of Shadows comes from even the 16th or 17th century is ridiculous. Also, most people would not have committed this information to writing. There were sumptuary laws about having certain types of things. Books were expensive articles, and it could have meant death for a rural peasant to possess one. Most people would have considered themselves Christian, at least in Europe. They might have done folk medicine or folk ritual. They might worship and talk to ancient divinities and try to placate them (the wee folk or the faerie, depending on the area). However, they would have considered themselves to be Christian. So I believe that what we've got is a reconstructed religion that probably was put together in as much as the last hundred and fifty years. I think that what makes us one with the ancient European Pagan cultures is that we follow and worship the Old Gods, we try to look at the world in a different way than what has been presented by Western culture, and we are more Earth-based and Nature-oriented.

MARY NESNICK: To a limited extent. I personally feel much was "modernized" in the late fifties from older teachings and traditions as well as other religious teachings into a practice that could and would find current acceptance.

ELIZABETH PEPPER: Yes, and I feel the resurgence of Witchcraft today is due to the fact that it's a centering-in on life right now, life on Earth. For the last twenty centuries, humankind has waged an unceasing battle against Nature. The Craft reminds us that nature is our ally, that we're all a family; an integral part of the Earth. Also, a spiritual vacuum has been created, and Nature hates a vacuum. Witchcraft fills a need for beauty, faith, romance, and a sense of the larger pattern. It's as simple as this: a sense of Witchcraft is as elusive as a sense of humor. It can't be defined or taught. But if you've got it, you know it.

PATRICIA POTHIER: Its basic principles are based on ancient writings, but many rituals have had to be reconstructed because there are immense gaps in the ancient sources. Much of the poetry and all of the music have been lost. It does not really matter. The core of the religion—man's place in the universe is an integral part of Nature, not separate from Nature. The good life is the life lived in harmony with Nature—has remained intact. The trappings would have been changed over time even if they had been preserved. Religion cannot become fossilized in the forms of the past.

TRIVIA PRAGER: I believe the Craft is a Mystery Religion and goes back as far as the time mankind began to realize there was more to life than mere survival. As a mystery, it can't be taught but must be experienced. We don't have an unbroken chain from the ancients, but some things can be reconstructed through research, trance and dreams. We come from the stars and are linked to the Gods and they are to us. We just have to remember that.

ROGER PRATT: I do. My mother had never adhered to the belief that Witches worked in covens. I was always taught that by nature, we are solitary observers of life around us, of Nature, of the seasons. I believe implicitly in the Craft's ancient origins.

RAOKHSHA: Anything "ancient" was not written. Anything written was probably lost. I think we have not really rediscovered as much as rein-vented the Witch. We've got a statue here and there, but no scripts. So we fill in the blanks. Gosh, I'd love to know that what I was doing when I raised my arms to the Goddess in an invocation was the very same thing my ancestors did on some moonlit hill in an ancient grove. I am, however, content to feel that I'm "coming close" to following in their footsteps. I sus-pect there was not so much vocalization in ritual. Working alone some-times seems more wonderful because I needn't speak aloud, but can "feel" my way through the ritual, and I think that this was the old way.

I do think that what we do is based on ancient teaching, but more in a manner of interpretation of a culture than of an actual oral tradition. If we can accept this dilution of the "teachings" through the centuries and go on to believe that we have captured the "essence" of Wicca and built upon it, I feel we will be on stable ground. Valid is valid, no matter how it was transmitted. Anything lost can be found again. Our insistence that all that we do is ancient weakens our argument for validity. The sooner we assert that we are reinvented, the sooner we can free ourselves of the "they think they're a bunch of Witches" stigma.

OWEN ROWLEY: I believe that the Craft I practice is based upon ancient teachings and principles. However, I harbor no illusions that I practice an unbroken ancient Craft. To me, Craft must be alive and relevant. Therefore, I like to rewrite and rework ritual elements until they resonate for me. Many times I have discovered magic techniques that I've never encountered anywhere before. Whether they arise because of my knowledge of ancient lore or not is of little interest to me. What is of interest is how it feels.

ZANONI SILVERKNIFE: Any teachings that I may be in possession of that are of ancient times are thoroughly private. These were given to me by my Elders and as such are to be guarded with my very life. I accept that they know from which they speak. I believe that whether or not these things were handed down in script or orally from one generation to another does not matter one whit. The kernel, the essence of those teachings given to me, rings true in my soul. My memories resonate in sympathy, much like the other strings of a harp will vibrate when the proper chord is plucked by knowledgeable fingers. Truth is truth. No amount of varnishing the truth or bending it to suit the religion d'jour is going to change what is. There are those things that we remember on a cellular level, genetically installed in our mainframe or, if you wish, by the blood of our ancestors. There are those things we can access through Spirit that are ours through incarnational genetics. All of these methods, written, oral, genetic, and spiritual history, are valid when building a personal philosophy.

SINTANA: I believe that we are just remembering all we are and all we have come from. Absolutely! I believe in the Ancient knowledge that has been directed to Earthly mankind. We find it within our traditional teachings; some teachings have managed to remain fairly intact, and these we treasure. But the bottom line is, as one of the masters said, "There is but one story and one story only. It is for those who have the eyes to see and the ears to hear."

STARSPAWN: When I first came into Craft I believed that everything was entirely based upon actual ancient teachings and writings. I, like my teachers, passed this belief on to students. Later we learned this was not correct. However, I always believed and continue to believe that the essential core of the Craft is ancient. I believe this is due to long-buried memories resuscitated by working in circle a.k.a. past-life memories. If this was all "made up," then why has it been such a central core of my being after more than twenty-five years of my life?

TANITH: Yes, in the broad sense. I believe the general theory and teachings are very old, but not specific writings.

THEITIC: I believe that what I do is a product of the worship and practices of ancient people. The writings have been interpreted by many and altered over time. Only the simplest and most basic teachings have remained intact (i.e., the raising of power to heal, bathing in Moonlight, accepting reincarnation as truth, etc.).

I believe that the natural laws of the universe can be viewed in many ways. The ancient teachings were given to the Wise in order to preserve the human race. These teachings must be adapted to society as each culture evolves through the centuries. If the teachings aren't adapted to the people, the teachings become stale and die. If the teachings are not adapted to the culture, but are only a product of the individual or group ego, they become muddied and unclear for future students. The spiritual leaders (meaning those who take these risks and challenges of this world and turn them into positive experiences) periodically need to re-evaluate the written and oral teachings. This is what keeps a religion alive and the people evolving.

TIMOTHEA: Yes, I think the main idea is there, but more so the basic observations, thoughts, and customs are preserved as myths and folklore.

JOE WILSON: What I do is based upon teachings that have been handed down word of mouth. I have no idea how ancient it is (and it really doesn't matter to me) though I suspect the principles go back thousands of years. The form it takes now is different than it was, but the force and the essence are the same. It is not based upon ancient dogma or writings.

How do you feel Craft today compares with the Craft as practiced in the sixties and seventies? What about the quality of teaching?

MARTHA ADLER: I feel today's Craft has strayed far from the way it was in the sixties and seventies. Some changes have been for the better, but teaching today also lacks important aspects of the Craft that students need to have in their training.

AYEISHA: In the sixties and seventies it was difficult to make a good contact for yourself. It wasn't a matter of just buzzing down to your local metaphysical store and being served up whatever you wanted. But serious-minded people found each other anyway. A magical search took place and people found the teachers they needed. And because it took that search and effort, and that determination to make contact, I think that people made better contacts for themselves. They often had to travel long distances to make contact. Everyone in Maryland who was traditionally initiated had traveled some distance, to New York, Connecticut, New Hampshire, or even down South. In the end, I think that they were the better for it. The groups were much more serious then. There were standards that you were expected to live up to. Each degree has an amount of knowledge and practice which results in some genuine understanding and wisdom. The system was set up to help you consciously accelerate your personal growth and to help you live in harmony with the world at large. No one thought that you could go directly to "page 42" and rule the world. In the pop-witch culture today, there's this idea that you can ascend to the throne very rapidly and that you don't need to do the first and second degree work. In public groups I often see people who come in brand new to the whole concept, attend public gatherings and then declare themselves High Priestesses or High Priests. They look at others in these public situations and often feel as though the public Witches don't know very much more than they do. Therefore, they don't feel the need to study. I think that people fall into a trap where they feel as though they can't start at the beginning and admit how much they don't know, which is a real shame. But the real flaw is that many of the people that they meet—the people who are beating their breasts and shouting, "I'm a Witch! I'm a Witch!"—many of these people have so little knowledge and understanding, that the people coming into those groups assume that's true everywhere. There really are good groups out there, but the new person tends to think that the fluff on the surface is all there is. In the sixties and seventies you didn't have all of this going on. You worked hard and then connected with a group, and that was a wonderful magical process. There was the ability to relax in the company of genuine practitioners, people who had taken responsibility for their lives and developed some real ability to wield magic.

MARSHA BARD: The Craft in the sixties and seventies: I was into it and not out of it, and therefore cannot have an objective opinion on how it really was. I was aware of the fact that outsiders were frightened by it all, and insiders were rebels by society's standards. Everyone who had ever heard the word Wicca was writing a book. A flood of material became available. Craft went public in a sense and in defiance of the social patterns. Probably the "free thinking" of the sixties opened the gate for this. There were some good teachings, but also a lot of drivel. One had to be very careful.

LORI BRUNO: I lived in Huntsville, Alabama in the sixties so I was well aware of the bigotry in the Bible Belt. My husband who was in the Army was stationed at Cape Kennedy. I was by necessity underground and played the game right under the noses of the bigots. Ave Marie, Ave Diana! You couldn't buy a Craft book; everything was underground. My tools were hidden in my house, and no one knew what I was doing. I moved back to the North in 1968, and I felt free once again.

In the seventies Spynis and Samuel Weiser appeared. You had to send away for books. There weren't any fancy chalices with engraved pentagrams. You made and inscribed them yourself. I remember having a wooden bowl that I made into a chalice. The wood was soft so I was able to inscribe the magical symbols on it.

I had a bronze blade as well as a steel blade. I made the bronze blade from a bronze name plaque and took it to a Sicilian man and asked him to cut it for me. He said "Ah ha, you're going to be cutting the wind with this aren't you?" and he hugged me and said "Strega." I had a piece of Rowan wood from a tree that had been hit by lightning, and this made a perfect handle for my knife. And if you look at that piece of rowan wood, it looks like a hoof. I made my staff from a gnarled piece of wood and put a crystal on the top.

RAYMOND BUCKLAND: In that it has spread tremendously and come to be generally accepted is an excellent move forward. A lot of the teaching today is excellent but there is an equal amount that is absurd! We have, for better or worse, reached a stage where anyone can claim to be a Witch and claim that what he or she is practicing is Witchcraft, and there are no real standards by which they can be judged.

CHAS CLIFTON: In the 1960's and 1970's, it was pretty hard to be a "party Pagan," as there were no big festivals with all-night drumming and that sort of thing. Nor were there Pagan coffeehouses, theatrical large-group rituals, or any official recognition of the Craft as a religion. Gerald Gardner's assertion (and Robert Cochrane's parallel one) that there was indeed an Old Religion passed down through the centuries was accepted uncritically because we wanted to believe that our circles were keeping an ancient flame alive.

As for the quality of teaching, it has improved in many respects, although some of my friends worry about an element of "mystery" (in the religious sense) being lost. I do think that it is harder to play the "She Who Must Be Obeyed" High Priestess, for instance, because people have more options today. Recently, on a Colorado Pagan E-mail list that I moderate, a case came up of a Craft teacher/occult shop owner who was allegedly charging for classes that would lead to initiation and forbidding her students to have contacts with any other covens. I heard a lot of astonishment that such things still happened, but they used to be fairly common.

On the other hand, I see that it is easy to be caught up in organizational stuff of running a semi-public religion. Some Craft teachers are calling for seminaries and ordination credentials that will enable us to meet on equal terms with the credentialed representatives of other religions. Others, whom I tend to be more in sympathy with, remain individualistic and small-group oriented. We all struggle to find a balance between the Craft as "practice" and as "religion."

DEVON: I feel that now, you can pretty much find a variety of methods for information. People, books, computers, lectures and study groups are commonplace. It certainly wasn't like that earlier. The quality of teaching and the availability of information can be quite good in some areas. What concerns me is the number of people who arbitrarily take from many baskets and proclaim that they've come up with something new and more real. Everyone knows a little about nearly everything, but I find that there are few who consistently remain viable as time goes by. I feel that groups and individuals should have a solid base of Craft work that has been proven to work spiritually and magically and stick with it. As the years go by, we all learn more and disseminate more, but that home base shouldn't change just because the wind starts blowing from a different direction.

ETIDORHPA: I think the students today are very fortunate for they have much more information to work with, but there was something special about us in the sixties and seventies. There was a dedication that sometimes is not there today. It was harder to get into the Craft then. You had to be very dedicated or you just didn't make it. Students today don't have to fight the battles we did. On the whole it's much easier for them.

ALEXANDRIA FOXMOORE: The Pagan community of today and the "Wiccan" have almost nothing in common with the Traditions of the sixties and seventies. The word "Witch" today, has a different meaning from what it meant in Traditional Craft. There is little training and for the most part, students are self-taught. Few traditional books of "Craft" still exist and many have been rewritten in common terms emphasizing the peripheral activities, losing the true essence of their original structures. If one decides to start a group, he or she does. Students today can buy all the tools, books, and Witch garb through retail stores and catalogs. The community of today is open, all-inclusive, and democratic. Many who have become disenchanted with Christianity have found a haven in Paganism. Today, one can read books and learn to read Tarot cards, carry crystals, and gather in groups to burn candles and incense, and do spells. All are welcome and for the most part there is little rule, regulation, or reverence. Paganism today is the grand fellowship of the "in vogue" youth, the socially protesting elder and the free spirit of our society.

Today, many proclaim self-initiations, read a book about Witches and overnight, they "are" one. They become elders at twenty-five and assume names from established Elders and covens from which they are not associated. Foxmoore has long battled the problem of imitations using the Fox name and people claiming association who were not part of

Foxmoore covens. The use of the Fox name is granted only by the Board of Elders to Foxmoore members in good standing. It has become commonplace to use the accomplishments and names of well-known Elders to gain recognition. Those who are true and sincere will choose to be known by their own deeds rather than cloaking themselves with the deeds of Elders they've met or read about. I believe it is also important for seekers to understand that true Craft does not proselytize. Beware of those who shout the loudest and advertise in bold wording.

The Witch of the sixties lived a religion. There was no thought of being public and the Witch would deny that he or she was a Witch. A sixties Witch was a naturally talented soul who was blessed with gifts and talents. Most were a part of the Craft because they went to great effort to seek it out and worked for their acceptance. The sixties Witch was well read, learned and lived a very disciplined life. They considered being a part of "Craft" as a subscription to making and crafting most all the things they used in their worship and workings. They made their tools, crafted remedies, sewed their own robes, and grew their own herbs; therefore bringing definition to the term, "Craft." They did not charge for their work, but rather bartered for exchange. They took life vows of honor, respect, and loyalty. They were naturalists, communicators with the animal kingdom, and people of the Earth Religions.

GWION: Today's Craft is looser. In the sixties and seventies one mastered a system. Today's Craft seems less concerned with mastering a system than inventing new ones.

JUDY HARROW: I think we've settled down for the long haul, with less emphasis on individual magic and more on Pagan spirituality. We are confronting life's hard issues, as all religions must, and recognizing that we need solid theological and pastoral skills.

HANS HOLZER: Well, there isn't an awful lot of Craft as it was anymore. A lot of people have gone away. They've gotten older and become more mainstream. I think that's a pity, especially when these people are successful, when they are in mainstream business. That's when they should stand up for the Craft. That's the time to do it.

CORBY INGOLD: Craft, as practiced today, seems a bit subdued, toned down as it were, compared with my memories of coven meetings in the sixties and seventies. For one thing, the drink flowed a bit more freely back then (it was after all, an era of excess). And while I can certainly agree from the standpoint of health, as well as growing societal awareness of the problems of addiction, that this move away from the excessive partying of a former era is probably a good thing. Personally, I miss the fun we had in the old days. This may make me a horrible, amoral old Pagan, but so be it. I remember that coven meetings, even in some of the 'robed' covens, often included optional skyclad dancing as part of the celebration following formal rites. So I think there was a more 'orgiastic' quality to many of the Craft meetings that I remember from back then, though in the covens I attended this was all quite innocent. It never descended into sordidness. Also, we did more things outside, ranging from peoples' backyards to big parks and forest areas. Sadly, much of this seems to have disappeared today. And I seem to remember far more magic working—Witches weren't afraid of it back then. After all, magic was what Witches did. It was commonly felt in those days that if you didn't practice magic you weren't a Witch, a view with which I happen to concur. Nowadays this view is regarded as politically incorrect. Before the days of Starhawk, et al, the Craft had nothing to do with political correctness. There are still a few Neanderthals like myself who feel that the fusion of Witchcraft with politically correct ideology, in addition to watering down the Craft, makes for a very unhappy marriage indeed.

JIMAHL: I can only make assumptions as I wasn't practicing that early. I would assume that people take the Craft just as seriously now as they did then. I would hope that the quality of teaching also endures.

CHRISTINE JONES: Craft was a lot more strict than it is now and a lot more private. I think entry is way too easy now, but I'm pleased that many more people are acknowledging the Mother Goddess. As for the quality of teaching—Oh well…

KERRY: The Craft was more an "underground" issue in the past.

LORAX: I don't believe the quality of teaching has changed much in the past twenty years, although the 1970s training was more rigorous than what is expected today. What has changed is the basic knowledge that a student can get from a book. The systematization of materials and even traditions has made it possible for someone to memorize verbatim the "what" of a ritual circle or moon. The ease with which this can be done has also minimized an understanding of the "why" and "how," as well as innovation within a context.

There are more good books, but there are also more bad books. Since quite a few of the awful books are written by a handful of people who often cite one another, this creates new myths and establishes some con-tra-factual histories that can only serve to confuse new students.

LEO MARTELLO: In many ways, the Craft is bigger and better. It is now a worldwide movement. Thousands of people can now join, learn, practice, and meet others of like mind at festivals, public circles and open spaces. Naturally, the quality of teaching will suffer, as well as the suitability of Crafters. But this, in no way, detracts from those who know the truth. Unfortunately, though I've always said that one of the first qualifications to be in the Craft is to be crazy, now we have the spectacle of the inmates taking over the asylum. Those of us from a hereditary or truly traditional path can be a part or yet remain apart from this.

MERLIN: I believe that the number of serious people in the Craft has grad-ually grown. I also believe that the number of dabblers has also grown. I'm not sure if that is good or bad. However, there does seem to be a lot of New Age practitioners offering what appears to be a quick path.

I do not have enough current information to compare those early teach-ings with today's, other than to say that people today do not seem to have the necessary patience and seem to be looking for the quick way, which is not consistent with the basic traditions and philosophies of the Craft. I do know that there is a good deal more information readily available today.

MORDA: This is very subjective. I think the Craft as practiced in the six-ties and seventies was more fervent and more intense. There was more dedication. People were more resourceful, especially since there wasn't such a plethora of written/instructional material.

MORVEN: The quality of teaching these days varies widely. In general I think it's improved. We all have access to so much more information, and we can ask students to do research projects without having them borrow our books for days on end. Because time is so short today, we practice time management and sometimes manage to get more accomplished.

MURTAGH: In the sixties and seventies the Craft was incredibly under-ground, and I believe there were a lot of good reasons for that. The Craft has always been a mystery religion, and to operate as a mystery religion there has to be an amount of secrecy. While we don't proselytize, we also have to make ourselves known, so we walk a very fine line. There were reasons for the secrecy. Craft, during that time period, was associated with sex, drugs, and rock and roll. If you told anyone you were a Witch, they immediately thought you were a Satanist. One of the better things that has happened over the past twenty to thirty years is that people have more understanding of Craft in the outer world, the mundane world.

Because we were a mystery religion, because we were a little more secret, because it was harder to get in, there were more rules on what to do. Protection of the people you were affiliated with was important. People used public names so that even if somebody found out what your "Craft" name was, they couldn't trace you back to your mundane self or your mundane activities. My feeling is that we were a little more dedicated and had more depth. You struggled to find the Craft and you struggled to do the Craft. The hurdles—the obstacles—were a lot tougher, or at least Craft as I was involved with it. We were on an initiatory path, and there were certain things you had to do to get through your degree levels. It was a hierarchy; we had degrees, and at the same time we were highly individualistic. We were on the path together. There weren't a lot of us. Today it seems as though anyone who reads a book is in Craft, or that's what most people put forth to me and, of course, that isn't how it works. To me, to be in Craft means that you have been initiated into a bonafide tradition, whether that tradition started five, ten, or a hundred years ago, doesn't make a difference. You have been tied into the current of that tradition. You could draw upon their strength and energy as much as they knew that they could count on you. In the old days Perfect Love and Perfect Trust really meant something because these were people who could have ruined you without it. At that time you were equated with a Satan worshipper or whatever, and if someone called your place of employment—well, people were not that sympathetic then.

Today, it seems like everybody reads a book and is an instant priest or priestess and starting a group. The other problem I see is that a lot of people are creating huge mega-structures of "churches." And I use that in quotes because they don't call them churches; they call them organizations. Many of these people become gurus. I don't find it to be so much a religion of individuals anymore as a religion of followers. One of the things early Craft taught is that you should not charge coin. What I'm seeing today is that some of these people who have been involved for a while are using newer people to support them.

As for the quality of teaching? Most of it is hodgepodge. There are books that are cobbled together from other peoples' books, sometimes even without a by your leave. Many of these books are being written more to make money than to spread knowledge or enlightenment. Prior to the sixties many books by people like Regardie and Gardner were done to disseminate information, and I believe they were done in sincerity. Now I'm seeing companies churning out these money books, and the quality of teaching has just gone downhill.

When I first arrived in Southern California twelve years ago, I found that people weren't even being taught basic magic techniques. They didn't know things like centering, meditation techniques, or visualization. Now how can you do magic without visualization!!! Now they make them write term papers and have pseudo degrees. I've seen some of these people who didn't even know the elements! People today seem more interested in collecting "stripes" and to see how much they can impress you. The show seems to be more important than the magic.

There is also the issue of the sacred and the profane. I feel that in older Craft there was a sense of the sacred, that what we did was sacred and holy. I think we are losing our sense of sacredness. Some will argue that we're making everything sacred, but I don't see them walking a sacred path every day. I feel we profane everything by shouting out on street corners and putting it all over the internet. I would go so far as to say that the more we disseminate certain things, the more we lose pieces of our soul and we lose the inherent qualities that made it magical. So in the end I think that the quality of teaching has gone downhill—period— no ifs, ands, or buts about it.

MARY NESNICK: From what I've seen, the current quality of teaching is pathetic. Practice in the sixties was very religious. Today it's pretty much an amalgam of seemingly everything depending on the desires of those in charge.

ELIZABETH PEPPER: Much of the lore and flavor is similar. Religion is far heavier a focus today than the Craft I grew up to know. That is not to say our work wasn't considered sacred for it was very serious indeed. The structure of beliefs and ethical considerations were of an entirely different framework.

PATRICIA POTHIER: Since one's intimate knowledge is only of one's own Coven (and the ones I belonged to gave excellent teaching), it is difficult to answer this question. However, from speaking to people at large gatherings, I get the feeling that they have read more books and know more facts, but have less real understanding than the students of my generation do.

TRIVIA PRAGER: When I first began studying there wasn't the Internet where you could find bulletin boards posting—"I am a thirteen year old High Priestess and want to talk to other thirteen year old High

Priestesses." You still had to work hard to find a teacher, and not all of the rituals were published. It was hard to find books; you had to go to specialized shops. Now all kinds of people read three books, self-initiate, and start groups. The beauty of the Traditional path is that you get to learn from someone with experience; you get the time to study, absorb and grow. It's a two-way street, you teach and you are taught. As Procol Harum said, "For the lesson lies in learning, and by teaching I'll be taught. For there's nothing hidden anywhere, it's all there to be sought."

ROGER PRATT: I am not terribly familiar with current teaching. I "feel" it was better, especially more comprehensive and more personal in the sixties and seventies.

The New Age seems to have fostered some popular, though erroneous (to my mind) ideas and beliefs. I prefer to know the "why" we do each and every thing.

RAOKHSHA: Traditional Craft has had the time to mature and create a body of knowledge and materials that comprise an excellent training manual. (On the other hand, the rest of the community is oftimes reinventing the wheel or may, at worst, be perpetuating a trail of misinformation.) In the early days there was an immediacy to "preserve the Craft." Since that time the "nuts and bolts" of practice have taken center stage, and techniques from other paths have entered (or been returned to) the Craft. I do believe that today's training frequently surpasses that of the 60's and 70's.

OWEN ROWLEY: Somewhere in the mid-eighties I lost interest in the public direction of Craft as it was shaping up. It felt hollow to me. There were too many people popping out of the woodwork with stuff they called a Witchcraft tradition, yet was their own contemporary work. Now, I occasionally come up with new things too, but the bulk of my working is based on practices that I know have at least some history. A tradition is a system but a system is not a tradition until it has some history underneath it. You can't just take scholarly research and revive pieces and call it a tradition (which I think happens all too often). Underlying all of this is the issue of borderline between religious practice and magic. Clearly, anyone can fabricate a spiritual/religious ritual and be completely satisfied with it. No one should fault that. But Craft revivalists who try to glean magical technique strictly from scholarship—and without connection to a genuine magical tradition—I believe are short-circuiting the process.

ZANONI SILVERKNIFE: Well, to be perfectly enigmatic about it, six of one and half-dozen of another. I have some pretty ambiguous feelings about the Craft as it is practiced today. While I am pleased that it is more open and accessible to people and that there are many good books out there for the reading, I am rather appalled at the lack of respect I see when I go to public events the "new guard" puts on. Is it true that each new generation has to drop the brick on their own collective toes, bang their loosely confederated heads against the same stone walls we learned years ago to avoid? Sigh. I guess they do. Frankly, I've been appalled by certain people of the last three decades who seem to view the Craft as an extension of their own groups and interests. I suspect that these people will fade away and leave a clean core of what the Craft really is for the next generation of newbies to frustrate.

As to the "quality" of teaching, I can say that quality has always been a scarce commodity, more so than quantity. The egotistical need of some people to be a Craft guru generates a hole to be filled by the gullible. These types form co-dependent relationships and give Crafters everywhere a tarnished reputation. How much actual "Craft style" teaching goes on is debatable. The want-to-be "I read a book" Witch evokes two trains of thought—one being that I am glad they found something of worth to work toward, the other springing from the deep knowledge that nothing can replace the experience that can be shared with guidance given from those who have already traveled that path and have gained wisdom on the way. Nothing beats the old one-on-one for a good measure of passing of the wisdom and power, the correctness of doing things in a way that accomplishes much more and is spiritually economical, rich in intensity of feeling.

SINTANA: There is no comparison; the teaching has totally changed. There no longer seems to be any emphasis on the spiritual teachings in today's Pagan communities. So many of their leaders are collectors of information, calling themselves Witches. They have become an intellectual, social grouping but have no real understanding and do not apply the teachings to their own lives. The underground network of communication between Elders that used to be so strong is, for all intents and purposes, non-existent. The Elders no longer come together for Witch Meets to discuss matters of common interest and share energy with their peers.

STOCK: The Craft and the people are essentially the same. In some ways the quality of teaching is better because a lot more is known and accepted today. In other ways, the quality of teaching is worse because many "bona fide" teachers have been replaced with New Age shamans.

TANITH: It's hard for me to make sweeping generalities, and some of the differences have to do as much with our changing culture as with the way the Craft itself has changed. Still, I think the major differences I've noticed have been the shift away from celebrating overt male-female sexuality so much, and the lack of emphasis on spell casting. This manifests itself as a shift away from practicing skyclad, ritual accommodation of same-sex relationships (changing of the wording of rituals with a resultant increased generic feeling). Also, the de-emphasis on learning or teaching any sort of spell which could actually effect a change beyond the most general sort (i.e., one must not cast a love spell to get a specific person, but only one to draw one's own true love, whoever that might turn out to be).

From what I've observed, the quality of teaching is probably about the same as it ever was. That is to say, varied, depending on the group one joins. All groups have slightly different foci; some are going to be more celebratory, others more historically or ethnically oriented. Whether an aspirant gets what he or she would find to be "quality" teaching would depend on how well-matched the group they choose is to their own needs and interests.

THEITIC: Much of the teaching has become sterile (notes, lessons, books to read, certificates to win). While it is true that a student will come away from the training sessions with the correct spelling of the zodiac signs, many of them still cannot go out into the night and find the North Star!

Personally, I have always felt that the Craft is meant to be taught in an apprentice-and-teacher format. There is no substitute for a one-on-one experience. Watching, learning and doing will also show the teacher that the individual has the desire to continue along the path. The ideal instructor is a priest(ess), counselor, parent, teacher and friend.

Teaching is not for everyone, and you aren't a teacher after you have a teaching certificate. You become a teacher when you have something to teach and when someone has a need to learn. At that time, a real teacher accepts not the responsibility of teaching, but the responsibility of someone learning.

TIMOTHEA: People were more dedicated to the Craft. They worked harder to get "in" and valued it more. They were more careful who was included and this eliminated many curiosity seekers and transients. Because it was smaller and had tighter controls, and many knew each other, "bad apples" were known.

JOE WILSON: The quality of teachings? What quality of teachings? I'm actually very disappointed. I had hoped that by developing a widespread Pagan movement, I would discover people who would be interested in the deeper philosophies and practices with which I am familiar. Instead we have a large mass of people who think that all they need is in a couple of books and they really don't have to work for anything. We have a "gimme" culture and the Pagan movement seems to have adopted the worst aspects of it.

Can you speak about the ethical and moral basis of Traditional Craft?

AYEISHA: Craft has one rule and ethic, the Wiccan Rede which is, "An it harm none, do what you will." Traditional Wicca is a religion of personal responsibility and personal growth.

Initiates take on, as part of the initiation itself, a particular obligation to their own personal development throughout their lives. They work very hard to achieve what we call true will, true will being the best possibility we can conceive for ourselves. Finding your true will isn't easy. It requires a lot of honesty, courage, and hard work. It is also very rewarding. Craft ethics are different in nature, and based in Nature, which makes them very different than the one-god religions that hand out a whole list of do's and don'ts. Having a hard system of do's and don'ts is difficult. You have a rule that says, "Thou shalt not steal." This is a good general rule that most people really ought to use, and it helps people to behave. But if you're in a situation where your children are hungry, and you've done whatever else you could do and still do not have food, at that point it would be totally appropriate for you to say, yes, we must steal. Wiccans have an extremely powerful ethical principle which we must apply in each specific situation, according to our best judgment.

In regards to understanding the Rede, it's very simple and elegant, and at the same time very, very complex. It is not "do whatever you want as long as no one is hurt." Finding your true will is difficult. Figuring out what is harmful rather than just painful or unpleasant is not much easier either. "An it harm none" is deceptively simple and incredibly complex because you have to judge each and every opportunity what harm is to whom, or what is good for whom. "Do what you will" is a challenge to self-direction. You're required to try to figure out what you want and not just what someone else wants for you. All of us are very much subject to tremendous role expectations and pressures that come from ourselves, our families, our friends, and society in general. It is very easy to just be molded, deceptively easy. On the other hand, you can become a compulsive rebel and, in reflex, do just the opposite of whatever "they" seem to want. Living by the Rede means accepting the responsibility to assess the results of our actions and choose when we will obey, confront, or even evade the rules. "Do what you will" is absolutely a challenge to action. You can't wait for someone else. You can't wait for Prince Charming or the Revolution, you can't blame your mother or the system. You need to make a realistic plan that includes all your assets. A plan that includes magic, the deeper insights and wisdom of divination, the focusing of your will and energy, all that comes from active workings.

Pagan myth as well as today's science and modern biology teaches us that the Earth is one interconnected being. We are a living sphere, a whole being where the actions of each affect us all. These actions are emphatically not limited to humankind. We are all connected to really intrinsic organic feedback paths. As our technology today really amplifies the effects of our individual actions it becomes increasingly critical to try to understand that these actions will have consequences beyond the individual. These are consequences that, by the nature of things, come back to the individual as well. It's important to understand that any refusal to decide or any action that you don't take are also decisions, and it becomes clear that all of us have to find our balance within the whole. Craft is the only tradition that teaches that all of life is interconnected and sees our incredible interconnectedness. Cooperation once was merely an ethical ideal. It has become a survival imperative. Judy Harrow wrote a piece about the Rede back in the late seventies that was published in *Harvest* around 1985. It was very well done, and I would direct anyone to read that for more information.

MARSHA BARD: My ethical and moral training in Traditional Craft set the parameters for my life. The moral and ethical codes of a society that I considered slightly askew did not take hold. I hold a belief in Karma and the Three Fold Law addresses that issue very simply and nicely. I also hold a belief in the natural instincts of the purity of the species. This is also addressed nicely in the Three Fold Law. Other things have been added to the codes as time passes, but at its very basic level, the ethic of "an it harm none" combined with the moral freedom to "do what thou will" has been the cornerstone of my life. I am free of guilt and full of experiences that others based in the Christian doctrine of "sin" dare not even think of (or do think of and that is the root of all their psycho-dramas and tragedies).

LORI BRUNO: The first thing I would say is that I may be a High Priestess but I do not expect my coveners to clean my house, or to pay my bills. We of the Sicilian Strega do not expect our coveners to do anything that would be disrespectful to their bodies, minds or souls for the purpose of achieving rank. Respect is all. If a High Priestess and High Priest do not respect their students, then they have no respect for themselves or the Gods, and the Gods will in turn disrespect them.

RAYMOND BUCKLAND: It can all be summed up in "An it harm NONE, do what thou will." Harm no one (including yourself); send out love and understand and respect all of Nature.

CHAS CLIFTON: Some people who claim to be Traditional do not claim to live by the Wiccan Rede of "An it harm none, do what you will" because the Rede limits them; they feel rather that "a Witch who cannot curse cannot cure."

Regardless of whether they claim to follow the Wiccan Rede or the law of threefold return or neither, I do think that most people calling themselves "Traditional" follow a lunar law of justice that does not make too many concessions to written law or conventional morality. We tend to be more like the private eyes of Raymond Chandler or film noir, who want things to work out in the end according to our own sense of justice.

DANA CORBY: "The ethical and moral basis of Traditional Craft is simple. It is total personal responsibility. And it is total personal freedom. You are accountable for the results of your choices, period. The Wiccan Rede, "An it harm none, do what you will," is well known but very little understood. It doesn't encourage acting on every whim; it demands that you identify your will and act on that. And it demands that you understand the meaning of harm in each context. But we must understand that "rede" means advice, not law. Another axiom is that no one is the keeper of a Witch's conscience. I'm disheartened by the youngsters coming up in the Craft who are so intimidated by the idea of getting "bad Karma" that they won't do magic and won't take responsibility for much of anything. Then why be a Witch? But most of us are conditioned to believe that "responsibility" means blame, when the true meaning of the word is "the ability to respond." A Witch responds to the events around her in an appropriate and sometimes magical manner, and this is as it should be. Responding with extreme violence is condonable in defense of the defenseless, but revenge is unforgivable.

It does a perpetrator no good to be permitted to go on as he is, and does great harm to his victims. Stopping him by whatever means necessary is within the Wiccan Rede. I'll grant you that what passes for a justice system in today's world does nobody any good either. When I'm being really cold-blooded on the subject I think that, since neither freedom nor incarceration does criminals any good, the most compassionate thing to do might be to execute them and let them be reborn to try again. But then I get real.

ALEXANDRIA FOXMOORE: "An it harm none do what you will..." began with never harming yourself. It meant no harm to our Mother Earth, its creatures, the plants, etc. It meant, too, that Traditional Craft was probably the staff bearer for animal rights. Traditional Crafters considered themselves caretakers of the Earth, healers, and buffers against evil or destruction. Respect was ingrained and loyalty was expected. There were rules about keeping your home, family and spiritual family well taken care of first before you entertained outside activities for yourself. There were the ethics of secrecy that protected the families. There were serious understandings that the Witch did not bring down the law of the land on his or her family or coven. Covens were a spiritual family with family ethics and morals. Witches, most of all, broke no law, moral value, or ethic not only of their religion but also of the society they lived in, so that they never brought undo attention to their brothers and sisters in the Craft. Besides the Ancient laws, the Rede (accepted Craft laws) and Pagan laws, the Witch subscribes to the "Tenets," which are a set of suggestions for leading an ethical existence. These Tenets are: the Tenet of a Balanced Life, the Tenet of Harmony, the Tenet of Trust, the Tenet of Humility, the Tenet of Tolerance, the Tenet of Learning, and one secret Tenet that remains unspoken and understood by all initiates.

GWION: All the chapters I could write on this can be summed up with "An it harm none, do what ye will."

JUDY HARROW: The Rede is an excellent and balanced statement of situational ethics. Beyond that, I think is the spirituality of immanence, the perception that we can find the sacred within this life, in these bodies, here and now. Flowing from this, a devotion to Mother Earth—to defend and heal Her.

HANS HOLZER: "An it harm none" is the motto. Actually, I have said it publicly and in my books that Christianity has taken over many of our Tenants, and why shouldn't they because their beliefs came afterward. Jesus was a student in an Essene monastery, and they stayed away from political rivalry and tried to steer a much more esoteric course. There is really no difference between taking the cracker and the red wine from the Christian priest and taking the bread and wine from the High Priestess. It is the same thing, the same symbolism.

CORBY INGOLD: I think that the ethical and moral basis of Traditional Craft is pretty well summed up by the Witch's Rede: "An it harm none, do what ye will." I don't personally believe the Rede pre-dates the 1950s, but it serves as a useful ethical guideline in the working of magic. And great and profound truths can often be expressed quite simply. Of course, to view the Rede through a slightly more sophisticated lens, we should bear in mind that, as a great Buddhist writer said, "Harmlessness is an ideal to strive for, but it is not always possible to live without causing harm to other beings."

JIMAHL: I teach my students that white magic and black magic are both unhealthy extremes. All magic is gray. As Witches we must learn to balance light and dark, to walk between the worlds. I instill a strong sense of ethics into my students' training so they can be well equipped to make the right choices.

CHRISTINE JONES: I wish all religions would relax and accept others. It would prevent a lot of wars if people could stop being afraid of each other. It is the fact that they don't believe in what they do that makes them so hell-bent on trying to convert others.

LORAX: The ethic of Traditional Craft, as I understand it, is that there is always something bigger that can eat you; the universe is not a dead thing, and others will notice any changes you make. It therefore behooves one to make good changes that minimize, if not eliminate the possibility of harm to others.

Any student smarter than room temperature will either learn painfully or quickly intuit that if he or she can work magic and change some parameter in his or her life, or the life of another, then others can too. Loud magic can attract an awfully big crowd in this world or the Akashic.

There is an elegant demonstration of the efficiency of ethical behavior in the game "tit for tat." The most effective strategy for survival is cooperation and mutual support with all the players in this game of life, and probably in the afterlife game as well.

LEO MARTELLO: I don't know about others but in the Sicilian Craft without a moral and ethical basis there would be no Craft. We'd all be dead. For a fuller understanding of this see my chapter on "Sicilian Witchcraft" in my book, *Witchcraft: The Old Religion*. We were sworn to silence, to each other, for life. In olden days it was literally a "life and death matter." In one important way we differ from the "lily white Witches" in that we feel a wrong in this life must be rectified in this life. We don't say "Let Karma take care of it." We are responsible for our own Karma. We don't bring an unresolved conflict in this life into the next. No one has the right to do us wrong. We all have the moral right to self-defense.

MERLIN: Traditional Craft has a very tribal, close knit, family orientation, generally based on a level of Love and Trust. From that all of the benefits and problems of a family are present in a spiritual setting and become part of the learning and the mysteries. Adherence to the basic family or tribal values (such as love and trust) are the ethical and moral requirements.

MORDA: I view the ethical and moral basis of the Craft as I know it to be extremely high. Most Craft people I know live ethically. What's good, is that there are no prohibitions in the Judeo-Christian sense, no repression, hence nothing to rebel against. I really like the concern for the environment and animal rights issues.

MORVEN: Our ethics are still "An it harm none…" We evaluate each situation separately, thinking about the ethics of our possible courses of action, not just now, but Karmically. I have heard discussions of non-Craft ethics that are very strict, so compared to them, we may be considered liberal. For example, I know people who will not perform a healing without having the person's permission. I would send energy so the person could use it to fight for his or her life, or use it to move on. For example, if you know CPR and someone has a heart attack in front of you, do you refuse to do CPR because you don't have permission? No! You try to save the life! Yet, I've known of people who refused to send healing energy to someone who's had that heart attack just because they didn't have that person's permission. I believe you need to examine your motives and use common sense.

MURTAGH: Traditional Craft had an ethical and moral basis. We were human and we had faults, but we really tried to do more than pay lip service to "an it harm none." And that's the bottom line. You can do what you want to do, but "an it harm none." When you're in a holistic system and you're in harmony with the universe, you will not do anything to harm anything or anyone. Perfect Love and Perfect Trust—they were attempts— and, again, we are human. We make errors. We have faults. But these were at least attempts to try to be in harmony with each other, to not hurt each other. Egos got in the way, but I think the attempts were made. Now I hear lip service. The original Rede that we have is 28 lines, and it has things to live by in it. We had reverence for life, but we also understood death. When we were asked to do healings, we did them because we were asked. If we sent energy to someone because they were in a coma or such, there were things to understand. The person could, on a spiritual level, refuse. I've been in healing circles where the person has refused. And everyone in the circle knew that the person had refused the healing and, of course, several days later the person passed on. But we understood that; we didn't force it. Traditional Craft was about enlightenment, being on a path. And being on a path there are certain ethical considerations that normally as "an enlightened being," you should know and come to grips with.

MARY NESNICK: I find similarities, and little or no conflict between the Craft and Tibetan Buddhism in that both believe in reincarnation and the idea of Karma, but I think that the teaching "an it harm none do what ye will" says it all for Craft.

ELIZABETH PEPPER: The first thing that comes to my mind is the deep and abiding love for animals. This is the one attribute every member of my family, all their friends, every single person we knew and associated with shared in common. I feel it is central to the recognition and practice of Witchcraft. I realize that this is a sweeping statement, certain to provoke dissent. However, I'm absolutely convinced of its truth. Second is a sense of humor. It's like a balance wheel. We should be serious in our work, or Craft undertakings, but not pious. "A Witch isn't self-righteous" is the theme. Third (there is always a third, which is a tradition in itself), you can never refuse a cry for help. And when a gift is given or a favor done, the recipient is expected to pass the goodness along—not to necessarily repay the giver but to respond in a similar manner when the occasion arises. Other than that, I can only say that I think Witchcraft is far more mysterious than anyone realizes.

PATRICIA POTHIER: It is inherent in the premises of the religion rather than "revealed" or specifically legislated. If you truly live in harmony with Nature, you will observe moderation and you will try to harm none. More than this is situational. But you must always accept responsibility for your actions. If your actions are not appropriate to your status as a citizen of the universe, you debase yourself.

ROGER PRATT: Only do, and allow done to others what you can condone within your own heart.

RAOKHSHA: The Crowleyan "Do what thou wilt shall be the whole of the law" has either been a license to create a lawless society or has struck a chord with otherwise moralistic individuals to be above reproach. I prefer the "perfect love and perfect trust" altruism.

I personally feel I should be a role model for my coven, my family, and others who might look to me for hints about doing "the right thing." I think that Traditional Craft people would score really well on a morals test. Either our "leaders" are ethical or they just don't get the press of the media's Christian fund-raisers. Our law of threefold return is a real temperer of roguishness, and the acceptance of reincarnation and/or Karma doesn't leave one an "out" after a bad showing this time around, does it?

The Charge of the Goddess adopted by most traditions today, offers a code of moral behavior within its guidelines for the successful practitioner. Love Her and honor Her, and you can do no wrong.

OWEN ROWLEY: "Eight words the Wiccan Rede fulfill; an it harm none— do what ye will." Beyond that, let's talk about morals in general. Morality is informed by values, and values are gained by experience and other educational methods. Those who claim to own a purchase on morality because they are informed by a document could not be any further removed from the truth of the matter. If the values and experiences which inform truth and morality are not earned by the individual then the truth of those values and experiences has not been tested by that individual. At that point it is all theory; they are values of no real value.

At the heart of the Craft is the concept of Perfect Love and Perfect Trust. Let me be clear—Love and Trust are already perfect. When we align our values and understanding to form a triangle with Love and Trust, we form a perfectly stable triangle—a structure of true wisdom.

ZANONI SILVERKNIFE: As I learned the Craft, there were definitive guidelines to follow, morays and morals to be observed, and ethics to be considered. One did not do a thing (magic) merely because one could. The responsibility you shoulder when you take an oath of initiation is substantial. With each degree taken, or elevation achieved, or spiritual plateau you reach, the responsibility increases in a geometric progression. The underlying universal laws of the way everything operates must be carefully taught and attended to. If you wish to get the appropriate results you must adhere to the proper approach, that specific method by which any good practitioner achieves results. Knowledge of the ethical and moral underpinnings of the Craft is very necessary to getting things done in a correct manner. True, you can twist things out of time, space, and natural shape and get what you want. The rebound, however, is rather spectacularly unnerving and nearly fatal to those who challenge the universe. It is rather like twisting an elastic band too tightly and losing control—it smacks you every time.

Ethics is one of the "holes" in the philosophical view and magical practice of people who did not get guidance in their early life or as a practicing "Pagan." I was given the Laws and Ordains, The Rede of the Wicca, Ethical Considerations and other like documents such as the Cosmic Laws and The Desiderata to guide me. One either has moral fiber or one doesn't. It isn't something you can catch like the flu. You can develop it with an effort of will. The laws and similar types of information are necessary for people who do not have an unerring sense of correctness. One must remember, however, that the Spirit of the Law is what counts here, not the Letter of the Law, though it doesn't do to interpret too loosely. I find that a great many people give lip service to the Ethics of Magic and the Laws of the Craft. When it comes to something they want, they will use any tool at their disposal to get it—damn the consequences and go full tilt. Snap! goes the elastic band!

SINTANA: We have our Ways to Grace, Tenets, and Laws which were passed unto our Sacred Keep. They give to us the boundaries we apply as we go through our individual experiences in this life. Our experiences will be provided as a direct result of what we have put forth, i.e., deeds, thoughts, words, and actions. We are responsible for all we are, and we have a sacred responsibility to all living members of our planet. This is very misunderstood by today's Pagans who use the term "An it harm none, do what ye will."

STARSPAWN: Some groups today charge money for the training, some ask even more than that, such as cleaning the leader's houses, providing a tithing, or even sexual favors. All of this is totally forbidden in the traditional Craft teachings. A student is taught as part of an oral tradition passed down since the beginning. It is a sacred duty for both the teacher and the student.

The majority of my teachings on ethics and morality of the Craft was done by example. I watched how my group leaders behaved within their groups and with non-initiates. I learned by example, "An it harm none, do what ye will."

STOCK: Traditional Craft is family…..period. Most important are family, tribal, or clan values: love, patience, understanding, argument, nurturing, and blind loyalty. Ethics and morality boil down to one statement—"I am part of a family."

TANITH: Traditional Craft, as I learned it, taught the Rede: "An it harm none, do what ye will," with an emphasis on taking responsibility for your actions. As a Witch you may cast any spell you like as long as you are prepared to deal with the results. You don't deliberately harm anyone, and you try to help people. It's about pursuing wisdom and truth. It's a pretty ethical, realistic religion.

THEITIC: "Mind the threefold law ye should, three times bad and three times good. Eight words the Wiccan Rede fulfill, An it harm none, do what ye will." Our ethics and morals are guided by our Rede and can best be summed up by these two stanzas. Although we understand Karma to be a natural law causing energies to "return to the sender," this is interpreted with a deeper meaning than simple "retribution." We believe that we make our own situations. There is no predestination. We are responsible for our actions and our own happiness.

The Rede says, "Mind the Three Fold Law…" It doesn't threaten the Witch. Our law only tells us to "mind" the law; know that it exists. Should you choose to take action because of personal choice, this is your right as a conscious being.

We do not believe in turning the other cheek (lest that cheek be slapped as well.) We are warriors for spiritual enlightenment and freedom. We are not slaves to a concept supposedly delivered to us by a dead god. Neither are we warriors for another's unjust cause. Our people do not believe in warfare for its own sake. We fight enough wars within our own psyche for one lifetime. These battles between our individual dark (ignorant) and light (wise) sides are a lifelong work, and this is where the Witch would be wise to dedicate effort.

I believe that when a person carries out his or her life, taking responsibility for his or her own actions, he or she lives a moral life. Remembering that no one has the right to forcibly impose his or her belief system upon another.

Many Pagans today seem to have a problem with Traditional Craft degrees and hierarchy. What are your feelings on this issue?

MARTHA ADLER: The coven I came from is of hereditary origin in England and did not utilize degrees. In later years I incorporated the degrees with at least a year and a day between each.

AYEISHA: I think that the concept of Craft is badly misunderstood by many Pagans. Craft is traditionally an initiatory path that relies heavily upon its oral tradition and the passing of magic from one person to the next. I would say that there is an ethic of mutual respect among any initiated Craft persons, regardless of degree. This is a teaching tradition, which essentially does teach people to grow up and be powers in and of themselves. It is understood that each person who is accepted into a coven is a person the rest of the individuals in the group feel is a serious student and practitioner. There's mutual respect right from the very beginning. On the other hand, any system of teaching and learning has to have markers. Traditional Craft is a systematic approach that guarantees that all of the people who come through it will receive a basic amount of information, a basic core of knowledge, and a basic series of opportunities for a person to do ritual and have experiential understanding as well as intellectual understanding.

In the Craft you have three degrees and go through specific levels of training. The first degree is the lunar degree in which you expect people to drink in a lot of information, to think on it, and to start the beginning of their practices. By second degree you expect them to have absorbed enough of the practices to be a real practitioner in the world, a person able to use his or her personal power to—first and foremost—make his or her life better, but then, secondly, to also benefit the world in some way. By the end of second degree you expect the person to be able to teach. Then in third degree you take on a lot of the larger responsibilities like the Rites of Passage, Wiccanings, Handfastings, and Deaths. When you achieve third degree, the understanding is that you are going to completely cycle through those degrees over and over again and that you're never really finished in your line of growth. It would be safe to say that Craft has a sort of benign dictatorship as opposed to total anarchy, which is what a system becomes when everybody can do whatever he or she wants at all of the basic levels.

Traditional Craft is a certain animal. It is not this, and it's not that, it's what it is. And what it is has these three degrees that a person is expected to, at the minimum, progress through and absorb that material. And if people don't want to do that, then they ought to go off and be something else and not call themselves Witches. In the principles of Wiccan Belief from the Council of American Witches, Rule Number Eight states that calling yourself a Witch does not make you a Witch, but neither will heredity alone, nor will the collecting of titles, degrees and initiations make you a Witch. A true Witch is someone who is formed from the inside out. If somebody has gone through the degree system in Wicca, you can expect that he or she has a bottom-line amount of opportunity for wisdom and growth. If people haven't gone through the degrees, they haven't received all of those opportunities, which is why I feel that if somebody abolishes those degrees, he or she is really cheating the people who come after.

Some traditional Witches have abolished degrees and have put all of the information into one book, tossing aside material that they no longer wanted or needed. The problem with this is that you deprive people of opportunities and information that they otherwise might have had. They forget that having gone through the degree system that helped to shape and form them, they are today the products of having had those opportunities and experiences.

The Craft is what it is, a traditional, apostolic succession system that presents to you "x" amount of understanding, wisdom, and opportunity to have experiential wisdom. It is, as so many people like to say, like any other kind of school. If you have a doctor and the doctor says, "I didn't feel like going to school. I did a little bit of reading on and off on my own, but now I'm ready to operate," people would feel very shy of that kind of thing. You know, these are learning systems, and if you don't go through the learning you're not going to be very useful at the end of it all. I think that because the terms, Craft and Pagan, are bantered about loosely, and because so many people just read a book and call themselves Witches, or come by it very quickly, everybody is looking to get right through. Whereas, everybody knows that you have to start at the beginning and work your way forward if you want to go anywhere.

MARSHA BARD: I agree with the concept of degrees but I have a problem with the political process in covens. To some, the elevation is a matter of self-esteem—to those I would bestow degrees for proof that the knowledge had been intellectually processed. To some the elevation is a matter of goal-oriented success—and to those I would also bestow degrees as proof of meeting those goals. But for some, the change from the ordinary world, as perceived by the non-Craft, to the extraordinary world of Craft, is a heart-felt wonder, and they see this as enough in itself. These very few I would make priests and priestesses. For I feel that Craft is a state of the heart. It can be learned and struggled for, and for that one would deserve a just reward. But for those who feel it is their heart, no learning, no lecturing could reward them more. It would be those people that I would send out to teach and hold close to me through a process of degrees, those struggling to open their hearts with their minds.

LORI BRUNO: My Tradition does not use degrees. We believe the Gods see your degree and your merit, and they are the true initiators. They touch you, and you feel the quickening in your body.

RAYMOND BUCKLAND: Some traditions have a degree system; some do not. The seeker should choose that which is comfortable without criticizing what is right for someone else. Neither is more correct than the other. If you have a problem with degrees—or with the lack of degrees—leave that particular tradition alone.

CHAS CLIFTON: I never went through a degree system. The nearest I ever came was that Stewart Farrar, who welcomed Mary and me into his and Janet's coven circle, referred to me as initiated "after the order of Melchizedek," (see Genesis 14:18), in other words, valid but of no known tradition. When we had our own group in Manitou Springs, CO, we basically performed a one-degree system.

I work in academia, where degrees of another sort are taken quite seriously, and I know how much work goes into a master's or doctorate degree if it is done right—not at some diploma mill. I have also seen academic degrees (or rather their lack) used as ways to keep people out of jobs that they might otherwise be well qualified for. So it is with Craft degrees. They can serve as recognition of dedication, achievement, and maturity on the Path, but they can also be weapons of snobbery and meaningless game-playing. Here the "congregational" or "temple" Pagans have a point: if you claim to be a third-degree, but you stay in your living room with the curtains drawn having small-group ceremonies, what is the point of it all?

DANA CORBY: It seems to me that some "seekers" want everything for nothing. Others, think they can pay for enlightenment, and that if they pay enough, they can have it instantly (or at least get it at a weekend seminar). I don't really care if someone has a problem with the way Traditional Craft works. This is how it works, and if you want what it offers, you'll do what's necessary to get it. During the process, you'll come to understand why it works that way, stop thinking of it in terms of "getting something" and begin "becoming," which is what it's all about. Obviously, I'm in favor of the degree system and use it. Properly used, hierarchy teaches respect in a culture which does not, while gradually increasing, not so much the initiate's rank, but his or her level of responsibility.

Our Tradition owes a lot to the older British Trads, and did not until recently have a third degree. Our system is somewhat different from many. We're of the "teach, then initiate" school of thought. There's a short course, combining basic energy working, simple spells, and a lot of theory, leading to Dedication. After Dedication comes the year-and-a-day time period leading to Initiation, followed by working through the degrees.

Lately, I'm finding a resurgence of interest on the part of the young people in Traditional Craft. They seem to be having problems—not so much with the structure of traditionalism—with understanding the difference between learning something and living something. They expect their teachers to be like their professors were, and have to struggle with the more amorphous approach to learning that is traditional. The dropout rate is fairly high, but some do make it.

DEVON: Yes, I use degrees and the requirements of learning, teaching and responsibility grows with each degree. I think that there is a hierarchy in every Pagan group whether it's acknowledged or not. If you don't have someone to keep an eye on things it can be very hard to make decisions. Everyone wants to be heard and everyone wants a say in what should be done. That's fine, but it must be managed in a way that is fair to everyone, and I emphasize "fair." The more people you have in a group situation the more important it is to have someone who is given all the information, the wants and needs of the group or the individual and the responsibility to act fairly in any situation. That's why there are parents, managers, team captains and presidents. Without some type of clear leadership there can be chaos. I think that is a fact that follows through in life, homes, and jobs. I also feel that sometimes one of the problems is that many people want to be leaders without taking the time to learn the skills, and in a Craft society that is extremely important. I don't like to see people taking in a little of this or that and then "teaching" other people when they don't have a completed system to work with.

ETIDORHPA: I think the degree system is still very pertinent and the degrees should remain. If an initiate is dedicated to his or her religion and studies, he or she should have to learn and reach a certain amount of awareness before being entitled to move on. If students don't want the degrees, they shouldn't take the initiation. They would do better to be Pagan and not Craft.

ALEXANDRIA FOXMOORE: Many Pagans today are not Witches and do not understand Traditional Craft. It is not important that they do.

GWION: I am traditionally based, therefore the degrees are a great part of my system. I was taught and believe that the degrees are magical steps/operations performed on the candidate. If viewed in this manner you might say that they are not really hierarchical. The degrees also act as a safety valve, allowing the initiate to progress in a measured manner without becoming overwhelmed.

JUDY HARROW: I sure do believe in using the degrees! Skills deserve recognition. Our requirements are too detailed to list, but they include real clergy skills, based on Pagan theological insights and values.

HANS HOLZER: I don't see any problems. We have three degrees. There are no restrictions. It is up to the Initiator to decide what level you have reached and what degree you are ready for. Other religions have their requirements. I believe the degrees to be an indication of what the person has studied and how far they have progressed.

CORBY INGOLD: I think that if you want Traditional Craft then the Degree System is part of the package. If you don't like the degree system and coven hierarchy, etc., then you can just make up whatever pleases you and call it "Wicca" if you like, but it won't be Traditional Craft. Nor will you have access, personally or magically, to the body of traditional lore handed down among initiates. You also won't have access to the inner plane contacts and practical magical keys that give Traditional Craft a great deal of its power. As older style British occultists like Dion Fortune would say, "The Craft is a 'contacted' system." This means that when you receive initiation into a Traditional Craft lineage, you also receive the keys to contact the inner plane power that is invoked and worked with within that particular initiated line.

Our requirements for the degrees are fairly standard to most forms of Traditional British Craft. We, like most traditions, require quite a lot of work from initiates. Each initiate must demonstrate a reasonable application to and understanding of the studies, appropriate to his or her degree, before being considered for advancement to the next level. Having said that, I want to emphasize that we really do want our initiates to advance. Our training takes place in a friendly and mutually supportive atmosphere. My High Priestess and I feel that our job is to support our students. We also strongly adhere to the idea that we are all students; we learn at least as much from our initiates as they do from us. Once you start thinking you know it all, you're dead.

JIMAHL: The Alexandrian Tradition follows a three-degree system. I feel very strongly about the degrees as benchmarks that the student will reach.

At the second degree, the student should be prepared to become a role model and teacher. At third degree, I encourage my students to form their own covens. The Craft must keep growing in order to survive.

CHRISTINE JONES—They have it too easy now. They don't want to work for anything. You have to earn your way.

KERRY: "Tough!" This was how I was taught. Even at that time some people had a problem with the hierarchy. It was "tough" back then too.

LORAX: I think the problem is less with hierarchy than the perception that the coven hierarchy somehow grants one powers and abilities far beyond the ken of ordinary coveners. It does not. Hopefully, one teaches out of respect for the materials and what it can offer, and not just to try and wield some sort of power over a small group of persons for a few hours a month. True hierarchy is a revelation of the sacred.

Since there are more groups now than there were in the past, a student can almost always leave and find another group to study with. This has, to some extent, democratized coven decision-making processes and diminished some of the potentials for abuse.

The downside is that a student assumes that simply because a book has been published with initiations A, B, C, and rites X, Y, Z, that memorizing or quickly reading through these rituals grants understanding. This is simply not the case. It may take years for a student to internalize even a few rituals and be able to actually "work the rite" or use the ritual cosmology his or her teacher is using. Until the student can spontaneously and creatively use what he or she has been taught, he or she doesn't have a working grasp of it.

LEO MARTELLO: Sicilians don't use degrees. Continental covens do. Degrees are "traditional" only to those covens that used them. Those who disagree with degrees can now join groups who don't use them. They have a choice. No problem. As I wrote years ago, "In the final analysis I still prefer a first degree person more than I do a third degree Witch."

MERLIN: Traditional Craft is generally initiatory. Initiation is a process that includes rites of passage. That concept alone requires levels or degrees. Who better to help someone with a rite of passage than someone who has done it before? Moreover, that is the way of family In Nature, elders help the younger ones until they can take care of themselves. In addition, Elders are the main resource of experience, clarification, and qualification of the teachings. Those who do not seek such a path are looking for something else. We do use degrees as prescribed by our tradition.

MORDA: I've learned it's better not to get hung up on the degree system. We keep our members at first degree for many years, and we avoid the trap of feeling "obliged" to elevate members to higher degrees. While we don't have formal requirements for the degrees, we do expect ritual competence.

MORVEN: Hierarchy is part of life. We can refuse to acknowledge it in our covens or use the coven as a place to learn how to make hierarchy work. We can learn to lead well and to be led well. Initiates need to learn to govern graciously and also how to accept authority without losing self. They should learn to question things that make them uncomfortable, but in a way that we feel comfortable with. That's a very valuable skill to have in this lifetime. A good Priestess must graciously and patiently answer the repeated questions of Neophytes or deal with emotional outpourings. Wouldn't those skills come in handy in interpersonal relationships, even parenting? I consider my role of High Priestess in a similar light as I did my role as Managing Editor of *Harvest*. It's not an absolute democracy; it's more a "benevolent monarchy." However, like any monarch, if I abuse

my power, I'm bound to be overthrown! I'm trying to train a group of people to lead in a very short time, and I need to be concerned about efficiency. That might not be true for others, but it is for me. Being a
Priestess is a lot like parenting; sometimes you have to be the "bad guy,"
and sometimes you make mistakes, but if you treat your coveners with
love and respect, it should all work out in the end.

I follow the traditional Alexandrian three-degree system with an additional grade of Dedicant. All new members begin at the Dedicant level.
After a time they are considered for initiation if suited.

MURTAGH: I believe degrees are necessary. While I went through a hierarchical system, I don't know if hierarchy in its original form is useful
because it does breed in some people an "I am better than you are" attitude, and even in traditional Craft I saw this. There are natural hierarchies in the universe, and they shouldn't mean that one is above
someone else. It just means you are in a different place—either on the
path or on the ladder or in the scheme of things. I do believe in organic
hierarchies—those that come about because they are natural, and they
change as people change. The way I perceive degrees is like college.
You're a Neophyte—a freshman. You come in with some knowledge that
you've gleaned from life, but the specialized knowledge you don't know;
you don't have the prerequisites for. You are no better or worse than the
people in higher degrees, just like in college. It has nothing to do with
power, it has nothing to do with energy, it has nothing to do with anything outside of the system. I think degrees are necessary just so that
you can gauge your progress. Part of the hierarchy here is a student-
teacher relationship. And what the teacher is seeing, or the Priest and
High Priestess is seeing, is development of someone within the system.

In Traditional Craft there are rules, and to be honest, I've told people
that if I initiated you and was training you, you would not like me because
there would be things I would expect of you. When I'm having a study
group or an outer circle group, well, if people blow it off, well they blow it
off. Eventually if they blow it off enough, they're wasting my time, and I
don't want to deal with them. Within a traditional degree system, I would
expect that after the first year of being a Neophyte that they would probably be around for the eight Sabbats and all thirteen moons. They should
understand how magical space is created, understand the components,
the elements and the tools they are using. They should know rudimentary meditation, centering, grounding, and purification rituals. They

should have an understanding of the mythos system and be able to make some sort of spiritual contact with divinity on a one-to-one basis.

Second degree is where you learn and hone your magical Craft. At this point you should be writing your own rituals; working with higher magical forms, probably have some kind of specialty that you've developed and focus on, and have a divinatory skill that you can call on that you know intimately. You also begin to form your relationships with god forms.

In third degree you should be, in my opinion, an expert in some form of your art. You should be an expert in some form of divination. You should be in a relationship with a god and a goddess. You should have an intimate relationship with some form of entity or entities that you can call on, that you can talk to, that you worship. You know magic is real, and you understand the inter-relationships of the universe. Then on becoming an Elder you have proven yourself and can go out and train others.

MARY NESNICK: The degrees and the hierarchy are an integral and necessary part of Craft as I know it. I think the system is much misunderstood by those who haven't had the training and experienced the system first hand. Hierarchy is a fact of life and is present in every walk of society in some form. Without it there would be anarchy.

PATRICIA POTHIER: The covens I have been associated with have used degrees. As measures of one's achievement in learning and self-mastery, I don't see how anyone can object to the degrees. The problem comes when the degrees become ends in themselves and turn into ego trips. But this a problem of the people, not the degrees. One passes from outer to inner court depending on one's level of knowledge and spiritual attainment. It certainly is not a question of how many times in a year and a day you have parked your carcass in the Covenstead! Do away with degrees and you have anarchy.

TRIVIA PRAGER: My tradition uses the three-degree system. In the first degree the students reflect the teacher and learn and grow with the help of the coven. In the second degree the student takes on more responsibility. Although students begin to teach in this degree, I waited until I received my third degree to teach. The third degree is given to those students who have come through the system with the necessary knowledge and dedication to begin a coven of their own, ensuring that the Craft will continue to grow and survive..

ROGER PRATT As a Gardnerian we used degrees as a designation of responsibility earned and skills mastered. I really felt my third degree "kick-in," so to speak, when I was about forty. I had opened an occult shop in New York City and had to "minister" to a wide variety of people in the community. It was then, and only then, that I actually felt the need for priesthood. In my own circles, we were all very much equal. I was ritually able, thanks to the training I received from my High Priestess. But I always felt that I am the Witch that I am today—the real "inner" nitty gritty, ritual aside, due to an inner "Witch spirit" inherited from my mother. She acknowledged only Witches and non-Witches. We had no degrees. I was taught to call the Gods only the "Lady" and the "Lord." When a woman was "with" the Goddess she was addressed as "Lady," but once the Goddess had departed, the physical woman was referred to only by her mundane name. My mum referred to High Priestesses who went around as "Lady this" or "Lady that" as "Lady Muck," a rather Scottish thing to say.

I do respect the degree system, but not when it goes to the person's head or creates an inflated ego. I suppose to me—a Witch is a Witch. And just that.

RAOKHSHA: The Neophyte has no clue to the essence of a system of magical knowledge! The books lump it all together and amazingly some "students" do survive.

The degrees are not flippantly handed out. No traditional High Priestess stands up to lead a coven and says, "Okay, Shirley, you'll be a first degree. and Bob, Gwen and Hal, you're second degrees. Francis, you be third degree. Any questions?" There are responsibilities and rights assigned to the degrees and each masters a body of knowledge that builds upon the prior body of knowledge. Rising through the degrees is not automatic.

The traditional year-and-a-day between degrees allows the teaching to be absorbed and the teacher to judge the progress of the student. There is no shame in remaining a first degree forever. It is a level of knowledge/experience that contributes specifically to the operation/workings of a coven. It's not a competitive sport, and it is the obligation of the Priestess to instill mutual respect among her coven members no matter what the degree. It is the "quest" that earns respect and not the "title," per se.

My oath prevents me from discussing the specifics of the degrees, but suffice it to say that our three represent the powers of the Goddess, the God, and the union thereof as defined by our tradition.

OWEN ROWLEY: This is a complex issue. My answer is that "it depends." The Craft that emerged from the shadows in the last half of the 20th century was difficult to find, obscure, and dominated by eccentric, often quirky, leadership. Interest in the Occult in general and, specifically Witchcraft, exploded in the post Hippy era, and the major publishers of esoteric books fed the resulting fire with hundreds of books purporting to reveal previously secret lore and ritual practices.

By the mid seventies you could buy paperback editions of Witchcraft secrets in just about any bookstore in America. You no longer needed to find an existing coven and work your way through the degrees; all you had to do was plunk down the $3.95 for Paul Huson's *Mastering Witchcraft*, perform the self blessing contained within it, and you were on your way. Over time, "book-taught" Witches have had an ever increasing stable of printed works to guide them through a myriad of variations on the Witchcraft theme. At the same time, the more easily found, more publicly accessible Craft traditions with hierarchical degree structures were also growing rapidly and becoming easier to connect with. This has resulted in a schism of sorts between the independent solitary practitioner form and the traditional coven form.

I don't think it can be said that one is right and the other wrong. It seems to me that each fits within its own realm. I've personally explored both and find that each has its own benefits and drawbacks. Of course, my own experience as a solitary is different than most in that I spent my formative years in the very formal hierarchical coven structure. I suspect an entire book could be written about this subject alone, and NO—I'm NOT volunteering for the project. Clearly, these are issues that depend on how you feel and what you are looking for in your spiritual quest.

ZANONI SILVERKNIFE: Frankly, it is their problem, not mine. It is rather like being angry that you can't be on a sports team merely because you want to, but do not have the skill-set and physical capabilities to do so. Go to a different playground, I say, where the rules are more to your liking. There are plenty of groups that operate with "facilitators" and decide everything by "consensus". They dish up palatable rituals that offend no one so that the spiritual nourishment is comparable to putting distilled water on your houseplants. If you don't like the degree systems then "dinna fash ye'sel." Not everyone likes peppermint ice cream. Choose another flavor.

My tradition has nine degrees of attainment. The requirements up to Elderhood are pretty much what you would expect of any traditionalist group. Study hard, learn the lessons, copy the Book, master certain practical philosophical and spiritual challenges, take the examinations in stride and BE! If you want me to be any more specific than that, you will need to ask for elucidation. Beyond Elderhood there are degrees that are attained only by Spiritual maturity and are not conferred upon one, but are decided by Spirit.

SINTANA: A number of Pagans today have little or no respect for any type of authority figure in general. Our prior Elders demanded respect by their very presence, for they taught with respect—respect for life and one another. We honor and give respect to those who give of themselves and who live the Old Ways, and by the wisdom of experience attained as they lived according to the Old Ways.

If one has not been seriously entrusted by qualified and learned teachers with the teachings of that tradition, and guided throughout their learning, then one is not of the Old Law. In my tradition, the year and a day is required for first degree only, and is the minimum. Thereafter it depends upon the individual and the personal commitment. Second degree generally requires a minimum of three years. We have some initiates who have taken more time, and this becomes a very individual accomplishment.

One is deemed worthy by the guidelines set down within our tradition, which states, "By their deeds they are known." Teachers at Ravenwood are generally second degrees. Third degrees are quite rare, as we believe this commitment requires that one truly become a servant and teacher, the Voice of God/Goddess to the people, and one must be willing and able to honor such a commitment. If you talk the talk, you must walk the walk. Our Craft cannot afford to produce and set free upon the vulnerable seekers fools bearing made-up credentials they never exemplified or learned. Our Law is, "Know this, seeker on the path, from where you enter in, there shall you ultimately withdraw." Therefore, your teachers should regard you well, for you are their inheritor.

STARSPAWN: I believe in a degree-based training as it allows for growth of the student to take place. So much of modern day life is stripped of the rituals of the changes in life. Where are the ceremonies marking the end of childhood and the beginning of adult life? Where are the ceremonies of first blood, of birthing, and of aging to elder? The degree-based system stirs these hidden cycles known for centuries within our souls.

I used to follow the three traditional degrees and still do but now have added a fourth, which is at the beginning of training. I really feel it is necessary for students to begin the process of training in a ritual manner.

This way they are introduced to ritual (before a circle is cast with them inside of it). This intro degree is of "dedication," where the student announces to himself or herself, to the teacher and others in training that he or she is serious about what is being given.

After Dedication there are the traditional three degrees. First degree is basically given to anyone who asks for initiation from me. As my tradition dictated (and Alex Sanders would teach), initiate a thousand, so maybe one would continue training. But initiating the other 999 means doors would open eventually for those others. Maybe not in this lifetime but the step would be taken at other times. I used to think this way as well, but now insist on the Dedication ritual as a pre-cursor to the first degree. Second degree traditionally occurs after one year of training. Third degree usually means the student "graduates" and would leave the coven at that point. The coven would then "hive" off, taking some of its members with it to join the new leader. In this way, a group would never be too crowded; with thirteen being a good working number. These days though, I have been in covens made up only of third degrees who work on a deeper level of the magic.

As with everything in Craft, one must find a balance within him or herself and then reflect that balance in the group he or she chooses to work with. As the Book of Shadows says, "If that which thou seekest, thou findest not within thee, thou wilt never find it without thee."

STOCK: People who have problems with Traditional Craft degrees and hierarchy are *not* Craft. They are the New Age Pagans. There is a *big* difference….Family! In Nature all families, tribes, and clans have hierarchies. That's the way it was intended, and that's the way it IS. If some of these people were initiated into Traditional Craft, they would know better. I use degrees as specified by Gwen Thompson.

TANITH: The degrees work as a system, but some people don't really want the sort of training and perspective one gets through a degree system. They only want to worship with like-minded people. That's fine too.

THEITIC: Not all Traditional Craft groups use degree systems. Some family traditions have no need for degrees—either you are initiated or you are not. My tradition uses degrees and I personally agree with this system. There is no guarantee that someone who is in the Craft for any period of time is better qualified to teach than a newcomer. But, I don't like knowing that someone with one year of experience (and who hasn't even had a Saturn return) is out there amongst the great masses claiming to be a High Priestess or High Priest! This is all too common amongst the New Agers. Brain surgery can't be learned in one year, and that only affects one physical life out of many that can be affected by a true spiritual teacher.

The three degrees are set up as reflections of life. The first degree is like the beginning years; learning about the world around you, understanding how much there really is to learn. The second degree is like the middle years of your life; working hard to understand and grow, forming relationships, and finding your place in society. The third degree is like the elder years; giving advice to the newcomers in life (Craft). I don't think it is healthy to skip degrees. And the Priestess or Priest that moves a Witch along too quickly isn't doing that person any favor, but rather an injustice.

TIMOTHEA: Degrees are necessary and desirable in that they guarantee that the initiate has been observed for a period of time and has the necessary knowledge to move ahead. The High Priestess who confers the degree then places her own reputation behind that initiate. The Ancients placed much time and thought into them as a result of years of study of humanity, and humanity has not changed. Degrees protect the initiate from handling power he or she doesn't understand; degrees protect everyone else by delineating their knowledge.

JOE WILSON: Many Pagans today have a problem with authority in general. They seem to be going through an adolescent rebellion stage, their purpose being to shock their parents rather than development of some spiritual understanding.

There are no degrees in my families, only growth and maturity, and the wisdom that comes with it. It's a slow process. As far as hierarchy is concerned, that's a family matter as well, with grandparents, parents, aunts and uncles, children and such, being given the respect due their age, wisdom, and position in the family.

It is said that all Witches are Pagans, but not all Pagans are Witches. How do you define the difference?

MARTHA ADLER: Witches are initiates who practice an ancient religion. Pagans who are not Witches may or may not practice a form of religion but do respect Mother Nature and all that pertains with reverence and respect.

AYEISHA: In Catholicism all priests are Catholic but not all Catholics are priests.

MARSHA BARD: I find a very definite difference in the terms "Witch" and "Pagan." One is a religion and the other, a world truth. Both are removed from the monistic system of belief, but the Pagan is more so removed and in a sense, freer in his or her belief system. The Craft has a certain set of value quotients, while Paganism is free to wander amid the many systems of polytheistic religions. "Pagan" is a term founded in Christianity. If you didn't believe in Jesus Christ and the one God, you were Pagan. It seems to me that at the time of its coinage, the term was more or less synonymous with "country dweller." Those close to the Earth understood what others did not. A Narragansett Indian was a Pagan by Christian definition, but certainly not a Witch. A Witch, by definition, would have to be a Pagan.

RAYMOND BUCKLAND: Paganism is a general term, covering Witches, Amerindians, Voodonists, etc., so, yes, all Witches are Pagans but not all Pagans are Witches. A parallel would be to say that all Baptists are Christian but not all Christians are Baptist.

CHAS CLIFTON: Not all Pagans want to be called Witches, because they see the "W" word as being about fear, cursing, persecution, and other negative things. I define all Witches as Pagans, however, if they claim to worship or acknowledge any divine force that manifests as multiple deities.

A lot of the problem comes back to the idea of "clergy" and whether or not Witches are clergy. Contemporary people (Pagans included) want certified specialists for everything, and as Pagan "clergy" become more visible we hear proposals for certification for us too. Unwittingly, we buy into a Protestant Christian model of clergy behavior which is to emphasize formal qualifications over devotion and is far removed from ancient Paganism. Here is where we can see how different we are from the Pagans of past millennia with whom we claim kinship. We see clergy as ministers to a congregation rather than as servants of a deity, which is the Classical model. Babara Watterson, author of *Women in Ancient Egypt*, observed that "Unlike, for example, a Christian church or cathedral, an ancient Egyptian temple was not a place in which a god was worshiped by a congregation led by a spiritual leader who was also a preacher and instructor of his parishioners."

Perhaps we are developing a two-tiered system of so-called clergy. One group will be the counselors and instructors. They will be adept at grief counseling, dealing with school principals aghast that so-and-so's child wears a pentagram. They will sit on interfaith councils and have reserved parking spaces at hospitals. At worst, they could become no more than social workers with pentagram necklaces.

Another group (and there is nothing to say that someone could not move back and forth) will be priests and priestesses in the Classical sense. For them, relationship to the Mysteries will be foremost. At times they will lay their lives on the altar of sacrifice, metaphorically if not literally. They will follow the soul into Other Places some times, and if anyone knows what the owl is or is not saying, they will. Some of them will call themselves Witches.

DANA CORBY: In the first place, that's not entirely true; I've known some good, Italian, Catholic ladies who were dynamite Witches! But seriously, I think it's a matter less of difference than of degree. Most of the Witches I've known over the years have been much more serious about their practice than most of the Pagans. With the exception of the Asatru and the Druids, both of whom—like Witches—see themselves as a priesthood. There seems to be a strong element of connection to the Ancestors among practitioners of these three Paths than among those who self-identify as generically Pagan, and a weaker element of political consciousness.

DEVON: We are all Pagans in our hearts. It is the spirit of Nature that we carry within ourselves. I believe that you learn to be a Witch. It is a process that strengthens and enlightens our Pagan form. It is easy to be a Pagan but in our society you have to explain being a Witch. It can be difficult and you must have the inner strength, the background and the self-confidence to be what you are without always being on the defensive. There are many public and well-known Witches in our country and they have been taking serious steps to ensure a compatible and safe place in this world for future Witches. But it seems to be a long and uphill battle with skirmishes well fought and won. Whether public or underground, every Witch does his or her part to help make things easier for all of us.

ALEXANDRIA FOXMOORE: Pagans are the people of the Earth who practice non-Christian religions. Witches are the believers of the faith of the "Wise," a type of Pagan religion. New Age Wiccans are a recent offspring of Pagans who have adopted many of the Witch traditions without the structure of Traditional Covens.

GWION: Witchcraft is a specific form of Paganism. All Witches are Pagan; not all Pagans are Witches.

HANS HOLZER: Wicca is an Anglo-Saxon tradition. The Strega Tradition of Italy is just the same in a different language. Pagan is a general term for people who are not Christian, Jewish or Muslim. Pagan is a group of religions in very general terms.

CORBY INGOLD: Some Witches, such as the late Robert Cochrane, made a distinction between Witches and Pagans. I think all definitions are crutches; as soon as you can get along without them, you should throw them away. I would agree that most Witches subscribe to what we could call a Pagan theology—multiple Gods, worship of the Great Mother, the practice of various forms of magic, etc. There are many forms of Paganism. The Craft is, in my view, primarily a way of working, of doing things. More than merely a belief system, it is a way of practice. As such, it is neither better nor worse than any other way of practice. It is a way that seems to work very well for people of a certain temperament. Part of this way involves the regular practice of magic, and the holding of a primarily magical view of the universe. Many people who find their way to the Craft seem to have this particular view innately. It is simply how they have always thought and lived. The Craft simply helps them to engage it more consciously.

JIMAHL: All Catholic priests are Catholic but not all Catholics are priests. It's pretty obvious.

CHRISTINE JONES: A Witch is a Witch is a Witch is a Witch. Enough said.

KERRY: I don't care for either types of nomenclature.

LORAX: I think the distinction between EuroPagan, Witches, and Wiccans, is fairly well drawn. Asatruar are not Wiccan. Norse Wiccans may share a lot in common with Asatruar, but they are not using the same cosmologies or working structures. Witches use a quartered circle, summon, stir, and conjure deities and/or guardians, and generally hold with the notion of a specific transmission of power that transforms an acolyte into a priest/priestess during an initiation ceremony. Witches work with bipolar or paired deities and generally, though not always, all Gods are one and all Goddesses are one Goddess.

LEO MARTELLO: Witchcraft is a specific theology with its own rites and rituals. Paganism as now defined embraces all the "old-time religions" prior to Judeo-Christianity, Islam, etc. All Catholics are Christians, but not all Christians are Catholic.

MERLIN: From the common usage of Pagan, I believe a Pagan is someone who sees Nature and Deity(ies) as the same. A Pagan is someone who uses Nature as the basis for religious belief and worship. Witches are usually Pagans who participate in a magical tradition, performing rites on an initiatory path or for some other purpose as prescribed by their coven. They are usually dedicated to exploration of spiritual mysteries.

MORDA: I use the terms interchangeably, but see Witches as those who are initiated and who have more of an inner, deeper tradition. However, the distinctions can and do blur.

MORVEN: To me, Paganism is the religion and Neo-Pagan means the new generation of Earth religionists. Nowadays I often use it interchangeably with Pagan. Neo-Pagans, like Pagans, are not always Witches. I define Witch to mean a "practitioner of magic." If people worship the Goddess and the Horned God but don't practice magic, I would not term them Witches. These are my personal definitions, and though we might use different or contradictory terms, the paths are still equally valid.

MURTAGH: Witches are Pagans. I define the difference primarily that to be a Witch means you have been initiated into a coven, into a Craft tradition, whether it is hereditary or initiatory, and are part of it, and have been trained in that system. Theoretically you have gone through some part of the system that says you are a Witch. You've been around long enough that you understand the system, the religion, and the magics of what it is to be a Witch. Paganism on the other hand, is kind of a generic term for anyone that follows a pre-Christian religion.

MARY NESNICK: All Witches are Pagan, but not all Pagans are Witches.

ELIZABETH PEPPER: I expect the word "Pagan" was originally used to define one who was not of the Christian faith, primitive, rural. I view Witchcraft as an art that requires discipline and the development of natural talent along with a firm dedication to attainment of knowledge and skill.

PATRICIA POTHIER: It depends on the time and the culture. In pre-Christian Europe, everybody was a Pagan, and a Witch was someone with supernatural powers. Today we think of Witches as Pagans who have gone through training and been initiated by another Witch.

RAOKHSHA: You betcha there's a difference. I define "Pagans" as the congregation and "Witches" as the clergy. Anyone can be a Pagan given a polytheistic belief system. It is the initiate/inheritor of the Craft who passes on the knowledge and conducts the rituals that cement the community together. A Witch is more precisely defined by each tradition as one trained and initiated, or born, into that tradition, and who practices its beliefs and follows its guidelines or Book of Shadows. I, myself, was never a Pagan. I was a Baptist and then a Witch-in-training.

OWEN ROWLEY: To me, Witches—and I prefer Wicces as a spelling—are clergy. Pagans are not.

ZANONI SILVERKNIFE: Pagan, in my understanding, comes from the Latin *paganus* referring to "peasants." Later connotations denoted a person who did not accept the Church of Rome or other branches of Christianity. Now, it means everyone but those who belong to Christian sects and denominations, Judaic, and Islamic persons. So, therefore Witches must be Pagans. It also follows that all Pagans are not Witches, since there is so much spiritual territory to cover in "Pagan."

To be more explicit, I would say that what we generally refer to as the "Pagan" community is not exclusively the realm of the Witch. By the same token, everyone who calls him or herself "Witch" ain't necessarily so. The Craft and the Witch are not even necessarily the same thing as the Wicca.

The Craft is a deep well of mystery that hides its secrets in the star-speckled pool, in the powder of a butterfly's wing and in the song of the whale. It is not found in books, nor in created rituals, but in the movement of bodies through space, the sounds of leaves dancing on frigid air. It can be found in the cold mud of Spring rains, in searing lava, and in bones on the desert floor. It is older than you can imagine.

Wicca is the system of rituals, rites, observances, and guidelines that humans have created to help guide them through life and spiritual ascendancy. Pagans practice "not-Christianity." Witches practice Wicca. That is the difference as I have experienced it.

I am Craft. I am not Wiccan except by my desire to have reference points to other humans. I am Pagan only by its most general definition. What I am is more truly a Unist. This is where spirituality is returning. You will find that among the old traditions of shamanistic cultures worldwide.

SINTANA: My understanding has been that to be a Witch is a defined, educational, spiritual commitment to be lived and applied in service as a teacher. This is achieved only by one's individual and spiritual commitment to learning and understanding the knowledge of the Ancients. This was then applied to the Witch's daily life—living the Craft.

I see no similarity between a Witch and a Pagan. You either are a Witch or you are not. You may be born to be a Nature lover and Pagan at heart, but you must be brought to the Gates of the Mighty Ones and properly introduced by one who is a Witch. You cannot birth yourself! Without training and acknowledgment from the hierarchy, you remain one who is "not of The Law."

It matters not what you call yourself. It is not what you do or know. It's what you are and become. You will be known by your own deeds and works of those you gather with. Calling oneself a Witch does not a Witch make.

STARSPAWN: This is a very controversial point and one that caused me some trouble due to my beliefs on the subject. My belief came about due to the plethora of Pagan Festivals begun in the late seventies, early eighties, and continuing to this day. Not everyone who attended these festivals was of the Craft. At one point I would say about 75% who attended were there for a good old Pagan time and not into the Craft at all. So I formulated the belief that:

■ If you were "of the Craft," you were a Pagan automatically.

■ If you were identified as a Pagan, this did not automatically make you "of the Craft."

■ I was taught that if you were Craft, you were a Priest/Priestess by rite of initiation, training, and belief.

■ Pagans had no formal training, no initiation and not necessarily any standard beliefs other than being as from the Latin for Pagan, "of the country," meaning of the Old Religion. Most Pagans I encountered did not want to align themselves with any coven, initiatory path, or deity system. Some just liked the title, others liked the Pagan gatherings with dance, drink, song and a free loving life style that at times came down to anything not Judeo-Christian.

STOCK: A Pagan is a person who deifies Nature as "God." To these people anything that clearly follows natural law is holy. Witches, however are Pagans who are schooled in traditional magical practice. Pagans assemble to worship Nature. Witches assemble to worship Nature but also carry out the magical itinerary of the coven.

THEITIC: Witchcraft is a way of life that most often incorporates a religion: Paganism. Its emphasis is on magic. Paganism is a religion that doesn't dictate a particular way of life, but rather, has emphasis on faith and deity. In both of these cases, the spirit realm and the seasonal cycles of the Earth play a major role.

In rare cases, there are some Witches that practice their Craft without the influence of religious beliefs. These are usually "individuals" or "groups of individuals" that have had little or no outside influences on their Craft practices for centuries. It is only in modern times that Traditional Craft practices have embraced religious beliefs.

Before Christianity, Paganism was the religion of the masses. There were shamans and sorcerers, but the majority of people were just plain Pagan! When Christianity became the major European religion, some people refused to convert. During the 1500s and 1600s these people were either persecuted or went underground to preserve their beliefs and practices. They were called Witches. Some practiced magic and some didn't, but they were all Pagan.

TIMOTHEA: Pagans love and work with the Earth and its forces. Witches serve, worship, and enlist the strengths of the Gods and other beings of Earth.

JOE WILSON: Oh well, here is a place where I can't avoid the word, "Witch." If I'm not mistaken, I was the first person to use that statement way back in the late sixties. What I meant by it was that Paganism is a general—if next to impossible to define—religious philosophy which anyone can adopt. But a "Witch" is a specialist within that philosophy, one who has specific training and "initiations" into sacred mysteries, the workings of magic, journeys, and so forth. A "Witch" in my families is much closer to a shaman, a "Technician of the Sacred" than to a priest or priestess.

It seems the term, "Craft" or "Witch" has been co-opted by many in the Pagan Community. What are your feelings on this?

MARTHA ADLER: If they are truly trained, initiated, or adopted Craft or Witches, they are entitled to use the terms. If they are not, then I think they delude themselves.

AYEISHA: I think that there's a lack of general understanding about what those terms "Pagan" and "Witch" mean. I think that people are pretty divided in their feelings, going from feeling generously tolerant to having high blood pressure and jumping up and down screaming, and that maybe we take turns doing those two things. On one hand, I feel as though if we just ignore them they will eventually go away. On the other hand, I'm cringing because when those people read a book and declare themselves Popes and speak to the public they are actually telling your neighbors who you are. Since they perhaps have a misunderstanding of what Witchcraft is all about, they are not very adequate at explaining who you are to your neighbors. Now that Wicca is a big fad, it will have lots of people who will sort of jump on the bandwagon in a general way without a deeper understanding of what the tradition is really all about. But, like fads, that interest will fade over a period of time, and then those persons will go off and do whatever is the fad of that time.

MARSHA BARD: I have no interest in what anyone would label him or herself, or others. I have the perception to see who or what people are on my own, and nothing else need be said. A label is something you offer or accept; it need not be correct or incorrect, just a matter of choice. I can respect that desire in anyone. If it is for malicious gain or information, I know that instinctively and make my own choices in return.

DANA CORBY: Grr! The problem, of course, is that they don't accept the Witch's definition of what a Witch is. They seem to think that merely being counter-culture is Witchcraft. Uh–uh. Being counterculture is a sociopolitical stance. Witchcraft is knowledge, a practice, and a way of living, all of which takes considerable work. By my way of thinking, if you haven't put in the work, you can't possibly know what you're talking about. Mere "book-larnin" doesn't cut it. Kindly call yourself something else.

DEVON—My feelings are that these have become popular phrases because they get a reaction. My experiences are that people who have been practicing and doing for a number of years—yes, even decades—have continued and will continue no matter what the catch phrase of the moment is.

STOCK: The term "Kleenex" has been co-opted by many to mean "bathroom tissue." Wishful thinking!

GWION: Pagans are not necessarily Witches. I think it just confuses who's who. Do we call all flowers roses?

JUDY HARROW: I have no problem with a self-initiate who has truly made the commitment and done the work. In fact, such people have to work far harder than I did—since they did not have the traditional teaching and support system.

HANS HOLZER: If they are Wiccans they had to have somebody initiate them. If they are not Wiccans then whatever they are, they are. But the term Pagan does not mean the same thing as being a Wiccan.

CORBY INGOLD: I think a certain amount of co-opting is inevitable. After all, imitation is the sincerest form of flattery! But this does underscore some of my ideas about the reasons for Traditional Craft secrecy. Once ideas, phrases, images, etc., get out into the mass consciousness, they become watered down. Words lose their original meanings and transform into something else. This is not necessarily bad; it's an organic process that goes on all the time. But once a particular word or image is swept into that swirling ocean of mass opinion, misinformation, and prejudice, much of its power is lost, or at least altered. That's why we traditionally retain certain secrets within the Craft which are only revealed to oath-bound initiates. Not because we are a bunch of emotionally immature adults playing at children's cloak and dagger games, but because surrounding an idea, phrase, image, concept, magical spell, or rite with a shroud of secrecy helps to preserve its power.

Words such as Craft and Witch were always in the public domain anyway. We ascribed to them our own peculiar and sacral meanings, but that certainly gives us no power to control how other people use or misuse these terms. I say "no power," but in fact there is one power that we do have, perhaps the greatest power known, the power of ideas. We cannot totally prevent others from using these terms in ways other than what we would wish (nor would I necessarily want to). We can, however, influence the perceptions of others through consciously introducing into the Group Mind certain powerful ideas about the ways in which we Witches traditionally employ these terms. Such ideas, though subtler by far than guns or legal statues, have definite and far-reaching effects, and this is how Witches have always worked to effect change—magically. Anyone who doubts that Traditional Craft has influenced modern culture since it first became public in the late fifties and sixties should look closely at the strongly Wiccan themes and images that run through much of modern fantasy and science fiction, as well as the paperback cover illustrations for such books.

JIMAHL: I don't pass judgment on anyone who calls their path "the Craft" or identifies with the word "Witch." I only concern myself with my own path and tradition.

CHRISTINE JONES: It makes people feel secure to claim the title, but if you haven't been initiated, it isn't yours to claim.

LORAX: I don't hear the term "Witch" being used in my area at all. The term "Craft" is not as commonly used as "Wicca," which now can mean anything at all.

LEO MARTELLO: My feelings are the same as those of a Catholic who hears all Christians calling themselves Catholic though not baptized, confirmed, or brought up in this faith. It's the same as Satanists who call themselves Witches. It's a form of theological undermining.

MERLIN: The Witches know the difference.

MORDA: I think it works both ways. I sometimes use the word Pagan to describe myself, especially in the mundane world. It's less of a loaded word.

MORVEN: Though I support people finding definitions that work for them, I would also caution that when people define the terms differently, it can cause communication difficulties. For example, I have heard of people joining Craft covens who didn't believe in the supernatural or spells and didn't want to learn invoking or banishing pentagrams because they were too "spooky." Likewise, I've heard of people joining Pagan groves who didn't want to learn about the Goddess. All they wanted to do was to learn to cast spells. Maybe we just need to remember to define our terms and not assume the words mean the same to everyone.

MURTAGH: I believe the words "Craft" or "Witch" specifically mean people that have been initiated into a bona fide group, whether that group was founded two years ago, or a hundred years ago. Basically, I just think that people are very sloppy in the use of their terminology. The word "shaman" has been co-opted and is used for everything. It's a catchall term, and people do not understand that it is a specific magical technology that evolved primarily in tribal cultures. And it is different than priest craft; and different from ceremonial magic. It is a specific magical technology that has to do with matters of the soul, whether it's the soul of the tribe or the soul of the individual. It is specifically used for going to the other world and bringing back information or energies, or in the case of soul loss, to help the individual come back from there. People feel "Oh, I went on a vision quest so I'm a shaman." No, everybody in Native American culture goes on a vision quest. People in many native cultures around the world have power animals. That does not mean you are a shaman. I feel that the word Witch has been co-opted similarly, and that it's just sloppy terminology.

MARY NESNICK: I think that if they want to call themselves "Witches" and say that they belong to "the Craft," they should make the commitment to study and become initiated.

ELIZABETH PEPPER: I don't think that rigid dogma belongs in the Craft.

PATRICIA POTHIER: I think there is nothing anyone can do about it. We owe a great debt to the Witches of the Middle Ages and those who kept the Old Religion alive through 2,000 years of persecution. But let us remember that it was the Inquisitors who called them Witches; they were Pagans. We seem to have come full circle, and perhaps the time has come to refer to ourselves as "Initiates of the Mysteries" rather than as Witches. It would certainly improve our relations with the Pagans of African and Native American traditions who commonly regard Witches as sorcerers.

TRIVIA PRAGER: There seems to be a lot more openness in people calling themselves Pagans or Witches. Personally, I'm waiting for the backlash. The extreme right in this country, the so-called religious right, are just waiting for the opportunity to burn us at the stake, or at least take our children away. The pendulum swings both ways, and I'm pessimistic that we're in a conservative swing. It's no accident that the Neo-Pagan movement took off when it did; it was a period of increased personal freedom and individuality. People were willing to try new things and reject the old ideas that didn't work for them.

ROGER PRATT: I believe that one who feels "Witch" stirrings within is a "Witch." I also believe that such a "Witch" benefits greatly from learning traditional techniques and lore of his/her forebears. Priest/ess training is valuable if one is going to be required to serve the community.

RAOKHSHA: To think that *we* have been trying to remove the sting from the "W" word and all the while others are brandishing it like a weapon. I've found that "Witch" is so often used for its shock value. "Craft," too, has a certain spookiness, as it carries more of a spell-caster imagery than does "Wiccan." Teens use "Craft" more than even the "W" word. Let's thank the media for so gloriously misrepresenting Wicca—from nose-twitching to talking cats. It's kicky and lends itself so well to adolescence.

A young initiate of mine (the son of my Maiden) studied Gardnerian Craft during his last year in high school. He told me how totally ignorant of the true Craft all the happy little self-initiated spell-casters at his school were. "It was so immature of them to claim they were Witches," he said, as he did his Traditional Craft homework and earned his initiation.

I use "Wiccan" and then go on to describe its beliefs, and I may, finally say, also called a "Witch." Years ago I simply said that I followed the Old Religion.

OWEN ROWLEY: The term "the Craft" has been in common usage amongst Freemasons for over a century—perhaps over two centuries. Our "the Craft" has only had a public posture for perhaps fifty years. There is ample evidence in the philosophical literature of Scottish Rite masonry, in particular the "Legenda" by Albert Pike that there is more than a passing relationship between Masonic Craft and Wiccecraft. The term Witch or Witche was in all probability originally Wicce or Wiccae which, in time, became Wicca (wick-ah). The hard reality of Celtic language is that a single "c" is pronounced hard like a "k" and a double "cc" is pronounced soft like "ch." For this reason I use the spelling "wicce" or "wiccae" for Witch and pronounce it "weech" or "weechah." I do not use "wick-ah" at all anymore.

ZANONI SILVERKNIFE: It used to irk me thoroughly that inappropriate people used those terms in conjunction with themselves when they had no realization of what it meant to be Craft or Witch. I felt that they were sullying something beautiful. Now I realize that everyone is striving for something more, something better.

It has been said that imitation is the most sincere form of flattery. I know now that we are all growing, changing. In one of my rituals I sing, "I am emerging, growing and changing. I am becoming who I need to be." It is a very powerful, evocative chant. Perhaps we are all just children playing dress-up. If we wear an adult's clothing, we will for a brief time become an adult. Emulation should not be scorned. As Elders, we should encourage positive behaviors in our junior Pagans and gently correct those behaviors that are not growth and result-producing.

To those who use the terms loosely, I say: You can call yourself whatever you want. A turnip is not a tomato, no matter what it labels itself. Just be yourself the best you can and look to Spirit for your guidance. Seek out those Elders who will share their wisdom with you. Don't scorn the Old Ways. That is the structure from which we all grow. If we and our spiritual ancestors had not clung to the way we do things, the newer generations would have had to build it all from scratch with little in the way of tools. Be grateful for those who have suffered ostracism and verbal as well as physical attacks to maintain your rights to practice your religion your way.

To those of us who are Elders and Traditionalists, I say: "Let the kids be kids." Providing they are not doing harm to themselves and others, let them grow and explore. Be there for them when they come to ask for advice. And when they become upset with the advice you give, remember what it was like to have your cherished beliefs and ways corrected by your Elders. We will only hear when we are ready to listen.

SINTANA: It matters not what you call yourself. It is not what you do or know. It's what you "be" and "become." You will be known by your own deeds and works of those you gather with. Calling one's self a Witch does not a Witch make.

STARSPAWN: Years ago, my first lover called himself a "Witch" as he was trained in the West Indies by his grandparents who were Witches in their village. He looked quizzically at my belief system of Craft as being nothing like Witchcraft at all. He saw it as being an odd branch-off from Christianity as we had pomp and ceremonies, bells ringing, swords flashing, calling of incantation oaths to the four corners and so on. I saw his Witchcraft to be completely at random, and more of what I thought of at the time as "folk healing," with none of the true seriousness of the Craft. It did not have any central belief system. He did not have to be initiated to be a Witch and his spell crafting was based on the winds. However, as time went by and he taught me some techniques, I grew to learn that many can call themselves "Witch," but it always comes down to the true inner self of being that dictates who is the true Witch.

THEITIC: They should call themselves what they are and be specific about it—eclectic Witches, Traditional Witches, "stole it all from books" Witches, country Pagans, Alexandrians, Druids, weekend Witches, TV/publicity Witches, family Craft, ceremonialists, Gardnerians, diviners, sorcerers, S.C.A. people, festival hoppers and the rest. I don't care what a person calls him/herself, as long as that is what he or she really does. I see the problem with definition in the general Pagan Community these days is that people don't understand what they are calling themselves. Definitions are important to those who are seeking. And we owe it to them to be clear about who we are and what we represent. We should not call ourselves something we are not, any more than a person working at a fast food counter can call himself or herself a chef.

TIMOTHEA: They are claiming membership which they have not earned. As no one has sponsored them, there is a possibility of them causing harm to individuals and to our Craft as a whole.

JOE WILSON: My feeling is that they have made the words as meaningful as a purchased degree from a diploma mill.

Do you believe that traditional secrecy has helped or harmed the Craft?

MARTHA ADLER: Secrecy has both helped and harmed. In times of persecution I most certainly feel it helped. Today, secrecy can hinder those who sincerely want to be part of the Craft, and these seekers should be helped to find a true source.

AYEISHA: I'm not allowed to say.

MARSHA BARD: This is a difficult question in that I see it harming and helping. The secrecy helped to build strength from within, yet did not allow for growth. The public-ness of it all has helped with regard to growth, but has sapped the strength from within.

LORI BRUNO: I believe you must undergo the spiritual and practical training to become a priest and priestess. I was not allowed to teach others until I was fifty-one years old.

RAYMOND BUCKLAND: Secrecy is what kept Craft alive for generations so it can only have helped. Whether or not it is necessary today is another question.

CHAS CLIFTON: A little secrecy is OK. There are some things that you do not do in front of other people. I don't think you talk about Mysteries in front of people who are not ready for or interested in them, not because the Mysteries will be harmed, but because your own Inner Self might get the idea that you do not take them all that seriously, and it is your own Inner Self (Dion Fortune) who is the Initiator.

DANA CORBY: I think it's done some of both. On the one hand it's enabled Witches to survive as Witches in times and places (20th century Alabama comes to mind) where they otherwise could not have. And on the other, it has caused knowledge to be lost, made Witches in trouble have to struggle alone and undermined our civil rights efforts. I think it's possible to be a presence in your larger community and still guard the Mysteries. Many other denominations do, such as Mormon, Orthodox Jew, Muslim, and many of the Asian temples being brought into our culture now. There's no reason we have to "bare all," and every reason to think that we may gain more respect by our reticence.

DEVON: My belief is that what you do is what you do. I would hope that there is never any intention to harm the Craft. These days secrecy is practiced for a number of reasons. One is that people want to practice their religion by focusing on the positive and to go about their lives privately. Some do not choose to be as private. So what! I say stop worrying about what your neighbor is doing to make the world healthier and more livable, especially when you can see that his or her garden is as green as yours.

ETIDORHPA: I believe in traditional secrecy and that it is still important. If we wanted to be evangelical, we would be just like any other organization or church. We're not, we're special.

ALEXANDRIA FOXMOORE: I believe that traditional secrecy should be in force today. Witchcraft was not meant to be an open gathering or modern church. It was the gifted wise who presented themselves quietly without ego.

GWION: I think secrecy in the Craft is misunderstood by the general public.

JUDY HARROW: Secrecy has helped in the sense of protecting us from persecution. It has harmed in the sense of allowing important knowledge to fragment and stagnate.

As technology is now, our secrecy is just an illusion. If there ever is another Inquisition (Gods forbid!), they will not need to torture us or even to ask us politely. All they need to do is subpoena our old phone bills and trace the links on the Internet to identify us. Personal confidentiality may protect us from prejudiced employers, landlords, or neighbors, but not from the cops!

Meanwhile, it reinforces two dysfunctional psychological tendencies. It fosters an unhealthy sense of isolation and paranoia, while also feeding a very pernicious and false sense of "specialness."

Although both our oaths and plain common courtesy forbid our "outing" one another, I think we are both healthier and safer when we come out of the broom closet. Our best strategy for safety in this time is public education. That will bring us more and more under the protection of the great American tradition of freedom of religion. The way the mainstream media portrayed recent extremist attacks on the religious practice rights of Pagans in the military bears witness to the benefits we reap from twenty years of effective public education.

HANS HOLZER: Secrecy is a relative term. I think that with proper education of the media, secrecy should not need to be an issue. After all, under the law Wiccans have the right to the same protection as any other religious establishment. I don't think secrecy is a good idea, but there is a difference between somebody being a Wiccan and somebody describing the initiation in great detail, step by step. That's another matter. That belongs to the initiate only.

CORBY INGOLD: I think I have expounded somewhat on my feelings about Traditional Craft secrecy already. Has it harmed or helped the Craft? In my opinion, it has done both. It has helped the Craft to survive, obviously, because it is an absolutely necessary component of Traditional Craft. Take it away and you don't have Traditional Craft anymore, you've got something else. Witches, like shamans, are by definition holders of secrets. It's a considerable source of power for us. To Know, To Dare, To Will, and To Keep Silent are the four sides of the Witch's Pyramid. All are absolutely necessary to the successful practice of magic. Also, secrecy can be a shroud behind which we may conceal ourselves during times of persecution.

On the other hand, the very secret nature of our rites and beliefs has kept many from even knowing of our existence. This has undoubtedly caused the number of real Traditionals to dwindle somewhat, or at least it's kept us from growing very fast. And, it's aided and abetted a certain lack of representation of the Traditional viewpoint in the world at large. Given our traditionally secretive nature, we are often somewhat hesitant to declare ourselves or to stand up and be counted when there is not a very good reason to do so. Because of the secret nature of Traditional Craft, many people who are drawn to Witchcraft, having no better information to go on, have assumed that some of the more watered down, generic, or "fluffy-bunny" forms of pseudo-Wicca being foisted on the gullible public today are the real thing. I feel sorry for such people. Many times they are really sincere seekers who end up in one spiritual cul de sac after another because of the spate of misinformation and "Witchcrap" books on the market today. I believe there is a middle way by which we Traditionalists may honor and keep our vows of secrecy and yet have some form of public outreach to dispel misinformation about the Craft and put sincere seekers in touch with those teachers and training covens that might be willing to work with them. There are several different groups doing this in my area, and I laud their efforts.

JIMAHL: I think it has definitely helped. Without secrecy, there would be no Traditional Craft remaining. In my Tradition, there still remains much oral teaching which is provided from teacher to student at the completion of specific degrees.

CHRISTINE JONES: Secrecy has been necessary to protect us. Even now, some work places still find ways to get rid of a person if they know the person practices Witchcraft. I've experienced this first hand. I was a guest on the Larry King Live show in 1992 and was subsequently denied a job because of it. I brought a lawsuit against the employer and won.

KERRY: Secrecy has helped.

LORAX: I think the traditional secrecy has been a mixed blessing but that it has protected more than it has harmed on balance.

LEO MARTELLO: Neither. One did what was necessary, given the climate of the times. My position is ambivalent. I was the most public of Witches in the late sixties and early seventies, yet I was also one of the most private. My Sicilian tradition prevented me from revealing our secrets.

MERLIN: I think it is necessary for the Craft, as it is an integral part of it. The mysteries and power of a magical tradition are lost without it.

MORDA: Traditional secrecy helps in that it keeps the enemy at bay. It makes good sense to be careful. However, the other side is that many who could profit by our teachings are denied them. It's a balance between the need to be cautious and the availability to the public.

MORVEN: Secrecy is a double-edged sword. Obviously, there's the possibility that some will use secrecy to hide unethical practices. The situation is similar to that which exists with a biological family; you don't want the entire neighborhood to know your family's business, yet in some families, secrecy has hidden abuse. One of the things I plan to do is to write a small handout for new students describing what's secret, why, and what to do if they feel secrecy is hiding something unethical.

Besides keeping secret some personal things (for example, people's real names and confidences), we have oath-bound material that we require members not to reveal to others. We keep it secret for the same reasons that Mystery Traditions kept material secret in Ancient Greece. Secrets involving the mysteries can and have helped the Craft.

MURTAGH: I believe traditional secrecy has helped us because it gave us the sense of being a mystery religion. It made us take it more seriously, it made us get involved in it, and there's something about it that stirred the heart. The way it harmed us is because we were a closed group, people could always throw stones at us. They said we were sacrificing animals, sacrificing babies, doing drugs, having orgies—they could make up stories because they did not understand what we were really doing. The other way the secrecy has hurt us is that we have had people want to be involved because they want to know the "secret." Then you give them a tidbit of a "secret" and they throw it back at you, and they don't get it.

MARY NESNICK: Craft is not for the masses. It is and always has been a "secret society," and this is not a bad thing. Even the Christians teach that you don't cast the pearls before the swine. Our teaching talks about preserving and holding that which is sacred. When the sacred is spoken freely to those who have no comprehension, it loses its meaning. All initiates take oaths of secrecy, and true initiates hold their oaths sacred and do not break them.

ELIZABETH PEPPER: At this point in time, I think discretion should be the key.

PATRICIA POTHIER: Well, after all, it kept us alive! Moreover, if we had continued to keep it secret, we would not have the problem of all the New Agers who call themselves Witches after a few visits to the local library.

ROGER PRATT: I believe secrecy has helped the Craft. I think it fosters confidence in the individual members of a coven, and closeness in the group.

RAOKHSHA: I recall a comment about the KKK—"They work by night because their purpose cannot bear the light of day." Unfortunately, our own predilection to hang out after dusk makes us suspect. But, on the other hand, if we had been truly secret about our work or existence from the beginning, we would be "invisible" and no one would be any the wiser and we could only benefit.

In the instance, however, of the despicables who use the ruse of "Craft" to extract favors from their fold, the secrecy works against the members. (But, then again, I hardly consider such as these to be "Craft" anyway, so it doesn't harm true Craft.

Being out of the closet, so to speak, brings a division of energies. One must spend time interacting with the questions and perceptions of "the masses," rather than just "being" a Witch. If you can balance both worlds, then do it—but realize that your magic will suffer. Shamans of old spent very little time on public relations.

OWEN ROWLEY: I am a strange hybrid. I am completely out of the "broom closet" in that I make no attempt to hide my Paganism. However, I believe that there is a benefit in remaining secretive. It's possible that what I really believe is that making Craft easily accessible devalues that craft.

A genuine secret is known only to one person, and when that person is dead the secret exists no more. Once a secret is passed to more than one person it becomes information. Information wants to be free, and must eventually pass along pathways which ultimately pervade the entirety of the Universe. Information has no real inherent value; any value is strictly in the sense which it is held. It depends upon how it is perceived; the value is added upon the act of perception. Enforced secrecy as a group practice to slow down or prevent information leakage must necessarily be an imperfect system and perhaps only an illusion that serves to conceal the greatest secret of them all.

Masonic and other Hermetic organizations often use obfuscation and purposeful deception at lower grades of initiation to prevent leakage from the secrecy system. This is aided by the heavy use of symbols which require long years of study to determine the ultimate meaning of the mysteries they "may" carry. Some symbols are employed as traps for the unwary to be ensnared and have no meaning whatsoever except to deceive and divert the fool.

The seeker who expects mysteries to be handed to them on a plate or who steals them from another is a total fool, and the so-called wisdom spouted by those who "steal secrets" is just so much babbling—not to be worried about actually!

The first line of defense in a secrecy system is the oath. Note that the operative term in our oath is "to keep sacred" the laws and secrets. As long as these are considered "sacred" those who honor their oaths will be motivated to keep them from being profaned. Those who no longer find a group's "secrets" to be sacred will either spread them as valueless or ignore them as valueless. The key is to keep the secret "sacred," not to keep the sacred "secret."

ZANONI SILVERKNIFE: Secrecy can be a shield, a weapon or a tool to be used for protecting, building or destroying. Who can say whether or not it has been helpful? In many ways the need for secrecy has passed away with other forms of behaviors that are out-moded. Particular secrets are maintained not to "hide" knowledge from the worthy, but to protect the ignorant and irreverent from harming themselves or others. When it is time for an individual to know a specific piece of lore or a method necessary to continue "the Work," that information will come to him or her by whatever means.

In historical terms, I believe secrecy has helped and harmed the Craft. It helped to preserve scraps and remnants so that we, today, would have something to work with—an informational object link with our spiritual past. This has been an invaluable tool for those astute enough to work with the pieces through intuitive process and methodical scholarship to obtain what we now have.

I feel that the harm that was done to the Craft during the time of the persecutions and beyond was that the mystique of the unknown was frightening to the unlettered and misinformed populace. To those in power, it was a direct threat to their sovereign reign in ecclesiastical matters and subsequent political infrastructure. Anything that is not known and under control by those in ascendancy is a threat to their power. Ignorance and fear, breeding superstition and hatred have ever been the prime tool for the oppressor. In order to control the populace, it must start in the deepest places of the psyche. It does not start with a conscious thought, but rather from an insidious whisper that grows and festers in the darkest fears of the human subconscious.

SINTANA: In our past it was deemed appropriate for our safety to be absolutely secret about our beliefs. With the exploding Witch craze that occurred in the sixties and seventies, a few Elders determined at the time, that indeed, it was important that good information on the Craft be available. This was because there were many charlatans abusing the teachings of the great Goddess in the name of Craft. These people were making themselves available through various publications. They exploited the vulnerable and eager seekers with mental, emotional, sexual, and spiritual abuses. This became commonplace. There lies within our teachings the understanding that there shall come a time when secrecy shall be laid aside, when we would be called upon to teach publicly, in order that the truth and beauty of the Old Ways be known. We believe that time arrived in the seventies, and we answered its call.

STARSPAWN: I think that different times dictate different ways. Years ago, traditional secrecy meant that some of the traditions were saved either from the burnings of the Inquisition or from those who were frightened by our differences.

In today's age of instant communication, the Craft has learned to continue to survive by adapting to the ways of the times. To a certain extent, the Craft needed to go public, but I believe its essential core will always be hidden from view.

STOCK: Secrecy has not only helped, but it remains one of the chief distinctions of Traditional Craft. Without it, there is no magic.

TANITH: I believe secrecy has helped the Craft. It has kept people safe while allowing them to explore and learn practices not understood or accepted by the general population. Not everyone is called to the Craft, and those who aren't, are afraid of what they don't "get."

THEITIC: Most likely it has done both. Each circumstance is different and should be looked at as unique. There are times when either philosophy could be the right one to embrace.

Having said this I choose to be generally open about who I am and what my practices are, but secret about how I practice and whom I practice with. In my case, it is sometimes seen as a matter of keeping secret that which is sacred.

TIMOTHEA: It has helped to keep the knowledge sacred. It has harmed by raising fear in the cowans. People fear what they do not recognize or know.

JOE WILSON: There is no "traditional secrecy" in my families. We take and make no promises of the sort, but only an understanding that we will be discrete. I personally distrust those who would make secrets since it appears that their secrecy is merely a cover for a lack of knowledge. As far as the topic of "secrecy and outsiders" is concerned, those who hide behind secrets merely give food for the speculation of obscene minds who use it as material for the rumor mills.

How do you define magic and does your tradition include the use of Ceremonial Magic?

MARTHA ADLER: Magic is the act of bringing together mind, soul, body, heart, ritual and tools to produce a desired result. I once used an ancient Etruscian spell to force a thief to return what he stole from me.

AYEISHA: Well, essentially, I would define magic as a change, or the ability to make a change. In a higher sense, hopefully, an understanding which also comes from knowing how and what change to make. Ceremonial Magic is definitely a part of what I do.

Most of the magic I do works. I've seen a lot of people healed from illnesses. I've seen people use magic to help them be more creative in their lives or on their jobs. I've seen people find each other, even though they were separated by a long distance. I use magic in almost all the parts of my daily living. If I'm going to go shopping, I do a little hum so that I'll be inspired to go to the sort of shop that will have what I need. I would never think of shopping without doing that sort of thing beforehand.

I read Tarot cards for people, and there's a lot of magic in that process. I'm able to tell them astonishing things, not only about what already happened in their lives, but chances, opportunities and circumstances that will happen. I'm able to give them good information about how to proceed in order for them to have the greatest happiness that they could have with the least harm to other persons.

So, magic is everywhere and happening all the time. Even the people who are drawn to come to me to have Tarot readings are drawn through a magical spiritual process so that I'm going to be actively useful to them.

Not only am I going to be giving them the information they need, but I'll be able to say it in a voice that they'll be able to hear. A small magic that I do in most of my readings is to pick up people's speech patterns, so if they use a specific term like "once in a blue moon," those words will come out of my lips, as opposed to "once in a great while." The "once in a blue moon" comes directly from speech that they use every day and understand so they can really identify with it. Magic is happening all of the time. It propels most of my life, and most of it works very well.

MARSHA BARD: I use Ceremonial Magic in everything I do. Craft is what I am. Ceremonial Magic is what I do. It is a talent of the intellect and a discipline of the Will. The tradition of symbolism is full and complete and I know where it comes from. I have a psychological agreement with the ancient magicians—I give over my mind to knowledge and they bestow it.

The creative processes of Ceremonial Magic make everything work. For me, it is the explanation of the Craft spell work, the healing circles, etc. It all works because of those things that the Kabala teaches. Craft is the tree in the forest and the spirits that behold its glory and magnificence. With Craft in my heart I can hold that tree, become that tree and feel as that tree feels, old and new, and at the same time—alive and dying all in the cycle. With Ceremonial Magic I am the process of photosynthesis, and the DNA that makes the energy at hand a tree. And in this knowledge I can understand the world of the tree in its very basic "treeness." This knowledge I can take back to the Craft ritual when I need it.

LORI BRUNO: Magic is life. The creation is magic.

RAYMOND BUCKLAND: Magic is making something happen that you want to happen. I have cited examples in my books, especially *Witchcraft From the Inside*. I don't personally use Ceremonial Magic.

CHAS CLIFTON: Magic makes things happen. Sometimes it's a form of "getting out of your own way." Here's a recent example:

During the summer of 1998, my wife Mary went to Philadelphia to visit her sister. Her niece, who was then in her late twenties, was trying hard to get her first professional job as a school psychologist after finishing graduate school. Mary came up with what she calls "a typical Harry's Occult Shop ritual," after a long established store on South Street in Philadelphia, near her sister's home. She bought some colored candles and some cheap, gold nail polish. Her sister furnished a bottle of wine. Jennifer, her niece, wrote out her desired job description on a piece of paper. They lit the candles, and then they role-played Jennifer being telephoned with a job offer. Jennifer dipped the paper in the candle flames and burnt it in a dish, and then they all drank wine and painted their nails gold "for prosperity." Jennifer got the desired job and, at this writing, still has it. It was "spoofy," as Mary said, but it probably was more effective because everyone was light-hearted and not worried about performing serious High Magic. Their inner selves got into the spirit of things.

DANA CORBY: I view magic as a continuum of phenomena from the simplest déjà vu to the most complex rites. For instance, a synchronistic "gift from the Universe" experience—meeting the right person at precisely the right time to make that life-change you've been needing—is magic that's outside your conscious control. Spending two weeks researching and gathering the correspondences for a powerful working while you wait for the optimum astrological configuration is magic that's not only under your conscious control, but until you start the working and cut loose, controlled by your intellect. The two examples couldn't be more different, but both are magic.

My own practice tends to the folksy and improvisational. For example, something needs to be done—a healing, a job-search working, etc.—and usually needs to be done NOW. I comb through my house and garden for what I need, and DO it.

When I was living in Idaho a new-age type friend was quite upset because his lady friend had been in a terrible auto accident; her pelvis had been crushed, and she might not live or might be crippled. I asked him if he'd like our coven to do a healing spell, and he quickly accepted. We used a small plant as an object link that could easily be disguised as an ordinary thing that could be put in a hospital room. We decided not to charge the plant directly because it could have caused the plant to prosper more than the patient. We used the healing energy of water, charging a container of it and then watering the plant. Natural respiration would make the plant's pores slowly release the water, and the energy, into the room, creating a "fog" of healing energy. At the end of our ritual, the candle in the Water Quarter was burned completely away while the others burned in a more normal manner. We gave the plant to him to take to the hospital that evening. Not only did his lady not die, but the doctors said they had never seen anyone heal that fast. She was home in two weeks.

ALEXANDRIA FOXMOORE: Ceremonial Magic is an integral part of Traditional Craft as I know it. The "High Ritual" of great holidays is celebrated with Ceremonial Magic. All rites of passage include Ceremonial Magic.

HANS HOLZER: Magic is the ability to obtain results that would not be available to those unfamiliar with knowledge of natural laws and forces. Magic is not miracles. Magic does not bend or change natural law; it works with it. I see Ceremonial Magic as a sideline. It is a talent, a pursuit of knowledge that can be included in Wicca but does not have to be.

CORBY INGOLD: I find some of the Ceremonial practices and the discipline required to practice them to be useful, especially as forms of training. The binding of the sigils, which we share in common with most British Traditions, is an example of Ceremonial Magic. So is the study of the various tables of Planetary Hours and the successful performance of the Planetary Rites which form part of the training of the student Witch. I'm aware of the current trend away from Ceremonial usage in favor of more purely Pagan practices, and this is valid too. Ceremonial Magic is not necessarily "Judeo-Christian" as some ill-informed individuals claim. Most of the Ceremonial Magicians I have known were Pagan. And in the old days, I don't think the kind of clear divisions we have today existed. The entire occult scene was much more fluid. Witches and Ceremonial magicians freely mingled and exchanged recipes and techniques.

JIMAHL: My teacher told me that true magic is the art of self transformation. I definitely believe in magic, and frankly I can't see the point in being a Witch without magic. It's sort of like owning a car without an engine.

I not only incorporate Ceremonial Magic; I have made it my personal work to restore many elements of Ceremonial Magic to traditional Alexandrian Craft.

CHRISTINE JONES: Magic is about tapping into the Universal energy. I use Ceremonial Magic and Angel magic, and I love doing it.

LORAX: My tradition includes the use of Ceremonial Magic. I believe magic is the art and science of causing change to occur in conformity with Will.

MERLIN: Yes. We celebrate Full Moon Esbats, Sabbats, Initiatory rites, social rites (marriages etc.), and other rites for training, healing and magical works. Magic is the causing of change in conformity with one's will. The change can be physical, metaphysical, personal, or spiritual.

We have seen many rites of initiation help to move people along a path to greater enlightenment, making them better Witches, better people, and better contributors to society.

MORDA: We use Ceremonial Magic. I view magic as on a continuum between old-style Craft magic and classical Ceremonial Magic. Magic is done to create a change internally (one's own mind, consciousness, experience, spiritual state, etc.) or to create an external change (healing someone, causing something to happen).

In 1972 when I decided to marry for the second time, I performed a Venusian ritual to bring the right person to me. It was early evening and getting dark when I began. I realized I needed more light to read a written text more easily. At that moment, a near-by floor lamp turned on of its own accord. I asked to be sent a man with the important requisites and attributes I required. Two days later this man materialized; three weeks later he installed himself in my apartment, and we've been married for twenty-four years. There were numerous other "coincidences" connected with this meeting and marriage.

MORVEN: Alex Sanders was very Ceremonial, and it shows in the rituals and studies of the Tradition. For example, our circle castings contain a lot of Ceremonial elements. In our branch of the Alexandrian tree, Ceremonial Magic is often utilized.

MURTAGH: My tradition uses Ceremonial Magic primarily as a means for personal enlightenment. We are trained in various magical techniques of Ceremonial Magic in the traditional system. I don't particularly use it nowadays; I use my own brand of Celtic Magic. I will train people in Ceremonial, and sometimes I'll fall back on it because it's something I know. Usually Ceremonial Magic is used to help us along the path. Change yourself and the world around you changes.

ELIZABETH PEPPER: Magic is making something happen that seems impossible—but I believe that the wildest dreams can come true through hope, faith in oneself, and the ability to match the rhythm, to be in harmony with the whole. One-third of life is predetermined by genetic and environmental factors, one-third has to do with the power of will, and one-third is subject to change, chance, and luck. In magic we're taking the two-thirds that seem a little out of our personal control and bringing them into control so that we can shape our lives. We can firm our will when it's shaky, find hope when we feel defeated, summon courage when it fails, and catch good luck. It's a way that understands Nature intimately and that opens up whatever intuitive powers we have so that we can use them.

PATRICIA POTHIER: Magic is the ability to turn ideas into reality through the expenditure of energy. You can find all sorts of magics that are worked on the stage at Lincoln Center or hanging on the walls of the National Gallery.

ROGER PRATT: Magic is the transcending of the ordinary. It is also the convincing of the self that a certain "thing" has occurred which then "mysteriously" manifests in the world of the ordinary. Our coven once attempted to heal a slipped disk of the brother of one of our members. The next day he decided to call us to tell us that we had failed. As he lifted the telephone's receiver, lightning struck the telephone line near his home. The resulting shock sent him flying backwards into the wall of his bedroom. He was unharmed, and the disk returned to its normal position. He was cured!

RAOKHSHA: We study the concepts of "low magic" and "high magic" but conduct ritual within the context of the Craft. Magic is the "creation or manipulation of reality by 'unreal' means."

OWEN ROWLEY: Magic as we know it in the 20th and 21st century is all somewhat ceremonial in nature. We simply need to differentiate between common folk sorcery and largely Medieval "educated" sorcery. I think it's the difference between folk music and classical music. In the case of the musics—the sameness is in the intent to entertain. How they do so is largely involved in stylistic differences and class distinctions surrounding where they have been maintained. I like both, but I prefer folk music. The same goes for magic: I like both, but I prefer folk magic.

"What you believe to be true—IS true—or BECOMES true within the limits of your experiences and experiments. These beliefs are further limits to be overcome—for in the realm of the mind—there ARE NO LIMITS." John Lilly, *The Center of the Cyclone.*

ZANONI SILVERKNIFE: Magic, to me, is simply the knowledgeable use of energy in patterns or with formulas that achieve a desired result. It is always done as a conscious act of will. A part of magic is as simple as sharing a spectacular sunset with your dearest.

My Tradition does use Ceremonial Magic. We also use some techniques that are the province of the Kabbalists. There is knowledge and discipline to be gained in the study of the practices of Ceremonial Magic. I liken it to the trellis upon which we grow our vines. The structure provides guidance to tender shoots that would otherwise sprawl on the ground and not achieve fullest potential. On the other hand, the trellis is only there to provide structure; it should not be used to cage the growing, exploring spirit and the magic of which it is capable. The truly deep magics, those that come from the depths of the soul, kin of the nascent, borning Universe, are not of the structure of law so much as from the chaos side, and do not conform to any specific tradition or set of "laws." This is what is called upon in dire emergency only as a survival mechanism, for its use is perilous and there is always a price to be paid.

STARSPAWN: I believe that magic is the ability to change consciousness at will. My refinement of that would be to change one's concept of reality at will. Alex Sanders, who founded Alexandrian Craft, was a Ceremonial Magician and as such, the use of this type of magic in our rituals was very common. Also common, though, was allowing coven members to experiment with magic in the course of learning their Craft.

STOCK: We use Ceremonial Magic in all of our rituals. I would define magic in the Crowleyan sense—the art and science of causing change to occur in conformity with Will.

TANITH: Magic is changing something through your will. We use Ceremonial Magic to some extent. How it's used depends on the individual coven's taste.

THEITIC: Magic is performing an action without using the physical. All ceremonies, meditations and rituals that perform an action and achieve a desired result are acts of magic. We use Ceremonial Magic in private workings as well as in our Esbat and Sabbat rituals.

TIMOTHEA: Magic is the use of mental powers, sometimes enhanced by ritual to concentrate the mind.

JOE WILSON: All of existence is magic; I make no separations of mundane and supra mundane. My Traditions do not use Ceremonial Magic. I am, however, trained in the process, have used it, and will again if the need arises.

What is the greatest lesson or gift the Craft has given you?

MARTHA ADLER: Craft has taught me to love, to try to tolerate and understand others who like me, are not perfect.

AYEISHA: This question stirred my curiosity and I asked several people about this. A common thing that people said was that they were given the opportunity to work with others who had the same ideas and interests, and that they had the opportunity to further their own knowledge and to have people who would be there as a support system for them. I would also say that Craft offers the opportunity to grow and the consciousness to help yourself find the right direction. Outsiders tend to think that Craft and magic are for making things simple, but in the end it actually complicates things more than they knew when they first came to Craft. Craft demands that you be responsible to the degree you are conscious. Even though life can seem more difficult at times, people are willing to bear with the growing pains to achieve the wonderful ability to effect change in themselves and the world around them.

MARSHA BARD: The Craft has taught me everything and introduced me to myself as a part of a cyclic nature. The Craft is the color of my life—it is the touch of the Goddess at the break of day. The Craft is the warmth of my breath on the frosty window of the world. It is the easy chair that holds my tired body at the end of the day. It is who I am and that is the greatest mystery and lesson one can approach.

LORI BRUNO: The Craft has taught me patience, tolerance and caring. I learned that being a Witch is defined as: W for wisdom, I for integrity; T for truth, C for the courage of your convictions, H for our honorable heritage which must be protected for those who come after us.

RAYMOND BUCKLAND: Understanding and love (of the Gods, of nature, and of life) are the greatest lessons I've received.

CHAS CLIFTON: Within the Craft, I feel no "science versus religion" dichotomy, nor does my religion end at the edge of town. Everything can be treated in a sacramental way, whether romantic love, ingesting entheogens, writing poems, going deer hunting, or gardening, something I had not seen achieved in either Christianity or Buddhism. My Craft is still philosophically open, however. I fear that some people today only read books with Llewellyn's crescent moon on them, when they could be learning more from the deep ecologists or the ecopsychologists or nature writers or others trying to overcome what I think might be the biggest issue of our time: how do we accept our own "wildness" and thus learn to love the rest of earth's creatures, instead of viewing the rest of nature as separate and in competition with us?

DANA CORBY Without doubt, the sense of the great beauty of the Universe, to lie in the midst of it, to be privileged to participate in it, and to some small extent contribute to it, is such a great gift that I, who am rarely at a loss for words, cannot adequately express my wonderment. The amazing thing about the Craft is that we seem to be the only belief system in the world (well, maybe Taoism understands) in which the Light and the Dark are equally beautiful and wondrous.

DEVON: The gift of being open and tolerant. Every individual or group is different—yet at conventions or get-togethers, I am always happy to see "all of us" working toward the same thing.

ETIDORHPA: Craft has given me a belief system and a way of life. If you are to be Craft, it is your life and you live it day by day.

GWION: The realization of divinity within myself and those in the world around me.

JUDY HARROW: Craft has been a central organizing principle or structure for my life. It has been an outlet for my creativity, and gives me the sense that I am doing something worthwhile.

HANS HOLZER: I've had the excitement of getting closer to the Universe, a better understanding of Nature, and a greater freedom of combining emotions with philosophy in worship. A religious expression that is not emotional does not work. Emotions are very important. Emotions are also where the psychic element enters in, and this is why I have very little patience with the restrictions that some groups put on their ceremonies. I think that today's ceremonies should be conducted as it was of old. If you really want the force, the ability to obtain the power of expression, you do not fool around with it; you leave it the way it is.

CORBY INGOLD: I think the greatest lesson the Craft has given me is a deeper understanding and appreciation of the hidden forces playing themselves out in the lives of men and women, and how these unseen forces relate to the turning cycle of the year. The mysteries of the Craft are deeply concerned with polarity, not in a mundane sense, but in a spiritual sense. To see the archetypal patterns of the interrelationship of God and Goddess in the lives of ordinary men and women, indeed, in our own lives, gives us a perspective which liberates us from the merely passing and temporal. More, it allows us to understand our lives in the light of a deeper mystery. We are part of this mystery, and the way in which it plays itself out against the backdrop of the yearly seasonal cycle provides a means by which we may not only feel a deeper connectedness with place, bio-region and planet, but with eternity. This mystery can never be explained in any book, it can only be lived. The Craft is a fully participatory mystery.

JIMAHL: It has provided me with a link to the Divine.

CHRISTINE JONES: Knowledge of beyond has transformed my whole life.

KERRY: The Craft has given me a sense of self-worth and a positive attitude.

LORAX: The greatest lesson the Craft has given me is the capacity to know what the saying "You cannot be a Witch alone" means. If one is a Witch, then one is never alone. We are surrounded by a sensitive, exquisitely beautiful flow of creation, birth, aging, death, and return. As one of the traditional medicine singers in the Northwest said, "It is not remarkable to be surrounded by spirits. What is remarkable is to either not know that, or to not care." Upon realizing what the Craft actually means, we can watch all of this unfold amongst us.

LEO MARTELLO: I relished my uniqueness. I lived my life my way without using other people in any way. The realization that a better world began with me. The guts to take on establishment religions and "authorities."

MERLIN: I view the Craft as a path of living and learning. Along the path I have had many lessons. They are the gifts. In addition, the Craft has helped illuminate that path and given me a direction that is part of my being. My wife, Bethany, feels that one of the greatest gifts she has received has been the ability to interact with all the familiar members of a far reaching family.

MORDA: The beauty of the rituals and the sense of being connected to all of Nature, the seasons and the yearly cycles.

MURTAGH: When I first thought about this, I was thinking of my relationship with my Goddess and some of my other non-physicals that I work with. Yet at the same time, some of them have been with me before I was in Craft. I feel that the Goddess has always been with me. I think in some ways the Craft has solidified those things for me. I feel I've been able to help people by doing things with or for them. I've been able to teach and give an example to people. I've affected peoples' lives for the better, and I think that's what Craft has given me, the gift to know that maybe in some small way I've actually made a change in the universe and the people around me. I think that entering into Craft was good for me because it gave me (even though I had been doing magic and such for over ten years before I got involved) some discipline in my life. It gave me some focus. I think that it made me help find myself. That's the greatest gift it's given me.

ELIZABETH PEPPER: The validity of hope.

PATRICIA POTHIER: A niche for finitude within the infinite—a sense of having a place in the universe, both in time and in space. It is very hard to put this into words because it isn't a word thing. It's part of the Mystery.

ROGER PRATT: Craft has taught me the lesson of empathy, of compassion towards all living creatures, and the ability to transform myself through this love.

RAOKHSHA: After years and years (!) of study and practice, the most precious lesson learned is that "the power comes from within."

OWEN ROWLEY: The opportunity to (1) grow in enlightenment and carry that light forward, (2) to refine the dross of my soul into a more refined form and share that with others who care to share with me, and (3) to reach out to that which is divine and find myself therein—and then praise all that is good and excellent.

ZANONI SILVERKNIFE: I would have to say the Craft gave me a protected place to be while I grew into who I needed to be. Like the cocoon that protects the unpretentious caterpillar, the Craft became my home, my shield, my transformative crucible. After twenty-five years of living the way of the Craft and giving service as a High Priestess, I jokingly say I am ready for my gold watch and testimonial dinner. In actuality, I am just transitioning into another stage of my development and leaving all the details to the younger crop of Craft teachers. The Craft fostered my left-brain abilities with a tender care and allowed those to recover and return to growth and strength.

SINTANA: The Craft has gifted me with the freedom to question, to explore, to find the tools to become empowered in my sphere of influence. Craft has helped me discover who I am and to celebrate my insatiable thirst for understanding the complexity and individuality of the human soul as I experience its diversity within me.

STARSPAWN: To always question. In my birth religion of Roman Catholicism, everything needed to be understood by faith alone. In Craft, I was taught to question anything I did not understand or could not comprehend. This questioning continues to this day, as I continue to grow in my beliefs.

STOCK: The Craft has given me a path in life where I am empowered, where I have understanding and, most importantly, control over my own destiny. *That* is the gift. The lesson is that "family" (Craft) values are essential to lead a fruitful and secure life.

TANITH: You can change things! You can perceive other realities, you can create, you can heal!

THEITIC: The sharing of a magical and religious experience with those I love. Helping to bring others into the fold of the Goddess and God. Seeing magic in everything.

TIMOTHEA: The conviction that my inner ideas were correct. The Craft had them already codified, so I am sane and sensible even though I am different from my contemporaries.

There has been a plethora of books and other information published in recent years claiming to tell all about Traditional Craft people and their practices. Considering everything that is public and available, do you still feel it necessary for students to work their way through the traditional system and, if so, why?

MARTHA ADLER: No published book tells all the necessary knowledge that a would-be Crafter is required to have.

AYEISHA: Many of the books that have been published are very surface books about doing specific rituals but have very little information included in them about the sense of the ceremony. The Book of Shadows is just that; it's only shadows and it isn't the main meat of it all. The wisdom in Craft comes from oral tradition. There's a lot of training in Craft about power, for example, not only about how to obtain power but also how to process it, how to internalize it, and how to use it well. So many people rush into rituals they barely understand. They get flooded with power, and the power energizes everything that is within themselves to begin with, their positive as well as their negative. In the oral tradition of Craft a person learns how to work with that energy and use it well. So many are just blown apart by getting in touch with any kind of genuine power because they haven't done a lot of the individual personal work. None of that oral tradition gets published in the books you come across.

In Craft there are mysteries and there are secrets. Anyone can publish a book and tell about the secrets. They can give you a particular ritual that was used, or even a particular idea, but secrets can easily be told and understood. Mysteries, and the Craft is a Mystery Tradition, are experiential. A good example of this is sex. Someone can tell you all about sex. Someone can publish books on sex with pictures in it, but no matter how much you've read or watched about sex, you don't understand it until you actually have sex with someone. At that point you really know sex in a very different way, no matter how many books you've read.

You know, it's an interesting thing to me that the people who publish these books are mostly all people who stood inside the Circle and took an oath that said, "I will not reveal these secrets" and then immediately ran out and revealed them. Not only that, they hardly ever gave credit for their information to the people they actually got it from. It's just plain wrong. It's very basic that if they are publishing what they swore in sacred space not to reveal, that doesn't give them a very good recommendation for doing a good and honest job of teaching you. There is no exchange for having real people who really care about you who will tell you difficult things about yourself, as well as positive things.

Traditional Craft is a specific animal. It is ideas and understandings and insights, and all of these need to be followed in a specific order to get the desired results. This is much like putting the ingredients together to make a cake. There needs to be specific ingredients. You have to have a raw egg; a pickled egg is not going to work, and egg salad won't do it, and deviled eggs won't do it. The egg has to be a particular kind of egg, and it has to be introduced in the proper sequence of time and events in order to get the result you want. You can't wait until the cake is in the oven and then try to blend in the egg, nor can you add the egg after the cake is taken out of the oven. Craft training assures that the people who have gone through the initiation and the training will speak the same language. Often, with public Craft people come in to the class, and they truly don't expect that you're going to have anything to say to them that they don't already know. In the end, they are totally flabbergasted! There's so much in the oral tradition of Craft that simply cannot be squeezed out of a book or a course. I think people should read as many books as they can, but that is no substitute for initiation and teaching. Calling oneself a Witch does not make a Witch, but neither does heredity, nor the collection of titles, degrees, and initiations. Everything comes from the inside out.

MARSHA BARD: Books simply impart someone else's experiences and knowledge. There is no replacement for personal experience. It is in the experiential process that one forms opinions and hopefully is able to alter his or her personal worldview. The psychology of the traditional degree system is consistent with the age-old process of spiritual growth in any given religion, but for very human reasons the system is abused and used for personal power rather than spiritual growth. I do believe a person can reach a state of self-discipline and achieve growth through a self-imposed degree system, without the stresses and strains of a political union of like minds.

LORI BRUNO: Training is important. Respect and responsibility are the cornerstones of the Craft that a book cannot teach. Books cannot teach students respect for those Elders who have gone before; books cannot provide the necessary structure.

RAYMOND BUCKLAND: It's not necessarily the right path for everyone, but I think there is much to be learned form "working through the traditional system."

CHAS CLIFTON: Is *Sacred Mask, Sacred Dance* one of those books? Wait until you see the sequel. All Is Revealed!

DANA CORBY: Oh, my, yes! I asked the other Mohsian leaders for their thoughts on the value of Traditionalism, and one of them articulated it better than I can: "One of the most important things about Traditional Craft is that it has Elders. Craft is not about knowledge. We have been indoctrinated into a society that is fixated on knowledge and cleverness, yet despises the wisdom needed to use knowledge safely. It has done everything it can to obfuscate and ridicule the path of wisdom. Elders are needed to ensure that we re-examine everything in our past in the light of new perspectives. The steadying influence of a wise Elder can keep one from becoming an obnoxious fool, alienating family and friends with one's 'knowledge'. The book-taught Wiccan has not been subject to an evaluation of his or her character, skills, maturity, and wisdom. Traditional Craft has an edge over book Craft because of the selection and training of its Elders.

However, even above and beyond the forgoing, I would emphatically state that you cannot get a hands-on initiation out of a book, and hands-on initiation is necessary. The wording varies from tradition to tradition, but a main function of the Traditional initiation is to pass on the power.

The passing of the power in the Initiation rite connects the initiate not just to his/her initiation, but to that person's initiator, and that person's initiator, all the way back as far as the line goes. It connects the new initiate to the ancestors in a way that not only gives them roots, makes them responsible to those ancestors, but gives them access to reservoirs of wisdom and experience far beyond the here and now. This is the true meaning of "Lineage."

DEVON: There is no experience like the experience of doing.

ALEXANDRIA FOXMOORE: As owner of two stores and a serious student of the Craft for well over thirty years, I feel I am qualified to say that the information that is available in no way "tells all" about Traditional Craft. However, I do think that there is an amazing wealth of wonderful New Age and Wiccan information available. As for students working their way through Traditional Craft, I think people learn in different ways. A disciplined lifestyle is only for the serious. Many Pagans today do not want or need to be a part of Traditional Craft. Pagans have choices today. They can belong, participate, and enjoy being a part of Paganism in freedom.

Traditional Craft is of interest to only a select few, just as it always has been. There is no way to read and learn how to live a "hands-on working Craft." One of the things that sets Traditional Craft apart is that it is a lifestyle of movement in rhythm with nature. Another aspect of Traditional Craft that cannot be self-taught is the actual "Craft." The ritual of repetition to create the crescendo of a chant, the art of blending herbal teas to taste, the development of sensitivity, and the balance of intunement are not acquired through reading. Masterful arts are learned from those who have mastered them. The ART of Witchcraft is an experienced practicum.

GWION: I still believe it is necessary for students to work their way through the traditional systems, despite all the books available out there. You cannot feel the magic through a book, nor can you ask a book questions. And, finally, you cannot be initiated through a book, and we view initiation as a magical process that the candidate must experience.

JUDY HARROW: It's one thing to read a cookbook and another thing to cook. Craft (and many other real things) can only be learned experientially; theoretically doesn't do it. These things can be learned alone, but it's easier and safer with an experienced person to guide and give feedback.

HANS HOLZER: Reading a book is not the same as learning the Craft live. Reading a book is just preparing you for the Craft, nothing more.

CORBY INGOLD: Yes, I still feel it is of value for students to work their way through the Traditional Craft system. The plethora of books you refer to only tell part of the story. As I mentioned earlier, the Craft is a mystery, and a participatory one at that. Thus, a large part of the mystery is experienced by participating in the Traditional training process. I don't care what these books purport to reveal, you simply cannot short-circuit this process. I am liberal minded enough to accept that there are deep spiritual mysteries in any genuine religious path. There are certainly levels of mystical experience within the Christian faith, however much orthodoxy may have tried to stamp it out. Now it is a fact that the Christian scriptures have been in print for a very long time. But merely going to a bookstore and purchasing a copy of the bible doesn't automatically open these deeper mystical elements within the church for you. Even so, in our religion, versions of the standard Gardnerian derived Book of Shadows have been in print since the sixties (I believe *Witch* by Rex Nemorensis was the first). But merely possessing such a book doesn't make you a Witch. That can only come about through an initiatory process. The Craft is an initiatory mystery religion. And yes, undergoing the rigors (and joys) of the traditional training system, however that may vary in detail from coven to coven, is part of the process.

JIMAHL: No, it isn't necessary for a student to work through a traditional system. But I do think it's a good system and one that works better for most students. There is so much information to get through on one's own that a guide is an obvious benefit. Also, the group experience of a coven is unparalleled.

CHRISTINE JONES: Yes. Whenever something is worth having, you have to work for it.

KERRY: If students are serious, they should work their way through a Traditional system. In my opinion, if they haven't been initiated, they are just dabbling.

LEO MARTELLO: Some of these books are being ground out like sausages and pursuing the Pagan party line. All of the authors reincarnated Rebecca of Sunnybrook Farm, wearing Blessed Be sunbonnets, carrying baskets full of lily-white rose petals which they strew over one and all, whitewashing Witches into some idealized version of a Christian Snow White! Where is the Wicked Witch of the West now that we need her? Without traditional training, without earning their way, all these nouveau Witches are cheating themselves of the true Craft. Better them than me.

MERLIN: Without a system the books and information just amount to data. It needs to be interpreted to be effective. The traditional system provides the necessary framework to apply the information. Students need to work their way through because that is the way the system works. The close knit, structured group working together in a cohesive system, experienced elders, oral traditions, clarification, and repetitive, consistent practice can not be found in books alone. Traditional Craft is not merely intellectual. It is more experiential.

MORDA: Experience is the best teacher. Too many Americans want/get everything out of books.

MORVEN: Books can never take the place of actually doing the work. Think about learning a musical instrument. You can read all about it, but until you actually play, you can't learn it. So, can you get a book and do the exercises, and do the magic? Possibly. Just like a person can teach himself or herself how to play an instrument, it's possible to learn magic on one's own, but it can be easier with training from a qualified person or when working with a group.

Once again, using the music analogy: A music teacher might know a tried and true way for the student to learn, saving the student time trying various methods that don't work. Still, a really gifted student can succeed, no matter what. Most of us, though, could use some direction and hints.

Also, whether you can get it all from books depends on what you want. If you just want the Neo-Pagan aspects, you don't need training. You can simply do what's in your heart. If you want to work magick, that's different.

MURTAGH: I certainly do believe that hands-on training is necessary. There's something that being initiated and working with a group will give you that you will not get otherwise. There's an energetic tie that occurs, and if you lose the link with other people then you just don't get it. You're working with a holistic system; with the universe, and how can you work with the universe and not be a part of it? And so, that means touching people (and not on your computer). I really think that it's necessary for people to be part of a system. And if the system's been around for a while and is a "traditional" system, then all the better because it has a proven track record. You know that if you do "X, Y and Z," you will get results. And when you're a student early on, you need to have that affirmation that it works. If you are a solitary, things could be happening but some of it could be in your head. There are people that do magic and never leave their heads. I remember when our coven was learning to work with the elementals. We had a discussion with our priest and priestess afterward about each element and what happened during each ritual. And as I talked about each element I could see them looking at each other and nodding and saying, "and then this happened," and I said, "Yes, that's right, how did you know?" And of course, they had done the workings and other people had been there before me, and so they knew that I had made contact because I got the right results. You really need to have people who have gone before you. Having a teacher is good, but being in a system like a coven gives you people to work with, who have different experiences.

You can read all the books you want, but they're only books. In some ways those books are like chains, like in Dickens' *The Christmas Carol* when Marley's ghost appears to Scrooge with the chains and the ledger books. Those were the weights Scrooge created in the world, and in some ways the books will weigh you down magically. People are very caught up in the idea of scholarship in Craft, especially in Celtic spirituality. They read primary sources and look for things and connections that no one else saw and such. But at the same time, they get so bogged down in the books, looking for what's right, that they don't try anything. I think that, eventually, the time comes when you need to get rid of the books and even the scholarship because they aren't going to help you. The books are only giving you half the magic. You can't get the oral tradition from books. It's from the people who have been trained orally that you learn magic.

MARY NESNICK: A scholastic degree without a mentor/instructor is unknown. Book knowledge has never been sufficient by itself, and this certainly holds true for the Craft.

ELIZABETH PEPPER: I believe we (when we have gifts) follow paths that appear before us. An inner voice declares what is correct for each individual.

PATRICIA POTHIER: Yes. Books are great for imparting facts and ideas from the mind of the writer to the mind of the reader. But no one ever learned a mystery from a book.

TRIVIA PRAGER: The advantage of a traditional path is that you don't have to reinvent the wheel; a lot of the work has been done for you. This allows you the time and energy to work on your own growth. Rituals have been tried and found to work, allowing you to tap into a reservoir of energy. You have a common ground to work with like-minded people.

ROGER PRATT: The differing view and opinions given in books can be confusing to the student. Teaching on a personal level is geared to each individual's personal developmental needs and speed.

On the other hand, the books can give the seeker an idea of what to expect from training, and a variety of paths to choose from. I value greatly my Gardnerian experiences. And I value that I had my mother's personal system as well.

RAOKHSHA: There is absolutely no "soul" to be found in the textbooks. And, if you consider the mercenary intent of many authors, the knowledge within these tomes is bastardized! The books out there today are twelfth-generation regurgitations of the primary source material. Anything written by "Vicki Starlight" is suspect. The worthwhile material has always been out there. The student who will not wade through Regardie and the like, but devours the fifty page treatise on controlling the universe is sorely in need of a traditional system (emphasis on system). The beauty of Regardie's, Gardner's and Crowley's work is the system! The authors of the how-to's out there now don't have a clue, but they parrot well.

You can get your "credentials" from any of the $6.95 "literary" experiences; just don't expect the rest of us to take you seriously

OWEN ROWLEY: I found it to be valuable to work my way through a traditional system—twice. I tend to think others would find it valuable to do likewise. It must be said, however, that not all traditional systems are going to provide the same value in similar scale.

Ultimately, I believe it is the seeker who does the work, that determines the value. But it's not outside the realm of possibility that some can be sidetracked by spending too much time and effort with fools masquerading as bearers of traditional wisdom.

My own experience was that I asked the universe to lead me to the place I ought to be in order to achieve my goal of enlightenment in this lifetime. I believe that if one sincerely and successfully makes that request it will be honored.

ZANONI SILVERKNIFE: Like the old sayings, "words are cheap," "the map is not the territory," or, if you prefer, an anthropological study does not give you a culture, it only describes someone's perception of that culture. Books can go on for chapters and volumes but the surface is only scratched and the essence is not touched. People will do as people will do, and those whose pride and ego tell them they can learn it all with a book or two and some cleverly written "rituals" can continue on their merry way. There is an indefinable event that takes place when two people undertake a course of study together as teacher and student. The transmission of information becomes purer, encoded in "soul-talk." This is not something you can get on your own with a book for guidance. There is a flavor of experience that comes with the teaching.

If I take you through the "rapids" correctly the first time, you will be able to negotiate your way through on your own the next time, and do it safely, gaining a lot of capabilities that would be denied to you if you were paddling like mad to keep from drowning. Each time through, you can allow yourself to notice landmarks and subtle changes in the terrain while still maintaining an intelligent and safe passage. If you bumble through on your own the first time, flipping the raft here, running up on a shoal there, battering yourself on the rocks in another place, you will learn the river, but each time you traverse that particular piece of river you will have nano-seconds of recall and a splinter of "freeze" before doing what you should be doing. That can be fatal in the case of shooting the rapids. In the case of magical workings it can sour the work, if nothing more drastic.

I do not think that everyone is meant for Traditionalist training. It is very demanding. There is a distinction made in who will be able to accommodate such a training, benefit by it, and pass it along to others who are capable of assimilating such a course of study. I do, however, suggest that anyone who is contemplating a magical path find a person with whom to share information. The person you work with should be incisively honest and firm, but kind. A no-nonsense approach is the best course to take because this is not "play," but very serious business. Avoid "yes" persons or those who fall in with your every suggestion. They are not good companions for walking the path of spirit. Always listen to your inner voice. Always take the path to your greater good.

SINTANA: Yes, it's all out there. Today the public can find a wealth of information on Craft, traditions, and magic. But I ask any older generation Elders; does this represent what we're about? Is this a true representation of your beliefs? You will get a resounding NO. Now of course there are exceptions. There are individuals attempting to put forth reliable information, but I ask you how can an individual without the guidance of a qualified mentor, teacher, or guide, discern and properly apply the teachings? We are not and never have been people of "the Book." Our teachings are quite individual and there are no two people who can learn and then apply at the same level; each will have a different perception, depending on his or her own experience. A book can only give you information. I know many who are collectors; collectors of all they can lay their (gotta get the magic) hands upon. Jumping from one group to another, hunting for the guru, the Elder of the moment, and collecting from them their magical books of knowledge. Most of them never really understand some of what they have and most of it is run of the mill and quite misleading trivia. It becomes a cycle and many are caught in it. They feed upon the vulnerable and become a mirror of their own egos. One must work their own path, and there are no short cuts. "Seek ye a qualified teacher who will lead you through the Web of Illusions that you may know and conquer the spider of deception".

Books are magic; they bring the experiences of others to our world and can give us great insight, but they cannot give us the experience that will bring wisdom. The Craft cannot be learned or applied or lived to full experience without direction, and especially spiritual direction. There is no way for one to be a Priest or Priestess unless their growing to knowledge has been witnessed and blessed by the knowledge, grace, and guidance of their Elders.

STARSPAWN: The Craft has always been an "oral" tradition. It's only recently that anything was written down and even now with all the writings that are available to the student, they learn more when sitting in circle, properly prepared and hearing the words from their teacher, in the manner in which it was taught to their teachers before them.

To clarify: You can be told what the color blue looks like, but if you were born without sight, you would not be able to fully grasp blue as a color. The same goes for Craft teachings. You can read about it, you can hear people tell you about it, but until you experience it, you simply do not grasp its full meaning.

STOCK: Yes, it is necessary to do the work because *that's* the way it's done.

TANITH: Yes, unequivocally. There's a lot of stuff you have to get through being around others. It is an apprenticeship as well as a simple memorizing of facts. It's a physical re-attunement and a group experience, even if the group is only two or three people.

THEITIC: Although I have seen numerous books claiming to "tell all about Traditional Craft people and their practices," I have yet to see any books that actually do.

If someone wants to learn Traditional Craft there is no choice except to learn by experience. Book knowledge must be put into practice. The actual "wisdom" comes not from performing the actions that are learned in books, but by feeling the changes between these actions. The religious or magical actions are a product of knowledge (from books) and wisdom is attained as the experience of these "in-between" actions as they become assimilated into the Magician's psyche.

JOE WILSON: The attitude that there's no longer a need for traditional training since so many fine books are available today is stupid. There are also many fine books available on medicine, psychotherapy, law, accounting, physics, agriculture, writing, music, art, sculpture, and literally every discipline that exists. Their availability does not eliminate the need for training. If anything, it does just the opposite. Traditional Craft as I know it has nothing to do with that which has been published in any book I've yet seen. You cannot learn anything real from a book; all you can do is learn about it. There is a huge difference.

Do you think the public is more tolerant toward Craft today than twenty years ago, and do you think Craft should be a mainstream religion?

MARTHA ADLER: I believe the public has become more tolerant, despite all of the Born Again Christians and fanatics. Many of our people have "come out of the closet" and are educating through books, lectures, radio, and TV to reach people. I believe with certainty that we should be a mainstream religion.

AYEISHA: Right now I think there's a little bit of a popular culture surge for Wicca and a lot of people are going through that kind of phase. But even so, I think that if you go under that pop-culture layer, if anything, people are more opposed to Craft than they used to be.

MARSHA BARD: I think that the Christian Coalition is the most dangerous organization on the face of the Earth. I think that because of the work of this organization there is far less tolerance for anything not white and Christian in today's society. I find their work to be the evil they write about in their books. We should be very wary of them and, if necessary, go back under cover. The Craft is in a very tender state; part of the religion is accepted on the basis of Neo-Paganism which is faddish right now, so we have the good will of some—but only until the next fad comes along. I think the tolerance level is geographical. We need to be open where we can be open and invisible where we cannot be open, and we need the guidance of the Goddess to tell us where we are.

I think that, given the state of this society, everything that Craft has to offer would suffer if it were to become mainstream. Let it lie in the soft moonlight until day breaks on its own. Don't force the light to shine on Craft; we don't have that sort of sunscreen, and we will all burn again.

LORI BRUNO: The public is more tolerant because we've had the "colgiones" to come out and be a formidable force to be reckoned with. We've "come a long way, baby;" we're on the internet; we are factory folk, farmers, doctors, judges, and politicians.

RAYMOND BUCKLAND: Having been there thirty years ago, I think the public is obviously much more tolerant. But I think that Craft should be accepted for what it is—an alternate religion. I think that's sufficient.

CHAS CLIFTON: Because I work in academia, I feel somewhat freer from persecution and ignorance than do many Pagans. The danger here might be more the marginalization that any religious person encounters—that old Enlightenment notion that religion is only for the superstitious and the uneducated. (Some members of my family, notably my father, think that way.) I think that those of us in religious studies still must fight an uphill struggle to see "Pagan studies" taken seriously. It has always been all right for Jews to study Judaism, Christians to study Christianity, and so on, but we Pagan scholars are occasionally accused of being "too inbred" and of wasting our time on a peripheral area. (Granted, if being employable was the leading criterion, I would have majored in New Testament studies.) I do think that religious studies as a field remains mesmerized by "texts" in the narrow scriptural sense, and since Paganism is non-scriptural, we just do not seem as serious.

DANA CORBY: I don't believe there is any more general understanding of, or toleration for, Witchcraft today than there ever was. There may be less. What there is, though, is an understanding that under our current legal system you can't get away with trampling on people's civil rights, however much you may believe it might please your God(s), because you believe they are "Satanists." I believe one of the reasons the radical Christian right seeks power in the Federal Government is so they can pass laws giving themselves the ability to outlaw "Satanic" activities, by which they seem to mean pretty much everyone but themselves.

I do not believe that The Craft should be a mainstream religion. The value of Witchcraft not only to its members but to the larger society is that it exists in the borderlands, those shadow realms which are neither of the light nor of the dark—or such an admixture of both that it takes training to tread the path through it. There is a deep need for walkers through the borderlands and for borderlands to walk through. If

Witchcraft is forced, as some now seem to be trying to force it, into the mainstream, the gates will be closed to us, as they closed to Christianity when it came out of the catacombs and seized power in its world.

On the other hand, mainstream or not, Witches should have their freedom of religion respected. We should not have to sneak into the hospital to minister to a sick covener. We should not have to defend ourselves against the attacks of the ignorant clergy of mainstream faiths. Our culture is learning to respect, or at least not to interfere with the religious beliefs of our many Asian immigrants, strange as they may seem. Immigrants from the Caribbean have had their right to perform animal sacrifice (i.e., to bless the food before they kill it instead of after it gets to the table) acknowledged by the U.S. Supreme Court. They did not have to become "mainstream" to get these rights because the Constitution guarantees them. This is a civil-rights fight, not a petition for acceptance. Keep that context clear and we can walk both in the borderlands and in the light of the sun.

DEVON: I don't know if the word "tolerant" can be given to the general public concerning the Craft. Yes, there is certainly more visible evidence that we are out there. Unfortunately, I think that as a whole it is a tad bit scarier in some ways. There is growing and extreme evidence that too many people are out there who shoot first and ask questions later. This is definitely a concern. People may listen a little better, but I feel that there is some distance to go before the general public is tolerant. I don't want them tolerant anyway; I want them accepting! I definitely feel that Craft should be recognized and accepted as a religion.

ALEXANDRIA FOXMOORE: WHAT?? The society we live in is Christian and is never going to be tolerant of Paganism, much less Craft!

GWION: I think that today there is more tolerance toward the Craft. I think this is due, in large part, to an overall tolerance evolving in society. I do not think that Craft could or should ever become a mainstream religion. The very nature of Craft is intimate and would be difficult to convey to the masses.

JUDY HARROW: I think the public is much more accepting, due to some of us taking on the job of public education. I believe that Paganism should be a mainstream religion. I envision a role like that of the Quakers, always a minority, but respected. And, as the Quakers have consistently spoken for social justice, we should consistently advocate for Mother Earth.

HANS HOLZER: I think they are not so interested in what Wiccan and Pagan people do. Now there's so much diversity in the other religions, and so much damage being done by their work that I don't see that they are that interested any more.

As far as the Craft being a mainstream religion—it IS!

CORBY INGOLD: I have always found the public to be pretty tolerant of the Craft where I live. Of course, I reside in a notoriously liberal city on the West Coast. Fundamentalists have never been the norm in my town. I've been more or less open about being a Witch since my teenage years (of course, I don't put it on my resume). I'm well aware that folk in other areas aren't quite so lucky. And in this city we have Witches serving on the Church Council (an interfaith organization). Even thirty years ago, in the swinging sixties, many people were remarkably tolerant. Due to the shrewd promotional instincts of people like Sybil Leek and Alex Sanders, among others, it became very trendy and hip to be a Witch. It was all part of the general sixties rebellion against the stifling stodginess of the preceding era. Of course, this also created a backlash in some areas, as people less glamorous than Leek and Sanders came out of the broom closet. It was one thing for Alex Sanders to appear in flowing ceremonial robes and silver pentagram at the local pub in London, and quite another for Joan or Joe Doaks of Peoria to announce to their neighbors and employers that they practiced the Craft. And this, I think, is where some folk ran into trouble, which in many cases provoked personal and familial tragedy, as in the well reported cases of Witches having their children taken away by the State. This is where the ongoing work of public education undertaken by numerous Pagan organizations has been of tremendous benefit to our community. As a result of their valiant efforts, I would say that, overall, the general population is far more tolerant towards Craft today than in previous times though we've still got a long way to go.

I would not personally like to see the Craft become a mainstream religion. If it did it would cease to be the Craft as we know it and become something else. Though there are those popularizers of the Craft who want to make it mainstream, we Traditionalists have always known that it is not a path for everyone. It is, in effect, an esoteric mystery cult working through small, autonomous groups and individuals. One of the real strengths of the Craft, in my estimation, is its independence from large organizational structures. You have, basically your coven and your particular Craft lineage (Gardnerian, Hereditary, etc.). Beyond that, we are quite independent of each other. We may choose to interact with other covens or traditions or not, as we choose. There is also a remarkable freedom, intimacy, and fluidity of working in a small autonomous magical group which is lost in a larger organizational situation. I believe that the Craft will always be a path for the few. Our strength is not in our numbers, but in our integrity. For all these reasons and many more, I hope Craft never becomes mainstream.

JIMAHL: There is still a "knee-jerk" reaction that people have to the Craft. I am very careful about confiding in non-Wiccans. A lot of their thinking is deeply rooted in their subconscious memory, yet they are afraid of us for all the wrong reasons. As far as the Craft being a mainstream religion, I would say, yes, in regards to bringing it out into general acceptance. But I think that's unrealistic. I would say, no, in that it would suffer so much in the translation.

CHRISTINE JONES: I think the public is somewhat more tolerant but still very fearful and NO, the Craft will never be mainstream.

KERRY: I don't really know if there is more tolerance today. I do believe the Craft should enjoy the same rights and privileges that other religions enjoy, but that the Craft should remain underground.

LORAX: I do not think that the general public cares much for any non-mainstream religion. I suspect that toleration varies by city block, occupation, and many other factors. I do not think the Craft can EVER be a mainstream religion in our culture. Maybe among Tibetans or the Burmese it could be mainstream, where people find it normal to send large numbers of children off to monasteries for religious study, but not in the West.

LEO MARTELLO: Definitely more tolerant as witness the hundreds of positive articles appearing in the press. The media is more savvy. Many in the media, if not Witches or Pagans themselves, are Pagan-friendly.

Craft basically is mainstream though not as yet organized as such. Look at the substrata of Catholicism as an example.

Why should we be religion's stepchildren? Why not have all the advantages of other religions? For those who prefer a more non-structured format they have a choice. That's the beauty of the Craft and Paganism in general; you can be organized, unorganized, or disorganized. We need them all. Has everyone forgotten the Inquisition? We are the spiritual descendants of those tortured souls burned at the stake, the living reminders of their guilt, the spiritual avengers of those innocents murdered because they were Witches, or were accused of Witchcraft.

MERLIN: The Craft would no longer be the Craft if it were a mainstream religion. Some forms of Paganism could do that and that could be good.

I feel the public Is generally more tolerant now because more information is available and the media has done more to expose the existence of the Craft. The world is a smaller place today. Familiarity has given rise to a degree of acceptance. However, I do think that under the right circumstances, this level of tolerance could change quickly.

MORDA: Yes and no. I personally see more tolerance, probably due to media exposure, and the fact that the Craft is more open than it used to be. In terms of fascism and the Christian right, there is less tolerance.

MORVEN: There's a big difference between tolerance towards Paganism and tolerance towards Witchcraft. In general, I think Paganism is much more accepted these days. You hear about the holidays on TV and on the radio, there have been great strides in protecting freedom of religion, and Neo-Paganism is more often recognized as a religion. I don't think Witchcraft enjoys the same acceptance. (I hear that in some parts of continental Europe, the opposite is true. People equate Pagans with Neo-Nazism, so people have to call themselves Wiccans and not Pagans.)

Also, I think acceptance still varies from area to area and social group to social group. For example, the Bible Belt of the South in the U.S. still isn't very tolerant towards Neo-Paganism or Witchcraft. A campus environment in southern California is still going to be more accepting than a small community in the Midwest. Educated people, whether they like the practice or not, might still be more understanding than uneducated people because they've been exposed to a broad range of ideas, not only those they agree with.

I don't think the esoteric teachings of Craft should be mainstream, no. Those teachings are part of a mystery religion. Neither do I think we should be teaching the general public how to work magic because we don't know what they would do with that skill. Do I think Neo-Paganism should be? I'm not sure, but I'm more open to them being mainstream than Craft.

MURTAGH: I think the public in general is more tolerant, but I believe it depends on the area. In certain parts of the country you can say you're a Witch and people won't even blink. In other areas you'll have rocks thrown through the window and burning crosses on the lawn. I think the tolerance has come about because there have been people out in public talking about it more, and people who are not as closed to it and who try to educate others. Hispanic friends of mine grew up with the very scary image of the Bruja, the negative-imaged Witch who does bad magic. It really bothered them to use that term. Because they were friends I really tried to do some educating and because they knew the kind of person I am, that helped them get over that hurdle. But I don't generally tell people what I'm involved in. I have a friend in the film business who tells people constantly and then can't figure out why she doesn't get called back for work. I think that especially here in California, there are so many New Age type people that most of it is seen as a joke.

As for being a mainstream religion—no, no, no, no! I don't believe the Craft should be mainstream. I have never believed it and never will. Craft was and is a mystery religion, and a mystery religion cannot be mainstream without losing the mystery. But now we see groups becoming non-profit organizations and using tax shelters. Some have set themselves up like churches and are getting paid by their followers by their (and I use this word) "flock" to minister to them. We have already seen the Christian evangelical sects having problems because of money and corruption in the system. I would just as soon remain a mystery religion that changes for the people and is more individualistic in nature than the mainstream religions that lose sight of people.

ELIZABETH PEPPER: Tolerance implies superiority, a patronizing attitude I can't accept from public opinion. True, cooler heads prevail at the moment, but "mainstream religion" would provoke storms. A subtle force like the current *Harry Potter* series will give Witchcraft a good name and not severely threaten the establishment.

PATRICIA POTHIER: I think that as the established religions feel increasingly threatened both by science and by alternative religions, they become less and less tolerant of all things that they do not understand and therefore fear and hate. The Craft should not be a mainstream religion. The "mainstream" wants to have a set of rules to follow so it won't have to think. It wants to be rewarded for goodness because goodness per se is not enough. It wants someone else to die for its sins. How can Craft be suited to become "mainstream" when it requires thought, has no rewards or punishments, and insists that one take responsibility for one's actions?

TRIVIA PRAGER : The Craft is a path of accelerated growth and is not for everyone. I don't see it as ever becoming a mainstream religion. First of all, it's too much work for the average person. "An it harm none, do what you will" makes you weigh all of your choices and take responsibility for them. There's no room for "the devil made me do it." You actually have to think for yourself. There are too many young souls out there who aren't ready for that responsibility. I was raised Roman Catholic, and some days when I'm feeling tired I think of those wonderful days when you could screw up, go into a box and say, "Bless me, Father..." and walk out forgiven. Now I know that if I screw up, I have to figure out a way to fix it. That doesn't mean that I think the mainstream religions aren't good for some people. For some, this gives them a moral code to live by, giving them the righteous life and support that they need.

The second reason I don't see Craft as becoming mainstream is that power corrupts and absolute power corrupts absolutely. The mainstream religions may have started out as mystery religions, but once they gained political power, they made compromises to keep that power. Rules were changed to accommodate the new reality and the spirituality got lost in the process. Then they had to build great structures to show how powerful they were. Before you know it, the emphasis is on maintaining the structures. I value the fact that I can teach in my living room and worship in my dining room, bedroom, back yard, the woods, or anywhere else I feel moved to do so.

ROGER PRATT: In general, more tolerant in Northern cities. I live in New York City and take a bus each morning to work where, every day I see several people reading Bibles as I travel. I am not sure just how tolerant people will remain. I think there will be changes for us ahead. As far as Craft becoming a mainstream religion—goodness, I hope not. It is, perhaps, too mainstream already. You know, Jesus leads sheep in a group. Pan leads his flock of independent, hardheaded goats!

RAOKHSHA: I think the public falls into three categories: 1) those who respect our scholarship, take the time to examine our beliefs, and accept us as equals; 2) those who think we're cranks and don't even worry about us; and 3) those who suspect anyone who is "different" and will lay the blame for anything or everything on us. Unfortunately, the first group is small and the second is easily persuaded to join the third.

I had neighbors who knew I conducted ritual in my home and/or yard. On the one side was a family that totally respected what I did and sometimes asked for healings. On the other side was a family that was bemused by me, but never harassed or threatened me. I am not an "in-your-face" Witch. If you ask me about the Craft, I will answer in a way I think you will understand. On the other hand, I make it a point never to confuse the fact that I am "allowed" to do what I do with the assumption that observers approve/accept what I'm doing.

For the most part, we are still an oddity and not exactly the primary concern of the majority of the population of this planet. There is, indeed, more quiet tolerance of the sincere Witch, and yet there is more intolerance of the antagonistic media Witch with an ax to grind. The latter erodes the former unless we rein in some of our grandstanding "public relations officers" in a hurry!

As far as becoming mainstream—No. We are what we are because we have worked against that dogma, hierarchy and institutionalization. We don't need a pope. We don't want a "diet of worms" to decide our tenets. What we need is a world where not being the majority is okay.

OWEN ROWLEY: I think the idea of becoming a mainstream religion is a two-edged sword. In one sense religion is a trap and in another it is a gift. It depends upon how you respond to the parts which are a trap and how you unwrap the parts which are a gift.

ZANONI SILVERKNIFE: Any decade has its ups and downs, periods of seeming acceptance and tolerance, and times of brutal harassment. Over the course of years that I have been involved with the Craft, I have been sought after by news reporters from the papers, radio, and television. I have been asked to speak on many panels and to many groups of diverse viewpoints. On the other hand, I have also been the target for such things as slander, dead birds nailed to my door, waste matter smeared on my vehicle's window, and I have been ostracized by community and family alike.

I think that there are now so many "alternative" modes of religious and self-expression that we are just one of many fish in a school. We are lumped in with others upon whom society looks askance. I do not believe, however, that we are done with persecution and ostracism. The hate-mongers will always hate, the "one way" people will only see their way, not "the" way. Do not be deluded into thinking we have actual religious freedom in this country yet. It may be the letter of the law, though the spirit is weak, and there are those who think laws are for other people. Always, always watch your back.

As for the Craft becoming a mainstream religion—no. It will lose its vitality, its cross-pollinating abilities. Leave it as it was meant to be—open to those who can hear the music of the pipes and the bough, those who can see the Roebuck in the thicket, and those who dare to be brought from behind the North Wind's mighty gale. I think the Craft should retain its philosophical and practical virtues. Things are changing and transmuting even as I speak these words. In another twenty years it will all be so different that you will scarcely recognize what the outer trappings of Paganism have become, though there will be strong threads of commonality that will be recognizable, with Traditional Craft sorts still being the trellis from which we can all grow and build. And the Craft is the Craft is the Craft, ever and anon. So mote it be!

SINTANA: Various Craft leaders, writers and educators have put forth much information on what we as Wiccans or Witches believe. They have all tried to be true to their own creeds to bring some enlightenment to the general public and especially to city leaders, media people, police personnel, and community and religious leaders. So much good work has been done. Blessed Be to all those who continue to represent our Craft, sharing our Tenets, beliefs, and presenting to the public a much-needed image of Witches as positive, productive members of society.

I know first-hand that indeed the public is more tolerant and accepting today than twenty years ago. It's been about nine years now since I've had a death threat. I believe the work is just beginning and the teachers and leaders and those representing the Craft to the public must be an example in our daily lives, within business, family, and society; they must live and exemplify what we teach. I believe there has been a genuine trend for various Pagan groups today to start policing their own and setting standards of behavior at public affairs. I believe those who present themselves and their groups as being Witches owe it to all of us to have some semblance of order and a modicum of decency.

The Craft as I know it is certainly not for the masses; the masses could not accept and apply the inner teachings and disciplines to their lives. There is long and individual training required, and it is individual, not group-oriented. To my understanding, the Craft is clergy. And certainly those individuals who wish to serve the Great Goddess and speak in Her name, should have serious training and a dedicated commitment for life. Those who represent us in teaching and ministering should demonstrate the highest of ideals, principles and character in their daily lives, and the most important and unswerving is a universal love for all. The clergy must be able to separate and divide from the ego, and they must be trained to touch the souls of those they guide, and not judge on raw personality alone. This is not a social club. We always have to remember that we have a responsibility to each and every one who seeks us out in the name of the Goddess, and for their perceptions of what we are imparting as teachings. We have to know where they are at in their understanding and on what level they can master. This is not easy and everyone is different. If one does not have the dedication to accept full responsibility for a student, one should never take a student. And we never attempt to train one who shows emotional problems. He or she needs counseling by professionals and perhaps a loose association in outer court training only. This, in itself, rules out the masses.

STARSPAWN: Recently I moved from my hometown of Boston to San Francisco and found that the Craft out here is widely accepted. I rarely have to explain anything after I say I am "of the Wicca." So the media mind-set here is much more open than my hometown, which would often immediately ask, "Are you a good Witch or a bad Witch."

Craft was never meant to be a mainstream religion. It is a personal path choice involving a spiritual, polytheistic system that places many demands on it followers. It has no central ruling authority, such as a Pope. It has no one priest in a congregation, as we are all Priests/Priestesses in our religion. Each group is autonomous, on its own, to decide for each member what each member wants to believe and follow through on. And even then, it's for each member to make the final decision with him or herself. This is very powerful, very moving, and to some, very scary. Some people need the assurances of another to dictate what, whom, and when they believe. The Craft teaches none of this. We are, each of us, total and complete unto ourselves, answerable only to our Gods, the ethics by which we were trained, and how we feel within ourselves as we continue on our journeys of the spirit.

STOCK: *Nothing* has changed. Gwen Thompson told me that we are warriors in enemy territory, and I firmly believe that this is true—philosophically, religiously, *and* magically. I believe that if the Craft were to become mainstream, it would soon perish.

TANITH: I think it depends upon where you live! I think the atmosphere in general is more tolerant. There has been a lot of demystifying, and many civil liberty cases have been resolved in our favor. There are still, and will always be, a category of people who remain intolerant just as there are still racists in our society. I think that Craft is a Priest/ess hood and should remain that way, although Paganism seems to be moving toward becoming more mainstream.

THEITIC: Some members of the Craft have entered the public arena while others have gone back underground. This is, in part, attributed to how their practices were accepted by the public. It comes as no surprise to most of us that many of our people in Florida, Georgia, Kansas, and similar states are fighting every day for their rights, while others in more liberal states like California or Hawaii are free to practice in public places.

As a religion, we have made major strides in being recognized by the government on both state and local levels. This has not been an easy road. Public tolerance has come in the form of laws. I hope for the day when tolerance turns into acceptance and we can practice our magic and worship our Gods freely and without fear of persecution or ridicule. Until then, we should not be naive in thinking that a law or two protects our kind. Silence and secrecy have been our best protection and defense for over 500 years. I wouldn't enter the public place unless I was prepared to stand up to ignorance and hostility because many of those who tolerate our beliefs won't be there to defend us against those who don't.

As far as the Craft becoming a mainstream religion—Never! That changes the very essence of what Craft is. Power is rooted in mystery and the unknown, and power is gained through the search for knowledge (the Fool's Journey). Wisdom is the proper use of personal power and leads to evolution of the race. We in the Craft are part of a very old and wise race, and we are an inquisitive race that seeks to know more. We are compelled to grasp at every thread of life's fabric. We search out truth in nature's creatures, the ocean, the stars.

TIMOTHEA: I think the public still fears us and are very intolerant.

JOE WILSON: With the advent of the shallow "white-lighters" in the New Age movement, the general public seems to be more tolerant towards Paganism today than it was. As long as the Craft is concerned, as long as people keep calling themselves by the magic word "Witch" that conjures into the general public's mind the evil, wart-nosed, child-eaters of the fairy tales, there will continue to be misunderstandings and lack of tolerance.

As far as Craft becoming a mainstream religion—no. That's what the Pagan Movement is for.

How do you feel about open circles and public rituals?

AYEISHA: I stand in a lot of places with this issue, as do many others I know. On the one hand it is an opportunity to sort of show people a little bit about what goes on. It takes away some of the darker and scarier aspects of things because you see these people, and they seem harmless enough, and they're just doing what they're doing. But at another level, I think that many of those things turn into a kind of freak show. I know people in my group have voiced this, that when you're putting on a show, and you have these curious onlookers, how valuable is that really in the long term? We were talking tonight about how a group of people could come and watch an open circle and say, "Oh, that wasn't so bad; they seem to be reasonable people," etc. But, if one of the participants in the open ritual were to go to ten of those people and say, "I can see through your aura (or your energy or whatever) that you have some sort of curse on you, and you're going to need to pay me "x" amount of money to remove that curse," eight out of ten would fork over the money because underneath, no matter how pleasant or how many white robes you wear with how many flowers, the bottom line is that people have a real fear and that doesn't go away by having any of these open circles. You might educate a few individuals, but by and large you are mostly going to entertain people who will only remember what you've said and done until the next negative thing they hear.

Having done lots of publicity myself back when I thought we should do this to educate the masses, I've learned that you really can't do that very well. So, looking at the public thing, on one hand you see all these metaphysical stores that seem to be thriving. On the other hand, take a look at the movies that come out, like the movie, *The Craft*, that was really bent around all the negative, horrible, and spooky stuff, and very little of it was light or promising or growth-oriented. I think that people are always going to be nervous around people who do things like magic. And, again, just like in all those books that get published, there's only so much you can say in a book. You can put out ideas in a book, but anything real is experiential that a person has actually internalized and that kind of knowing can't be put out in a book or a television show or any of that other stuff. The major religions are all very much based on the concept of fear, and I don't think that will lessen or disappear. People who come to the Craft are doing something that is out of the ordinary anyway. Many people are perfectly satisfied to go to work, come home, and eat their meals. They don't wish to pursue much more than that, and they shouldn't be pushed to do so.

MARSHA BARD: I have attended public rituals and done public rituals. I enjoy both parts as spectator and participant, but retrospectively I don't know if it was such a good idea. A lot of joy was present in the "happening," but a lot of sorrow followed. I would prefer open discussions about ritual followed by a more concise circle of like-minded individuals for the performance part. I have no qualms about a non-Crafter (but an interested, free-minded human) attending a circle or ritual. I think that can be beneficial to all if all are comfortable with it. But to publicly do a ritual amid the closed-minded would at this time in my life make me uncomfortable.

LORI BRUNO: I think that open circles are alright within limits providing that they educate non-Craft people who may be there. As far as being a mainstream religion, we are, and that stream runs long and wide.

RAYMOND BUCKLAND: Excellent, if done for the right reasons, well-organized and presented as religious rituals and not just for show.

DANA CORBY: Open circles and public rituals are a valuable channel for newcomers. They build community by giving us a shared liturgical year outside our own Coven or Tradition. They allow Crafters and Pagans to come together and exchange ideas in safe space. They provide a venue for our activities to cross generation lines, as well, since (at least in the Seattle-area Pagan/Wiccan communities) most rituals are planned to be child-friendly.

Out here we don't have the truly public events that I understand are common on the East Coast—no Full Moons for 500 in the park, that sort of thing. We tend to use the term "Community" events, rather than "public." They are advertised only in local publications appealing to Pagans, and/or by flyer. Festivals are more widely advertised and more open, but locations are usually not divulged until after you've signed up and agreed to confidentiality (though some have been held yearly at the same location for so long now that the "secrecy" is a joke).

A number of years ago a group of Craft leaders, including myself, formed a group to sponsor Full Moons and one-day seasonal "mini-festivals" called the Earth Religion Cultural Association (ERCA). We wrote guidelines for public rituals that were so successful that local event sponsors, several years after the demise of ERCA, are still essentially using it. The cornerstone of our philosophy was that Community rituals are different in essence from private ones, and that intense energy work was not only inappropriate but also irresponsible. You can't know the backgrounds of your participants in a public ritual like you can in Coven. On the whole, it has worked well, and paid a dividend in getting Elders and community leaders of all stripes talking to each other regularly and exchanging ideas.

DEVON: I think that public events and open circles can be very beneficial. It gives the general public a chance to see something of how our religion works. It also opens the door for individuals who may not be ready to join a group the chance to be with and practice with people of like mind.

ALEXANDRIA FOXMOORE: I don't care what others do. I would not participate, nor would I attend.

GWION: I think that public rituals are important in an informative way and that most Pagan Ways are a good forum for open circles. Aside from the obvious reasons for not performing our rituals in public (the uninitiated are unprepared in many ways), I think that to be constantly involved in a circle that holds open rituals is disruptive to the energy necessary for high magic.

JUDY HARROW: I think they are very important, both for general public education and for allowing "our own" to find their way home.

HANS HOLZER: I think that demonstrations and documentary films are necessary to teach people about the Craft. Demonstrations, lectures, and documentaries are two-dimensional. But I think that open circles should only be held for those who have a genuine interest in becoming initiated. This would be a first step in that direction. It should not be for thrill-seekers.

CORBY INGOLD: I think open circles and rituals can be a very powerful means of outreach and service to the community. I used to lead them regularly in the early eighties, but now I generally lead a semi-public Samhain rite for friends and their invited guests. Most who attend are not Craft, but sympathetic, spiritually open people who want to commemorate their ancestors in a traditional manner.

JIMAHL: I think they are of great benefit to many people. Personally, I don't have time for them.

KERRY: I do not like them.

LEO MARTELLO: The more, the merrier! Hereditaries and Traditionalists can have their own closed circles. They can also participate in the open ones. Why should other religions have a monopoly on this?

MERLIN: They are fine for Pagan religious groups, but not for Craft.

MORDA: I do believe in them and participate in them whenever possible. Several years ago at the Parliament of World Religions in Chicago, there was an open outdoor Pagan/Craft ritual that was beautiful, open to the public and well-received.

MORVEN: I sharply divide Neo-Pagan practices and Witchcraft. I'm okay with open Neo-Pagan rituals at Neo-Pagan gatherings, shops, and so on. I think opening rituals to the public at large presents a lot of logistical problems, but if organizers are prepared, and are willing to deal with this, that's up to them. Worshipping the Old Gods and celebrating the seasonal festivals doesn't have to be limited to just initiates.

MURTAGH: While I think open circles and public rituals have their place, I don't mean doing them for the general public. I don't really cotton to the "everybody come, we're having the Beltane on the hill and the whole city's invited." Open circles, as opposed to public ritual, is a little more intimate. I held open circles, but the only people that came were people who people knew, and I always talked with them before they came. Even when we had an outer order in TDD, people came because they were invited to come, and then people got to know them. If somebody was disruptive or shouldn't have been there, he or she was asked not to come back.

Public rituals are a little different because there it's not so intimate and you do have a lot of people. But again, I think it can be handled. People get invitations or directions from someone, so they're somewhat screened. And if you have them at festivals which are public, again there's a screening process in that people have to go out of their way to send in money or get the directions, and you know there's a process there. I'm not against open circles or public rituals. I just think that the energy level there is very different.

MARY NESNICK: I think that open circles should not be "performed" for the general public. The general public has no idea who or what we really are, and to allow non-initiates to participate in open circles only invites disaster. The Craft has never been mainstream, and I don't believe it will or should become mainstream.

ELIZABETH PEPPER: I believe they invite ridicule.

PATRICIA POTHIER: I don't see how any good can come of inviting unprepared people to participate in something they can't possibly understand.

TRIVIA PRAGER: I have mixed feelings about public circles. I've seen some done very well and some that were showcases for someone's ego. I've seen the public being respectful, and I've seen harassment resulting in police being called. My sense of religious freedom believes that if the Pope can conduct a mass in a stadium, we should be allowed the same space for ritual (albeit at a different time). The public-service announcement part of me wants to educate; after all that's what I do for a living and that's what I do as a Priestess. However, I'm not so sure that the public is ready for us or in any way, shape or form tolerant of us. My need for personal spirituality and personal connection with the Gods outweighs my need to show off or attempt to educate the masses.

ROGER PRATT: Hmmm—they aren't really for me, although I have conducted open weddings and invited selected friends. Open rituals may serve as a good tolerance factor for the public, but secrets should still be preserved.

RAOKHSHA: Public rituals are sideshows, and were probably designed to be. "Look at what I am getting away with!" Open circles are multivalued. They can be a means of providing an entry into serious Craft or they can be meeting places of the dregs of humanity looking for a drug deal or a quick fix and generally creating a sham of a ritual.

In my world, "open circles" are opportunities to invite initiates and trainees of other beloved covens to join in a common celebration. Sometimes candidates for training are invited, once they have been "qualified." By now you might have detected my crotchety perspective on "non-serious" Craft.

OWEN ROWLEY: I think open circles and public rituals fulfill a need and that they can be very positive experiences for a great many people. I also feel that only a small subset of people who are "heathen-minded" or "Pagan-spirited" have the drive and inner-calling to set foot upon the Path of Light.

ZANONI SILVERKNIFE: I am all for them. There are enormous amounts of people who wish only to skim over the waves of religious practice, to taste the goods and not have a deeper commitment. This is fine; this is where they are at right now. Public rituals, when done with cautionary safeguards are fine for this, and many good, serious people have been gleaned from these gatherings. I have been involved in many such rituals both as participant and as the High Priestess. I have seen the value of open circles, and this also allows the superstitious a chance to have a peek at the "oh, so eerie world of the Witch."

SINTANA: I have very little to offer on this. I hope people who share their space with others would have some background and understanding of ritual and realize that the larger the group the more organized you need to be. Generally these should be handled in a Pagan outer-court structure and be able to create a positive experience for all.

STARSPAWN: For this day and age, I feel positive about open workings, as long as they reveal none of the sacred or oath-bound teachings. The public workings are great for networking, sharing information, and raising the consciousness of the cowans or non-initiated.

STOCK: I think they are fine if you are a Pagan, but not so if you are Traditional Craft.

TANITH: I like open circles and feel they answer a real need.

THEITIC: Much good has come from open circles and public rituals by allowing the curious to participate in seasonal rites and experience them first hand. This gives the newcomers more information when making their decision about working with a group. Although I don't believe that it was wrong for many of us to come into the mysteries "blindly," as was the case in the sixties, I do feel that today there is a need for more information before making a commitment to do the work.

On the other hand, I have rarely found a public ritual or open circle that I felt comfortable in. Things are done too loosely, and energy is rarely focused, but rather scattered. This may not be evident to everyone who attends, but the rules of magic are strict for a good reason (i.e., as above, so below; the Powers of the Pyramid; to know, to will, to dare and to keep silent).

TIMOTHEA: Open circles are the best way to teach the cowans that we are not evil. Those circles should be simple, generic, and reveal nothing much of importance to allay fears. This also allows those without contacts or a "home" to share in our worship, fun, and activities.

JOE WILSON: I have no problem with them. I was performing open circles as early as 1970, with authorities from the military, local government and churches invited. This was one way of dispelling their fear of the unknown.

What role, if any, do you feel Traditional Craft should play in the Neo-Pagan movement?

MARTHA ADLER: I believe it is up to us to maintain our honesty and stability while maintaining on the Path so that we are able to guide and help those who come to us for the right reasons. We should be as elder sisters or brothers giving sound advice to the best of our abilities.

AYEISHA: I think that we should take a much smaller role. I think that we should be much more private and less available to any fool who comes along. People get these things confused, you know. Christianity or any of those other major traditions of the day demand people be a part of it or else the person will suffer eternally. If you believe that you're going to burn in some hell if you don't ascribe to a particular tradition, you're going to think twice before you leave that tradition. In Craft, we think that this is a path, but it is a path for a select few. We don't think that it's a good idea to try to convert people or try to make them follow this path because this has to be a path of choice. So in Craft we don't proselytize. However, in some other traditional paths it's not enough that you become a member of that tradition; you're also not allowed to let other people do what they choose to do. Some believe they can be sent to "hell" for failing to convert their neighbor, and it's a big incentive for people to try to make you become a part of their path, or else. So in the traditions that are newer, the movement is on to press people into membership, and everybody gets accepted regardless of their level of personal growth or commitment to growth.

Too many people in the Neo-Pagan movement want to take the term Craft and make it apply to whatever it is that they happen to be doing. The

Craft is a distinct animal in and of itself. If you look at the degree system, you can see that the Craft is a system where you are expected to absorb "x" amount of personal understanding and knowledge. You are also expected to become a practitioner and be able to direct your life in order to make your life better. The decision to be positive in Craft comes from a very pragmatic view, the understanding that if you don't find harmony within yourself, then your life is going to be miserable. It's not about a far-off torture date. It's about living right here, right now, in the moment. This means that some power outside of yourself isn't going to be responsible for punishing you, or even rewarding you. Rather, you are very much in charge of the good things that come to you as well as some of the bad things. So, all together, I think that Traditional Craft would be better off to be a little more traditional instead of putting up seven copies of your phone number in a local metaphysical shop that says, "Please call! Oh please be a member of our coven!" But I do think that you might post a P.O. box with a brief line that says, "Interested parties may write." Then those people will need to make a real effort to get in contact with you.

MARSHA BARD: I think that Traditional Craft should have its corner in the Neo-Pagan movement. Everyone has a right to information, to distribute it or to absorb it. I think Wicca can gain a lot by close association to Neo-Paganism in the sense of this incredible universal energy that currently surrounds it. I think that Neo-Paganism has a lot to gain from Wicca in softening some of those strange "terrible two's" type antics. Wicca can bring history to Neo-Paganism, while Neo-Paganism can download some interesting concepts to Wicca.

LORI BRUNO: I believe we are clergy and can provide foundation to the Neo-Pagans.

RAYMOND BUCKLAND: It *is* part of the Neo-Pagan movement, probably initiating that movement.

DANA CORBY: Of course, the role I'd like to see us in is that of Elder Statesmen. We led the way, stuck our necks out and used the "W"-word when it was a very scary thing to do, and some of us paid the price. My priest and priestess were shot at through their own front window when the neighbors found out; I've lost jobs and been forced from my home and subjected to harassment by the deranged, and my brother doesn't speak to me. Several of my friends, over the years, have had to fight for the right to raise their own children, as any Christian or Jew just assumes they can, in the faith that gives them such joy.

It would be nice if those for whom we smoothed the way gave us a bit of respect. It would be wonderful if they sometimes turned to us for the knowledge, experience, and wisdom we have gained so painfully, but they won't. Part of it is the general equation in our culture of Elder =old = irrelevant. Part of it is the fate of all revolutionaries, to be disregarded when the revolution is over or passes to the next generation. It was our way to liberate those we taught, not to make them dependent on us. Conforming the sarcastic "law" that no good deed goes unpunished, we're reaping what we sowed. They think they don't need us.

DEVON: I think that Traditional Craft can show Neo-Pagans a practice of continuity. You can bend with the wind and savor its sweetness without moving to a different place every time the wind blows against you.

ALEXANDRIA FOXMOORE: I would hope that Traditional Craft would have a respected voice and a place within Neo-Paganism. There is room for all of us. Just as the Christians have different denominations within their movement, Paganism has many diverse thoughts. The idea is that we honor and respect one another enough to allow for difference.

GWION: I'm not sure that the Craft should have a role in the Neo-Pagan movement.

JUDY HARROW: I see Traditional Craft as a dedicated religious order within that world, providing clergy services, creating, performing rituals, scholarship, art, counseling, whatever is needed.

HANS HOLZER: I think the Craft is the grand old party of the Neo-Pagan movement; it's the center, the heart of it.

CORBY INGOLD: I still think, as some did back in the seventies, that we Witches could act as clergy to the Pagan community if so called upon. Of course, we should never be so arrogant as to seek to impose this role on others. All we have to do is make it known that we're available in that capacity if people want us. We should also realize that other Pagan faiths have their own clergy now too, such as: The Church of All Worlds, and some of the Druidic Orders, etc. But there's room for all of us. We should, of course, serve the entire community, not just self-proclaimed Pagans, just as Witches did of yore. We should serve our neighborhoods and communities as healers, herbalists, midwives, seers and diviners, ritualists, counselors, etc. This is part of our purpose as Witches: to strengthen the bonds of community and to serve our people.

JIMAHL: Traditional Craft is one of many paths. I think it is important to stress that all paths eventually lead to the same place. Each may choose his or her own path to that common end.

CHRISTINE JONES: Traditional Craft plays its own role, not other peoples'.

KERRY: It's up to the individual and not the institution.

LORAX: I feel that Traditional Craft has not had much to do with the Euro-Pagan (to distinguish us from the Santeria, Voudon and Candomble revivals that are sweeping this hemisphere) movement for about the last fifteen or so years. We are a minority, or so it seems. Let us assume for the moment that there are 50,000 self-identified Euro Pagans in North America. Let us further assume that ten percent of these are Witches or Wiccans who have trained within a coven structure or system more than five minutes old. Of these, I doubt that more than ten percent are Traditionalists not off of the New Forest groups.

The main trend now seems to be towards churchification of Paganism. There is a call for professional clergy, service workers, and big open, eclectic rituals. While I feel this can happen without doing violence to the benefits of the small intimate group dynamic, most of the leaders articulating this vision seem to want to replicate the Protestant church down the block or become Pope. I think that Voudon and Eastern polytheistic religions can offer better models than this.

LEO MARTELLO: Traditional Craft is the bedrock upon which all the others are based. They exist. Those seriously interested in pursuing their own spiritual path, who realize that they need and want something deeper, who are sincere and qualified, have the security of knowing that there is something else besides what they have been exposed to as "the Craft." We all have a role to play.

MERLIN: It should only provide some participation, theosophical information, and guidance drawn from experience in Traditional Craft. It should end there.

MORDA: Our role is to serve as teachers, guides, leaders, and consultants when appropriate.

MORVEN: The Craft should continue, as it has, as a valid path for those who choose it. I think there's a lot of work to be done preserving what information we have, passing on information to new generations, doing research and study to fill in the gaps and corroborate what we have, doing work for altruistic causes like world peace, stopping violence, and so on.

MURTAGH: I think Witches should be available. As we enter the millennium we're going to start seeing more people looking for real (and I know I shouldn't use that word) Traditional Craft for traditional training. I made a prediction in the mid-eighties that we were going to become a fad as we got closer to the millennium, that a lot of people were going to jump on the Neo-Pagan band wagon, and that it was going to get watered down. Well, it's years later and it has. But, at the same time, there are younger people becoming interested, and they want something with "meat" on it, something that's real. I don't mean to diminish what others are doing, but the younger seekers want something that speaks to them. I think we should be available for when the fad is over so that people can find us and know that we really exist. They'll know that we have something to offer that might, at that point, be very different than what they are used to.

ELIZABETH PEPPER: I think we need to remain quiet and stay behind the scene.

PATRICIA POTHIER: I think we should be available for serious seekers who are looking for religion instead of fun and games. But they should come to us, not us to them.

ROGER PRATT: We should serve as a source of information and as a voice of reason.

RAOKHSHA: I use Neo-Pagan as a synonym for "hedonist." That being said, I would prefer to let the happy little "Neo-Pagans" light candles, magically charge pink feathers and red candies, and find lovers. I would hope that Traditional Craft could stand just far enough away as to be available when the perceptive former "Neo-Pagan," after some little time, realizes there might be something more substantive than "getting naked and laying in piles."

OWEN ROWLEY: I think that traditionalists should make themselves quietly available and perhaps even establish some public "outer orders" which can serve as conduits for true initiates to find their path to the Northern Gateway.

ZANONI SILVERKNIFE: Many Traditionalists are autonomous and underground, but there are others who are more open. The Traditional Craft is still the backbone of the broader Wiccan and Pagan movements. There will always be died-in-the-wool, strict traditionalists, thank the stars! They carry on a less adulterated line of our teachings. The "Neo" people explore new avenues and approaches that are viable and should be examined for any good that they may bring. Balance is the key. We need order and growth, law and chaos, balance.

STOCK: None. Traditional Craft is what it is. The Neo-Pagan movement is temporary, and at best only a mere "reflection" of the tenants and underlying meaning of Traditional Craft.

TANITH: I think that everything is evolving on its own, and there is no "role" for anyone to have to take on.

THEITIC: None. The Neo-Pagan movement is moving into the New Age Movement (much like taking off the brown gloves and changing to a pair of yellow ones). But, Traditional Craft will forever be my hands.

TIMOTHEA: We should be the ones others turn to, examples of training, knowledge, and personal character.

JOE WILSON: I don't know that Traditional Craft has any role in the Neo-Pagan movement any more. Because of my efforts, along with a couple of others, Traditional Craft was its mother and father. Now the child has grown to rebellious adolescence and will have to further mature on its own. A few of us old-timers may find it easier to find one or two people with a driving thirst for knowledge, the forerunner of wisdom, within the hordes of Neo-Pagans. I hope so.

What do you feel the future holds for Traditional Craft?

AYEISHA: Because Craft adapts itself to the times, because everything about Craft is open to the possibility of growth, because the Craft is very much about the magic of taking charge of your life, and being in tune with the rest of the world, I think that Craft is always going to be a very viable tradition. I think that there are always going to be people who aren't content to be sheep, that there will always be people who want to take up authority and power, but those people are not going to be the majority of any civilization that I expect to see on Earth for the next fifty to sixty years. So I think there's a wonderful future for Traditional Craft but it's not all that much larger than membership was twenty years ago. There will be these groundswells of popularity where you'll have a lot more people saying that they are Craft than there used to be, but that will even out again. But when you look at genuine Craft, people who are really coming from a tradition of apostolic succession, which is that one teacher teaches a student who becomes a teacher who teaches a student who becomes a teacher, then those numbers will pretty much stay the same. You might add on a few, counting the increased number of people in the population, but the ratio would be about the same.

RAYMOND BUCKLAND: Slow, but certain growth and acceptance.

LORI BRUNO: Excellence and the love of the God and the Goddess!

CHAS CLIFTON: If we see ourselves as servants of the Old Ones, we have a future. If we are "social workers with pentagrams," we don't.

DANA CORBY: On the one hand, the current political climate terrifies me. We may be forced to go underground along with everyone else the junta defines as Satanic. On the other hand, apolitical backlash is forming against the radical right. How successful it is may determine how free we remain. And there is also a segment of young Pagans seeking a more Traditional teaching and environment. We are not dead-ending, though we are being forced to change with the times.

DEVON: Traditional Craft will always be here.

ALEXANDRIA FOXMOORE: I think it will die with we who are Elders ... and then everyone will try to buy our books.

GWION: I think the Craft will continue to grow. I also think we will eventually move back to our traditional roots.

JUDY HARROW: Growth and deepening (if our Earth survives).

HANS HOLZER: I think that in the future there will be further integration of the Craft into the mainstream.

CORBY INGOLD: I'm not really sure what the future holds for Traditional Craft. I don't think we'll ever get really "big," in terms of a mass movement. I suspect that Traditional Craft will remain something that appeals to individualistic people, not to someone looking for mainstream values or pat, easy answers to all their spiritual questions. I'm aware that mainstream values have moved closer to those of the Craft over the last thirty years, but I still think that Craft requires just a little too much work and self-reliance for most people. Let's face it—you have to be a little bit different to be a Witch. And actually, our quirkiness and individuality, those qualities which place us a little outside the mainstream, are the very qualities I find most endearing in Traditional Craft. Blessed Be!

JIMAHL: It is getting stronger again. The old teachers are returning; the new students are taking up the flame. The Craft is as strong and resilient as it ever was.

CHRISTINE JONES: We will play a big role; we are the religion of the future.

LEO MARTELLO: It will be stronger than ever. The non-traditionalists will seek it out. When I went public in 1969, I envisioned a worldwide movement. But even in going public as a Sicilian *stregone*, I never broke my vows. I held to my traditional hereditary Craft. As a public Witch, I pursued goals that did not conflict with this in any way.

MERLIN: I believe it will dynamically continue as it generally has. If tolerance declines it will become more underground and continue as it did in times past.

MORDA: I think it's watering down, and there will be more of a growth explosion in Pagan groups that will be more suited to the masses. I think that anything, once it is more widely accepted, loses some of the original intensity and creativity.

MORVEN: I see a difference between the people I call Witches, and the Neo-Pagans. I think Neo-Paganism will grow exponentially. It will probably become tamer so it can be more palatable to the masses. Since Witches are also Pagan, you'll probably still see them join with other Pagans at festivals, but you might see them become more private with their coven activities. I hope that the two groups will continue to respect each other's paths as valid, and I know that I, as a teacher, plan to continue to teach that. However, I don't plan to give up some of the more powerful aspects of Craft just so we can "perform" in public places.

MURTAGH: I think Craft will always be there. I think it will change. I think it has changed in the last twenty or so years because we have evolved. We have certain things we will maintain and keep, but I think that in general we will grow and change and find different ways of doing things.

MARY NESNICK: All things change and all things remain the same. The Craft will continue on as it has in the past. The Wheel doesn't need to be reinvented.

ELIZABETH PEPPER: I believe that the Craft will continue for as long as humans respond to its magic.

PATRICIA POTHIER: Everything depends on whether we keep our Craft pure or water it down to make it palatable to the mainstream and the New Agers. We have kept the old truths from falling into oblivion for 2,000 years and we must continue to do so. It is a hard road to tread, and a hard road will never be a popular road.

TRIVIA PRAGER: I believe there is a future for the Craft. There will always be seekers of truth who are not satisfied having a priesthood telling them how to honor the Gods when their own hearts, minds, and souls tell them otherwise.

ROGER PRATT: Craft will continue. My mum's tradition perhaps, if I train one or two persons to pass it on. The other traditions will continue because there will always be those who need and require secrecy.

RAOKHSHA: I feel that there must be a time when the Craft truly believes in what it stands for and stops "letting the water run." (I want to throttle those who casually wash a set of dishes in fifty gallons of running water!) There is a crisis on this planet, and the Gods need us as much as we need them. Without mutual support we cannot survive. It is the Traditional Craft that will have the body of knowledge and understanding to utilize a system that creates change in the current natural imbalance. That body of knowledge is tested and fine-tuned, and it is not a spatter gun of "tricks."

I envision a coming of age for the Craft, wherein we take up major causes with civil action as well as magic to correct the wrongs, both corporate and personal, that have nearly destroyed our world...and us. We can work behind the scenes, as is our forte, but we must work!

OWEN ROWLEY: We exist in all times and in all places. If the light is extinguished in one place it will spring up in another. I "know" I was involved in treading my path for many lifetimes, and it doesn't matter one bit to me how I find my way back each time.

ZANONI SILVERKNIFE: It holds whatever we shape it to hold. I believe there will be those who will keep pure the Old Ways until there is no longer a need for such, when the world is more sane and accepting. As I tell my fledglings: Keep the old and invent the new. Use them judiciously and with great feeling.

SINTANA: I do not see any true respect for what we term Traditional Craft, or their Elders, and I find this incredibly sad. I believe we need to separate the chaff from the wheat. Of course, this could change in the future when the pop-Wicca craze is no longer in fashion. That will leave the serious who desire and respect order and tradition, who have genuine regard and respect for knowledge and the true will to apply it to life; they will be living the Craft, not on an intellectual level but one born of true consciousness. From this caliber of individuals will come those who possess a serious dedicated desire—to *be* and *become* the Wise, the Keepers of the Ancient Mysteries, for generations to come.

STARSPAWN: Just as Craft survived "the Burning Times," burrowing deep into the darkness, hidden within families as legends and passed quietly from one to the next of "like mind," so I would like to believe that

Traditional Craft will survive. It may never be within modern Wicca structure, accepted as commonplace, but it will survive. There will always be the select few who will crave more in their studies than learning from books, internet, email, Dungeons and Dragons Pagan groups, and public gatherings can offer. Those of a serious mind will always seek out a serious religion, and it is my hope that the Keepers of the Flame will be there for them.

STOCK: It will remain the same as it has been from the beginning. Again, it *is* what it *is*, and it will *be* what it is.

TANITH: The same as always. Craft will wax and wane; information will be lost, changed, and rediscovered in a new form.

THEITIC: I cannot even attempt to guess what the future may hold for Traditional Craft. I have come to learn that tomorrow can bring things we never expected in our wildest dreams.

I can hope that Traditional Craft will be a source of inspiration to future generations, and that it will always hold the mystery that was there for me when I began my search for Wisdom and Truth.

TIMOTHEA: The same as ever—A tight core of privately operating initiates and many followers who understand, participate, and believe on lesser levels, enjoying festivities without spiritual conviction or growth.

JOE WILSON: It will either grow, change and adapt to the times while retaining the seeds of wisdom, or die.

Contact List

The Witches listed herein are open to contact from readers. Their preferred method of contact is given. Inquiries to those not listed may be sent to the authors for forwarding.

ALEXANDRIAN

Jimahl
www.home.earthlink.net/~Jimahl

Morven
E-MAIL : morvenharvest@yahoo.com

Starspawn
2261 Market Street, #292
San Francisco, CA 94114
E-MAIL: handsontouch@yahoo.com
www.handsontouch.com

CELTIC

Christine M. Jones (Athena)
Apt. D155
50 Berkeley Street
Satellite Beach, FL 32937

GARDNERIAN

Raymond Buckland
c/o Llewellyn Publications
P.O.Box 64383
St. Paul, MN 55164-03837

Roger Pratt
www.rogerpratt.com

KEEPERS OF THE ANCIENT MYSTERIES (K.A.M.)

Trivia Prager
Mid-Atlantic K.A.M.
P.O.Box 33426
Baltimore, MD 21218

MOHSIAN

Lorax
inisglas@home.com

NEW ENGLAND COVENS OF TRADITIONALIST WITCHES (N.E.C.T.W.)

Marsha Bard (Lenura)
E-MAIL: lenura@nectw.org

Owen Rowley
E-MAIL: owen@nectw.org

Theitic
c/o N.E.C.T.W.
P.O. Box 29182
Providence, RI 02909
(401) 273-1176
E-MAIL: theitic@nectw.org
http://www.nectw.org

RAVENWOOD

Sintana
Ravenwood Church & Seminary
P.O. Box 5586
Atlanta, GA 30307
(404) 289-6126
E-MAIL: ladysintana@hotmail.com
www.ravenwoodchurch.org

STREGA

Rev. Lori Bruno
Our Lord and Lady of the
Trinacrian Rose
33 Everlyn Avenue
Medford, MA 02155
(781) 395-9297

TUATHA DE DANANN (T.D.D.)

Merlin Ambrosias and Bethany Lambert
Apple Grove
E-MAIL: BEAnMEatAPPLEG@aol.com

Murtagh A. AnDoile
11684 Ventura Boulevard, #479
Studio City, CA 91604
E-MAIL: Tagh@worldnet.att.net

Stock & Kerry
OakGrove
E-MAIL: OakGroveRI@aol.com

OTHER TITLES FROM
OLYMPIAN PRESS:

The Rede of the Wiccae

The Goddess Minerva

Botanicals and Their Cosmological Attributions

If you would like to be on our mailing list
to be kept informed of the release of the above titles,
or if you would like to order additional copies of this book,
please fill out the order form below or visit us on the web at
www.OlympianPress.com.
All mailing list information will be kept confidential.

TheWitchesAlmanac.com
Phone/Fax: (401) 847-3388
Toll-free Phone/Fax: (888) 897-3388

Sales@TheWitchesAlmanac.com

The Witches' Almanac LTD.

The 2007-2008 edition celebrates the element of Water. Its theme embraces the magic of sacred wells and charms for Neptune's favors. We explore the water rites of Fiji, the tarot's Death card, seashell charms, gypsies, freemasonry and much more. This issue also proudly boasts an interview with the late Elizabeth Pepper, founder of *The Witches' Almanac*.

Arcane symbols and intriguing graphic images are always a part of every issue.

$9.95 Paperback, 136 pages, 6" x 9"

2007 – 2008 The Witches' Almanac
____ (Quantity) @ $9.95_____
Shipping & handling _____
*(One book: $3, each additional book add $1)*_____
7% sales tax (RI orders only)_____
*Total*_____

SHIP TO:

_____

_____

_____

_____Zip _____

FORM OF PAYMENT:

☐ Check   ☐ Money Order   ☐ VISA   ☐ Mastercard   ☐ Discover/Novus   ☐ American Express

Account number (all digits) | | | | | | | | | | | | | | | | |

Signature _____   Expiration date   ___ /___ /___
(required of credit card customers only)

The Witches Almanac Ltd. Post Office Box 1292, Newport, Rhode Island 02840